# THE
# MORAL ECOLOGY
## *of*
# COLLAPSE

Essays on Inequality, Complexity,
and the Instability of Democratic Societies

LAWRENCE R. KUNKEL

ISBN: 979-8-218-92096-8 (Hardcover)
ISBN: 979-8-234-00610-3 (Paperback)
ISBN: 979-8-218-93017-2 (Digital)

First Edition.



This publication is designed to provide accurate and authoritative information in regards to the subject matter covered. It is sold with the understanding that neither the author nor the publisher is engaged in rendering legal, investment, accounting, or other professional services. While the author has used their best efforts in preparing this book, they make no representations or warranties with respect to the accuracy or completeness of the contents of this book and specifically disclaim any implied warranties of merchantability or fitness for a particular purpose. No warranty may be created or extended by sales representatives or written sales materials. The advice and strategies contained herein may not be suitable for your situation. You should consult with a professional when appropriate. The author shall not be liable for any loss of profit or any other commercial damages, including but not limited to special, incidental, consequential, personal, or other damages.

The design and typography were done by The Moral Ecology Press.

Moral Ecology Press
140 West 69th Street, Suite 78B
New York, NY 10023

# Contents

# Forward

Inequality is expanding, democracy is failing, the environment is getting worse, and morals are getting worse. These are all major challenges of the twenty-first century. People in a culture that has conflated technological advancement with human flourishing do new things. We created our political and economic structures on the premise that efficiency and reason are linear. Now, though, they work in a world that isn't linear, with feedback loops, tipping points, and networked fragility. The traditional maps of equilibrium economics and atomistic individualism are no longer useful. They come from a time when people didn't understand how the economy worked as a complicated adaptive mechanism.

*The Moral Ecology of Collapse* is a new way of thinking discussed in this book. The primary premise is that markets, societies, and moral awareness all change together in a network of knowledge and ecosystems. Dynamic feedback and adaptive learning help the biosphere arrange itself. A fair economy must also thrive through mutual wisdom, which I define as a moral ecosystem of prosperity. In this view, people are not separate individuals seeking the most out of their own lives. Instead, they are part of a network of meaning, trust, and interdependence that is always changing.

Standard neoliberal economic models, predicated on atomistic utility maximization, perfect information, and equilibrium, fail to illustrate the perpetual evolution and expansion of human civilizations. Complexity economics, on the other hand, says that emergent order doesn't come from control but from interactions, specifically from the spontaneous coordination of different agents who are all limited in the same way and have adaptive expectations. When we add moral, psychological, and cultural factors to this mix, we begin to see that economic outcomes are not just the result of incentives and information, but also of collective consciousness. In this manner, being prosperous isn't only about having a lot of money. It's also about maintaining a healthy balance among what people need, how institutions are set up, and environmental constraints.

This book takes this idea beyond economics. It says that a functional social order needs to combine moral psychology, cultural evolution, and systems theory into one story about why people exist. This framework, which draws on concepts from game theory, Jungian psychology, virtue ethics, and chaos theory, conceptualizes moral progress as a manifestation of self-organization. When feedback loops among empathy, fairness, and agency are strengthened rather than broken, societies move toward coherence. When those loops break down, when inequality and collective delusions skew the flow of information, complex systems become places where people grow increasingly polarized, resentful, and authoritarian.

The essays in this book look at these dynamics from many angles. For example, they discuss behavioral game theory of trust and moral signaling, the phase transitions that turn stratification into oligarchy, the collective illusions that sustain inequality, and the cultural and artistic movements that reveal the chaos of our economy and politics. Each chapter examines the nonlinear interplay among the mind and the market, ethics and equilibrium, perception and authority.

What emerges is not a novel ideology but a new epistemology that perceives the human predicament as a moral ecology in a state of perpetual flux. It advocates for a change from the idea that competition never ends to the idea that collaboration is always changing, and from the idea that sharing is good to the idea that materialism is bad. The way to long-term prosperity is not to be more efficient, but to be more understanding; not to regulate complexity, but to work with it.

In the end, *The Moral Ecology of Collapse* is a diagnostic and a guide for society, grounded in a clear political philosophy that spans many fields. It calls for a new level of awareness at the systems level: an economy based on moral intelligence, a politics based on shared truth, and a society that is humble enough to learn from its own nonlinear traits. There is order in the chaos of geometry, survival in the logic of cooperation, and the ultimate measure of wealth in the progress of consciousness.

## The Author

Lawrence R. Kunkel is an economist who studies game theory and complexity economics. Kunkel's work exemplifies what may be termed interdisciplinary systems humanism. It brings together economics, philosophy, social psychology, chaos theory, and art history into a single way of looking at and improving society. He envisions a future in which economic institutions are designed not only for efficiency and growth but also to enhance individuals' freedom, fairness, stability, and resilience. Mr. Kunkel earned his bachelor's degree (B.A.) from Providence College in 1978. Every student is required to take a two-year interdisciplinary course on the Development of Western Civilization, which covers philosophy, history, theology, literature, and art history. He earned his master's degree in the Division of Social Sciences at the University of Chicago. He studied in the Graduate School of Economics, the Business School, the Law School, and the Committee on Social Thought. From 1978 to 1981, Mr. Kunkel served as a research assistant to George Stigler, who won the Nobel Prize in Economics in 1982. He also learned about pricing theory from Gary Becker (Nobel Prize, 1992) and monetary theory from Robert Lucas (Nobel Prize, 1995). This is his first book.

# Chapter 1

# Complexity Economics and Emergent Order

## The Moral Ecology of Prosperity and Human Growth in Complexity Economics

### Abstract

This essay explores how complexity economics influences our understanding of wealth and human well-being. It asserts that economies are not only mechanical engines of efficiency, but adaptive moral ecologies in which values, norms, narratives, and institutional arrangements co-evolve. Prosperity does not derive solely from material wealth; it emerges from cultivating institutions that promote meaning, dignity, reciprocity, and relational depth. A moral framework that emphasizes complexity shifts economic policy from maximizing totals to maintaining the dynamic settings that foster the development of diverse human capabilities.

### Introduction: From Mechanism to Ecology

For a long time, orthodox economics has believed that models of rational optimization, equilibrium, and efficiency can help us understand how economies work. In this approach, growth in output, consumption, and other financial indicators is used to measure prosperity. People are viewed as distinct entities seeking to maximize utility, with market transactions serving as their sole means of interaction. People see institutions as fixed structures instead of dynamic forces in societal change.

In the 21st century, on the other hand, the world is not like a machine always seeking equilibrium. It is marked by social fragmentation, climate instability,

1

concentrated wealth, digital hyper-connectivity, and global interconnectedness. It works like an ecosystem that is continually changing. It is nonlinear, path-dependent, sensitive to initial conditions, adaptive, and molded by feedback loops.

Complexity economics doesn't just give us new tools; it also changes the way we think about things. It views economic life as a network of relationships among individuals influenced by their histories, cultures, ethical principles, and hierarchies of power. In these systems, material outputs alone do not define wealth. It is more correctly described as the emergent quality of resilient moral ecologies—systems that promote dignity, agency, mutual trust, and collective significance. The task of our time is not simply to generate greater wealth but to cultivate, sustain, and restore ecologies conducive to human flourishing.

## II. The economy is a Complex System that changes throughout time.

There are a few key features of complex adaptive systems that have an impact on social and economic life:

- Interdependence: What happens depends on how people work together, not just how they act alone.

- Feedback Loops: Even small adjustments can lead to major issues.

- Emergence: You can't break down system-level patterns into individual goals.

- Path Dependence: What we can do now is affected by what has happened in the past.

- Adaptation: Agents learn, plan, and adjust when things change.

This viewpoint asserts that the economy is not a limited optimization issue. As time goes on, it evolves because of culture, psychology, technology, institutions, and power. In financial markets, expectations and outcomes reinforce each other, strengthening them. Identity, position, and institutional design influence labor markets as significantly as supply and demand. Networks of collaboration, imitation, and rivalry drive innovation, not individual "entrepreneurs" working alone.

That's apparent what that means: the quality of the connections, institutions, and rules that regulate interaction is what makes people rich, not the amount of stuff that is traded. So, the question switches to "How do we get the most out of our work?" How can we retain the things that help people develop and change?

## III. Beyond Utility: The Ethical Dimensions of Economic Existence

When it comes to values, traditional economics seeks to be impartial. But the structures it makes must have values built into them. A market that prioritizes shareholder profits over worker safety and health follows a moral logic of disposability. An unstable, watched-over work structure shows that dignity is neither guaranteed nor permanent. An innovative system that relies solely on private ownership of public knowledge undermines cooperation and shared goals.

From a complexity perspective, moral norms are the building blocks of functional infrastructure. Trust makes it cheaper to do business. Actions are organized by shared meaning. Fairness makes people want to work together. People are stronger when they help each other. When these rules don't work, systems get weak, split, and unstable. This shows that prosperity isn't only about money; it's also about morals and institutions. A society that values efficiency over dignity encourages growth that doesn't lead to prosperity. A community that encourages meaning and belonging, even if it implies slower or lesser material growth, develops prosperity that lasts longer and is deeper.

## IV. The Moral Ecology of Money

A moral ecosystem is the collection of cultural standards, institutional systems, social ties, and shared tales that determine our identity and behavior. Just as a natural ecosystem can be healthy or ill, varied or monocultural, robust or weak, a moral ecology can be the same.

Some crucial features of a healthy moral ecology are:

- Dignity means recognizing that people have value in themselves, not just because of what they can do in the market.

- Reciprocity: Responsibilities that both parties have that maintain trust and unity intact.

- Agency: The ability to do things, make things happen, and influence your environment. Belonging implies being part of groups that share a common objective and a sense of meaning.

- Temporal Stewardship: A responsibility to future generations and the safeguarding of historical continuity.

People can do well even when there isn't enough of something if these factors are there. Even having a lot of money can make you feel stressed, lonely, and not confident while you're competing. It's a tragedy that many modern economies have prospered by losing the moral ecologies that give life purpose. Too-competitive job markets break up groupings of people. In a society of consumption, performance is more important than identity. Digital platforms make people more jealous, angry, and worried about their standing. When wealth is concentrated, working together becomes a fight for position that has no winners. We have been getting economic growth by taking things from the land and using it up in ways that are bad for the environment.

## V. Human Flourishing as an Emergent Co-Creation

It is impossible to achieve human flourishing solely through top-down policies. The market doesn't automatically make it happen. It is a property that emerges when people, communities, and institutions work together dynamically.

Flourishing means:

- The improvement of one's skills.

- The sense of having an impact.

- The feeling of being linked to other people and a goal.

- The ability to envisage and work for bright futures.

This needs places that are helpful in terms of culture, psychology, and things. It requires time and freedom to research, think, and generate new ideas. It requires social structures that see people not just as producers or consumers, but as active members of a moral and civic community. In a nutshell, relationships are what make life good. We don't have wealth; we create it together.

## VI. Building Institutions for Moral and Economic Power

If prosperity is ecological, policy must shift from attempting to regulate outcomes to fostering appropriate conditions. This entails making institutions that:

- Put justice and giving back into practice.

- Give people authority so that no one person has too much.

- Give communities greater freedom and make them stronger.

- Make sure that shared items don't change over time.

- Help people understand things and feel like they belong in their community.

Some examples are democratic workplaces, cooperatives, community land trusts, participatory governance, universal public goods funding, and shared innovation infrastructure. These institutions not only create wealth but also teach people how to be decent and maintain good relationships, which makes wealth worth having. The goal is not to do away with markets, but to ensure they work within and are shaped by moral ecologies that are good for people.

In conclusion, we are making progress toward a moral science of prosperity. Complexity economics urges us to view prosperity as fragile, social, and emergent. It shows that markets aren't fair; they're moral systems that shape identity, meaning, and potential. People need more than just growth and efficiency to succeed. They also need social institutions that foster respect, give-and-take, freedom, belonging, and taking care of others. This kind of system isn't something that people want; it's something that people need to live. A society that doesn't care about the moral ecology of wealth will always be weak, unequal, and full of problems. It makes a civilization robust, flexible, and able to thrive together. Wealth in the future won't be mechanical. It is excellent for the planet. That's correct. We all have a duty to nurture it.

# The End of Competition and Market Concentration: How Complexity Economics and the Monopoly Can Charge More

## Abstract

Since the end of the 20th century, there has been a lot more concentration in many areas of the US and world markets. These areas include technology, banking, agriculture, and healthcare. Traditional microeconomic models see competition as a self-regulating system in which high profits encourage new businesses to enter the market and reduce market dominance. Nonetheless, the persistent existence of oligopolistic enterprises in platform sectors and the emergence of quasi-monopolies signify the impact of more profound, systemic pressures. Complexity economics, which views the economy as a dynamic network that adapts to changes rather than a stable equilibrium, offers a more thorough comprehension of how market concentration can become self-reinforcing, suppressing competition and innovation while simultaneously elevating prices and economic inequality.

## 1. Self-Reinforcing Dynamics and the Economics of Complexity

Neoclassical models only have one equilibrium, but complexity economics looks at route dependence, feedback loops, and emergent order. For example, in digital marketplaces, network effects (the value of a platform growing up as more people use it) produce positive feedback that helps the people who are already in charge stay in charge. These impacts, together with switching costs, data advantages, and algorithmic learning, can make it so that one company wins most of the time in various industries. Joseph Schumpeter's idea of "creative destruction" is based on the idea that new ideas replace old ones. However, complexity models demonstrate how established firms can manage disruption through the acquisition of startups, the patenting of pertinent technologies, or advocacy for advantageous policies. This keeps the frontiers of creativity from moving forward.

## 2. Concentration as a Complex Adaptive System

The market shares of individual companies do not add up to the market concentration. It is a quality that happens when businesses, regulators, customers, and investors all work together. Financialization makes things worse by letting major institutional investors own shares in several competitors (common ownership), which makes it less likely that they will compete. Without anybody saying so directly, algorithmic pricing can bring markets together. These are attractors, which are stable patterns of behavior that the system tends to move toward. When an industry gets bigger, things like political lobbying, economies of scope, and data collecting make it even bigger. The industry probably won't become competitive again until something happens from the outside or the government acts.

## 3. Outcomes: Novel concepts, inequity, and democratic governance

It is possible to measure how high concentration affects productivity growth, wage shares, and political power. Empirical studies demonstrate that mark-ups and profit margins have risen during the 1980s, notwithstanding a slowdown in business dynamism (firm entry and leave). The system's ability to adapt is lower since there are fewer experiments, less diversity, and more systemic instability. This makes it less complicated. Monopoly power also makes inequality worse by shifting money from labor to capital and letting landlords take rent through platform control. Lastly, when economic power is concentrated, political power is too. This can lead to regulatory capture, which makes it harder for democracy to keep firms in check.

## 4. Policy Implications: Beyond Static Antitrust

Conventional antitrust tools, which focus on short-term price effects and narrow market boundaries, are insufficient for complex adaptive systems. A complexity-aware strategy would emphasize:

- Instead of fixed market shares, use dynamic competition indicators like entry rates, innovation variety, and data-access asymmetries.

- Systemic risk analysis, including detecting weak spots and choke points in supply chains and platforms, is like financial regulation.

- To reduce network-effect lock-in, we need infrastructures that encourage competition, such as data portability, interoperability requirements, and public digital utilities.

- Supporting worker cooperatives, open-source platforms, and decentralized finance as tools to fight against corporate centralization is what institutional diversity entails.

## Conclusion

Market concentration is not only a deviation from idealized competition; it is the anticipated outcome of self-reinforcing dynamics within complex systems. Policymakers can set rules that bring back diversity, resilience, and real competition if they understand how these things work. If we don't take these actions, the "death of competition" could lead to a new sort of economic feudalism, where monopoly power acts as a self-organizing attractor in the modern economy.

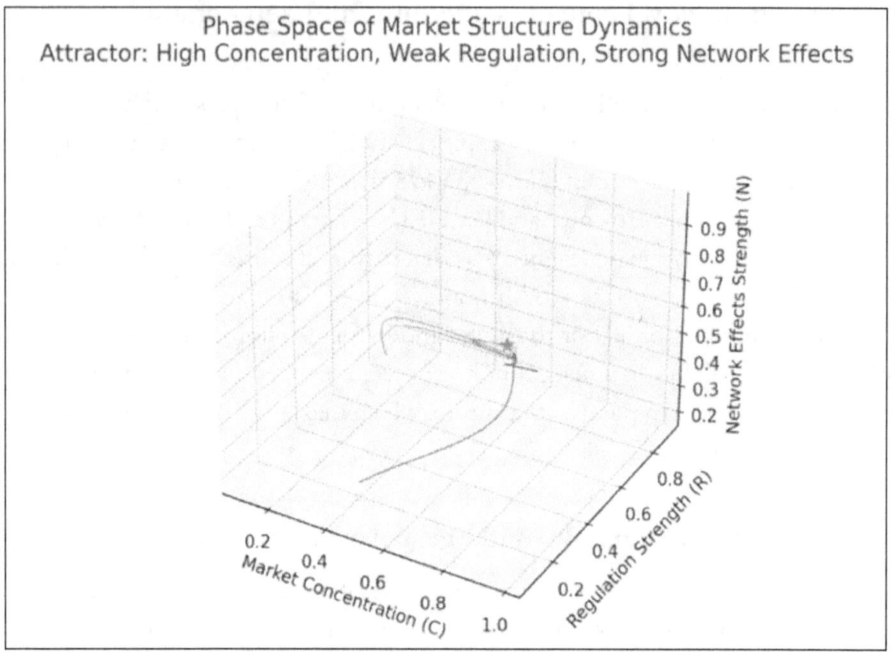


The above figure illustrates potential variations in market concentration over time, influenced by distinct policy and network-effect frameworks. It illustrates the concept of attractors in complexity economics: one attractor characterized by significant concentration amid poor regulation and robust network effects.

# The Economics of Emergent Despair: How Systemic Dysfunction Leads to Group Psychological Collapse

## Abstract

This essay investigates the nonlinear, systemic interaction between economic dysfunction and pervasive psychological decline, referred to as "emergent despair." The thesis, grounded in complexity economics, systems psychology, network theory, and political economy, posits that despair transcends individual mental health issues and manifests as a collective phenomenon arising from institutional failure, economic instability, societal fragmentation, and information overload. During structural turbulence in economic systems—marked by stagnant wages, reduced mobility, concentrated market power, precarity, and the decline of democracy—psychological disintegration becomes a pervasive phenomenon affecting the entire populace. The essay discusses the origins of the new pessimism, its nonlinear spread, and its implications for political stability, social cohesion, and moral order.

## I. When the economy becomes a machine for despair, this is how it starts.

A lot of people in America are feeling hopeless right now. The incidence of sadness, anxiety, addiction, suicide, violent extremism, and existential disengagement has risen considerably. However, individual psychology alone cannot completely clarify these phenomena. Modern despair is not merely individual; it is social, structural, and emerging. Economic systems affect people's identities, what they expect, how they make sense of things, and how likely they think their futures are. It's normal to feel despair when these systems fail.

Conventional economic models regard psychological states as external variables. Complexity economics, conversely, recognizes that psychological collapse stems from systemic economic dysfunction. Despair emerges when economies no longer provide dignity, stability, or mobility, and when institutions fail to cultivate trust or coherence. Despair basically becomes the new balance point of a system that isn't working.

The main idea is simple: when an economy is going down, it casts a mental shadow called "emergent despair."

## II. The Structural Roots of Hopelessness

### 1. Stagnant Wages and the Loss of Economic Importance

One of the worst things about modern capitalism is that productivity rises faster than wages do. For years, most workers have had less money to spend, less freedom to move about, and less chance of achieving the "American Dream." When hard work doesn't lead to safety or a better life, the economy no longer makes sense. Work goes from being something to be proud of to something to be ashamed of. When structures stop changing, emotions stop changing too.

### 2. A Constant State of Precarity

The shift to gig employment, just-in-time scheduling, contractor labor, and corporate power that is too great for one business has made precarity a permanent element of working life. This leads to long-term stress, lower cognitive ability, shorter time frames, and poor decision-making. Precarity also erodes trust. People who are worried about their money are more likely to think in conspiratorial ways, engage in zero-sum identity politics, and give up on everything.

### 3. The Loss of Things that are Good for Everyone

The roads, schools, and libraries that the public utilizes have gotten worse. Public areas are getting worse. Institutions that work together become less strong. People are beginning to view society as a competitive arena rather than a collaborative environment.

Public goods are important for mental health. Without them, people feel more alone and hopeless, which is the most common emotional state.

### 4. The Extraction and Financialization of Hope

People who take short-term risks, hunt for rent, and drive up the value of their assets are rewarded under financialized capitalism. Taking money out of the economy is what makes wealth rise, not making things better. It gets harder and harder to pay for a home, school, health care, and retirement. This has a significant impact on people's minds, making them feel left out. Most people believe they cannot access the engines of prosperity. When cultures don't let people speak out, hopelessness becomes a necessary part of the system.

## III. The Mechanism of Self-Amplifying Despair in Complexity Dynamics

Despair spreads through nonlinear feedback loops, just as disease, information cascades, and financial panics. The three most important mechanisms are:

**1. Problems lead to a lack of trust, which leads to not working together, which leads to more dysfunction.**

People lose trust when institutions fail. Cooperation declines as trust declines. As collaboration declines, the ability of institutions to do their jobs declines even further. This cycle runs from what one person does to what the whole country does.

**2. Inequality leads to relative deprivation, which leads to tribalization.**

Not only does inequality produce problems with money, it also causes problems with mental health. People compare themselves to elites who are getting richer and richer, which makes it hard for them to grasp how affluent they are. This makes people mad, splits their identities, and drives them to extreme beliefs. Tribal identities are becoming increasingly important as established social identities fade.

**3. Too much information → Cognitive fragmentation → The end of reality**

Digital capitalism produces money by making people mad, terrified, curious, or puzzled. The final effect is a story that doesn't make sense, too much information for the brain, a breaking apart of a common reality, and a loss of trust in knowledge. Without a common reality, people can't work together. Systems can't fix themselves unless humans work together. Next follows despair.

## IV. The Psychology of Systemic Failure

**1. Learned Helplessness in a Population Context**

People who can't modify their conditions eventually stop trying. When many people are going through hard times with the economy and politics, it's normal to feel helpless. Some indicators are not caring about politics, thinking that everything will end badly, being addicted, and feeling horrible when you stop using drugs.

**2. The End of Looking Ahead**

Healthy societies are built on the idea that the future is important. People can't plan for the future when institutions don't keep them safe. This is seen in fewer infants being born, less savings, short-term thinking, and a desire to escape.

**3. Social Resonance and Emotional Contagion**

Despair moves from one person to another. People show how they feel about the people around them. When many people are feeling pessimistic, the mood of the whole society becomes hopeless. This is called a self-fulfilling emotional equilibrium.

### 4. Loss of Identity and Lack of Meaning

Meaning comes from things that don't change, such as roles, institutions, stories, and communities. Identity falls apart when jobs are precarious, institutions aren't trustworthy, and stories don't fit together. Identity disintegration is a breeding environment for despair.

## V. Effects on Society and Politics of Growing Despair

### 1. Populism and a shift toward authoritarianism

People seek easy storylines, strong leaders, and someone to blame when they are down. Sad people often turn to authoritarian attractors. Populist demagogues utilize people's hopelessness to destroy the rules of democracy.

### 2. Disunity, Violence, and Extremism

People become more extreme when they are hopeless. Societies marked by psychological deterioration exhibit increased gun violence, fanaticism, domestic terrorism, and inter-racial strife. These are not isolated disorders; instead, they are anticipated emerging results.

### 3. Institutional Paralysis and the Loss of Legitimacy

When people are hopeless, institutions can't get them to obey rules, trust them, or work together. Governance becomes a symbol rather than a means.

### 4. The Economy isn't Doing Well

People who have little hope don't come up with fresh ideas, don't work together as much, and pull out more. The economy is becoming worse, which is making things worse.

## VI. The Moral Economy of Being Hopeless

Economic systems confer worth, dignity, and significance indirectly. A moral economy is one that gives individuals peace of mind, stability, and opportunities. People feel hopeless when systems give them shame, instability, and exclusion. Emergent despair is not merely subjective; it serves as moral evidence of systemic failure. Economies are like moral buildings; when they lose their moral foundations, they also lose their ability to work.

# VII. Pathways Out: Building an Economy That Gives People Hope

## 1. Get the economy back on track

- Everyone should have access to health care
- Strong protections for workers
- Good social security
- Affordable housing
- Minimum amounts of income

## 2. Put money back into things that are good for everyone.
Public goods bring back the basic ideas that help people live together.

## 3. Restore the Effectiveness of Institutions
You need to see that someone is fair and good at what they do before you can trust them.

## 4. Take Charge of the Cognitive Environments
Democracy demands a common understanding. We need to control cognitive pollution and algorithmic amplification to keep civilization stable.

## 5. Give Everyone Access to Power
Action is needed for hope. You need power to have agency. So, society needs to break up big firms, give workers more influence, and shift economic decision-making power away from the center.

# VIII. Conclusion: Despair as a Systemic Indicator

Despair is not random. It means that a system is no longer stable, dignified, or important. The economics of emerging despair demonstrate that when a political and economic system begins to deteriorate, individuals are prone to losing their sanity. We need to alter the economy, restore institutions, and rebuild the moral core of the social compact if we want to turn despair around. To turn rising despair into rising flourishing, nations need to make structures that protect human dignity.

# The Strange Attractor of Inequality: Nonlinear Feedback Loops in Wealth Concentration

## Abstract

This essay analyzes wealth concentration through the lens of chaos theory, suggesting that inequality operates as a strange attractor within a nonlinear economic system. It uses complexity economics and systems dynamics to view inequality as a self-perpetuating feedback loop involving the accumulation of wealth, the capture of institutions, and the decline of social mobility. When these forces work together, the economy becomes chaotic, with new order forming, initial conditions being important, and the economy getting caught in unstable equilibria. The paper examines these dynamics to place inequality within the moral and structural framework of complex capitalism. It suggests that sustained redistribution requires changes to the feedback architecture itself.

## Inequality's Changing Nature

For a long time, capitalist regimes have been known for having a lot of economic disparity. But in the late 1900s and early 2000s, its dynamics began a new phase that was very different from the past. The steady separation between the rich and the poor has transformed into a nonlinear feedback mechanism, which is a convoluted system that turns little disparities into enormous structural imbalances. The chaos theory metaphor of the odd attractor provides a convincing framework for understanding the self-stabilization of inequality, even when it seems unstable.

## The Feedback Structure of Wealth and Nonlinearity

Traditional economic theories assert linear causality: enhanced productivity leads to higher pay, and competition and market entry mitigates excessive accumulation. Complexity economics, conversely, regards feedback and nonlinearity as integral components of actual systems. Positive feedback loops, such as reinvesting capital gains, network advantages, and political capture, produce exponential outcomes instead of proportional ones.

## Emergent Order: The Strange Force in the Economy

A weird attractor appears in dynamical systems when deterministic rules lead to behavior that is both chaotic and organized. The wealth dynamics of the economy, driven by profit reinvestment, capital mobility, and institutional feedback, exhibit a trajectory like an attractor within the realm of inequality.

## Phase Transitions and the Separation of Chance

When inequality reaches a certain point, even tiny shocks can trigger systemic bifurcations, which are changes in how the economy and society work. These bifurcations, like those observed in fluid turbulence, demonstrate transitions from stability to chaos. Historical evidence demonstrates that periods of pronounced inequality often precede crises and populist uprisings.

## The Entropy of Power: Institutional Lock-In and Rentier Dynamics

Over time, the concentration of wealth causes institutional entropy, making systems less flexible and less able to generate new ideas. A small group of people with a lot of economic power creates a network of behaviors that seek rent, political capture, and cultural justification, which keeps getting stronger.

## For a Moral Ecology of Giving Back

We can't merely tweak the settings of the feedback architecture; we need to reinvent it to move away from the weird allure of inequality. Complexity economics aligns with moral philosophy: we should view success as an ecological state rather than a mechanical one.

## Conclusion: Staying Away from the Attractor

The weird attractor of inequality reveals that the economy's fundamental mechanisms stabilize by making things chaotic. The concentration of wealth is not a random distortion; it is an emergent trait of nonlinear feedback systems. You need to adjust the feedback loops that make up this path to change it.

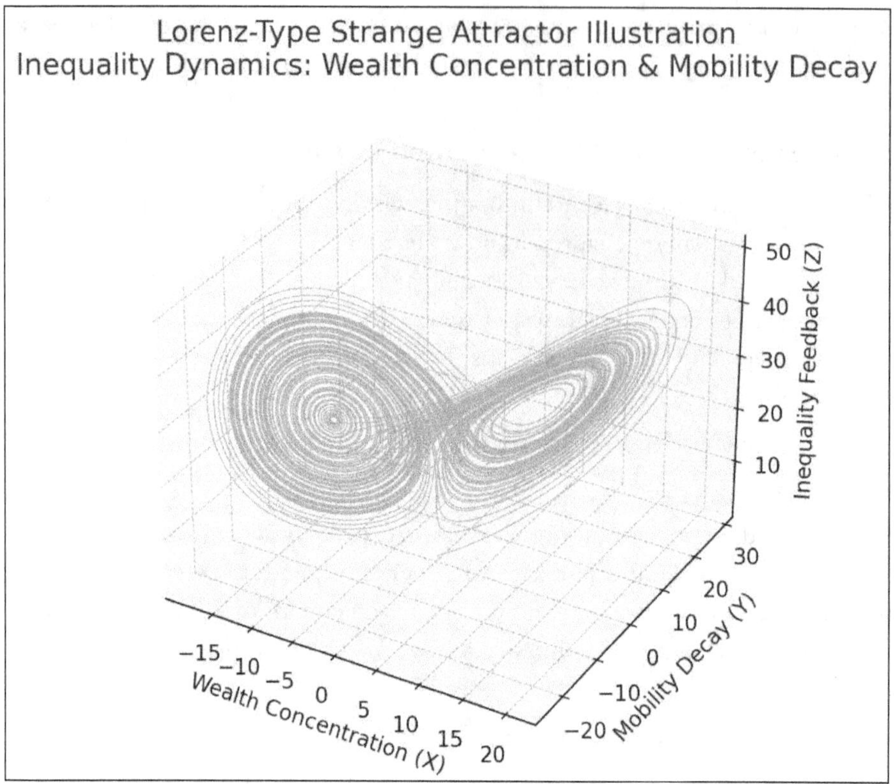


This is an illustration of a Lorenz-Type Strange Attractor of Inequality Dynamics: A simulated phase space showing how wealth concentration and mobility decay.

# The Rise of Oligarchy in America: How Complex Adaptive Systems Ended Equal Opportunity

## Abstract

The persistent existence and resurrection of oligarchy, governance by a small, wealthy elite, represents a conundrum for modern democratic nations that profess a dedication to equitable opportunity and social mobility. Oligarchic dynamics appear to be not outliers but enduring outcomes of socio-economic growth, from ancient Athens to modern America. Complexity economics and the study of complex adaptive systems (CAS) offer a powerful way to understand how wealth concentration, institutional feedback loops, and adaptive social behaviors slowly make it harder for everyone to have the same opportunities, keeping elites in power and hindering social mobility.

## Oligarchy as a New Trait

Within the framework of Complex Adaptive Systems (CAS), oligarchy is an emergent trait that develops from the interactions of agents (individuals, corporations, governments) in a system defined by nonlinear feedback loops. Like ecosystems that are mostly composed of a few highly adaptive species, economies tend to generate substantial wealth through compounding returns on capital, network effects, and policy capture. Thomas Piketty's "Capital in the Twenty-First Century" illustrates how $r > g$ (the return on capital exceeds economic growth) exacerbates inequality and reinforces oligarchic tendencies. Oligarchy doesn't emerge just because one person wants it; it happens when different adaptive techniques, such as corporate lobbying, dynastic wealth preservation, and financialization, work together to modify the rules of the game in their favor.

## Path Dependence and Loops of Feedback

Path dependence and positive feedback loops are two essential principles in CAS. When wealth concentration reaches a certain level, elites can have a significant impact on politics. This can influence tax policy, regulatory structures, and labor markets in ways that maintain them in power. This generates a self-reinforcing attractor state: political power comes from inequality, which makes inequality even worse. This dynamic can be thought of as a phase transition: societies can go back and forth between relatively open, competitive conditions and oligarchic supremacy. This is because of shocks like wars, revolutions, regulatory resets, and rapid innovation. Without these kinds of shocks, the system evolves toward a steady state in which upward mobility slows, and everyone has the same chance to succeed.

## The End of Equal Opportunity

Fair access to education, markets, and political involvement is necessary for equal opportunity, which is the foundation of liberal democracy. A CAS study shows that when inequality exceeds certain levels, mobility stops working. Kids born into poverty stay stuck because of structural impediments, while the rich get ahead by going to prestigious schools, inheriting money, and making connections through social networks. This looks like a coordination trap in game theory: people who act rationally make things worse because it costs money to change things without improving the system. The result is a collectively suboptimal equilibrium, an oligarchy that persists despite widespread belief in meritocracy ("pulling yourself up by the bootstraps").

Some examples from the past and now.

During the late Republic in ancient Rome, the rich took control of territory, troops were loyal to generals instead of the Senate, and power eventually became centralized in the empire. This was a path that favored a small group of people. During the Gilded Age in America (1870–1910), industrial monopolists like Rockefeller and Carnegie demonstrated how oligarchy can grow through political lobbying, technological advantage, and the suppression of worker organization. Since 1980, deregulation, globalization, and financialization have enabled the top 0.1% to capture an unfairly large share of the country's income. At the same time, intergenerational mobility has decreased to record lows.

Complexity, chaos, and lack of stability.

Chaos theory and CAS say that systems locked in unbalanced states become weaker. Extreme inequality is related to division, a lack of trust, and societal unrest. Oligarchy is an odd attractor in terms of phase space. It is steady but unstable, and if slight adjustments push the system past certain thresholds, it could break down (into revolution or populist authoritarianism).

## Conclusion

The end of equal opportunity and the rise of oligarchy are not moral failures, but rather the result of complex adaptive dynamics. When we see oligarchy as a natural part of CAS, it changes how we think about it from a failure of democratic vigilance to a foreseeable, almost unavoidable, systemic tendency. The challenge for societies is to establish adaptive governance mechanisms—such as antitrust laws, wealth taxes, campaign finance reform, public investment, and expanded social safety nets—that periodically readjust the system to counter oligarchic influences and foster greater equality of opportunity.

The following image shows how the rise of oligarchy (on the y-axis) and equal opportunity (on the x-axis) are linked across time. As equal opportunity decreases, oligarchic dominance becomes the stable attractor, while systems with strong equal opportunity feedback tend to stay closer to democratic equilibrium.

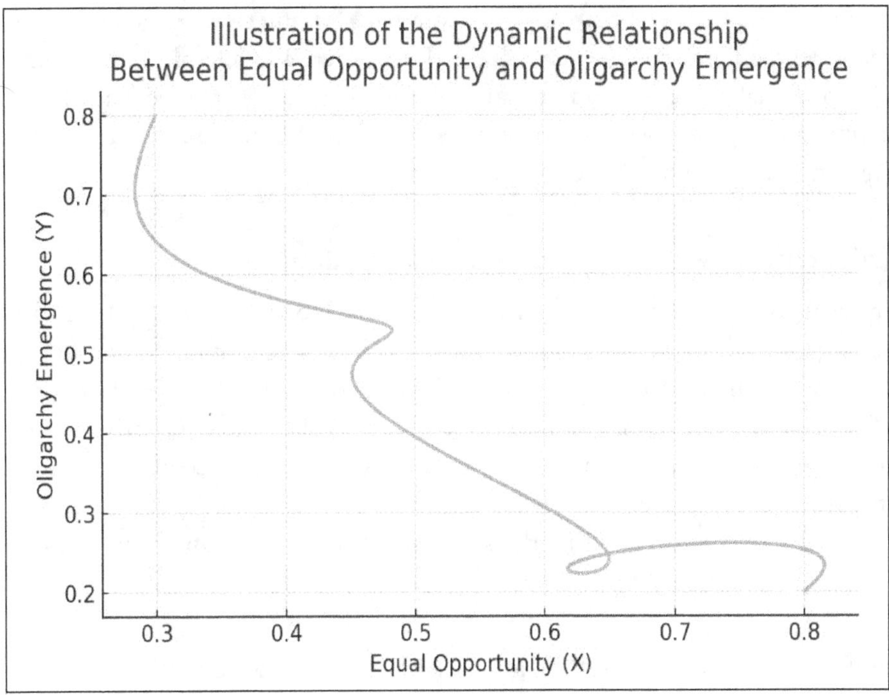

# The Emergence of Oligarchy as a Complex Adaptive System: Self-Organizing Inequality in American Society

## Abstract

Oligarchy, in which a small group controls a lot of money and political power, often happens not because someone planned it, but because decisions are made in a decentralized way. Complexity economics defines political economy as a complex adaptive system (CAS) consisting of interacting agents, whose micro-level adjustments generate macro-level order. When legal, financial, and informational systems promote capital accumulation, positive feedback loops connect wealth to policy power and back to riches, generating a cycle of inequality that perpetuates itself.

## Oligarchy as a System That Adapts and Changes

In terms of CAS, households, firms, platforms, lobbyists, and regulators are all adaptive agents that are connected by markets and institutions. Local optimization, such as reduced taxes on capital, regulatory arbitrage, and network effects, makes the benefits of incumbency even higher. Selection mechanisms (earnings, campaign wins, attention) reward techniques that centralize authority, which cause route dependence and lock-in. Rich-club development and preferred attachment in networks shift influence toward hubs, where minor advantages accumulate over time.

## Self-Organizing Inequality and Oligarchic Attractors

Inequality tends to rise empirically when after-tax gains on capital exceed growth rates, when market power escalates, and when union density diminishes. In these types of administrations, wealth concentration acts like a magnet: once trajectories join it, internal feedbacks (campaign money, lobbying, media ownership, philanthropic policy) keep the pattern stable. The Gilens-Page finding that economic elites and organized corporate groups are powerful predictors of policy change while common citizens have little effect on their own is a good example of this attractor on a large scale.

From the perspective of nonlinear dynamics, even slight parameter changes (such as loosening campaign finance restrictions or lowering antitrust thresholds) might push the system over the edge. Responses are very sensitive to the first conditions and shocks that occur near these thresholds. Institutional degradation and polarization can suddenly accelerate, triggering crisis cascades and swift changes in administration.

## Examples from history and comparison

Historical examples, from the late Roman Republic to the transition after the Soviet Union, show a trend toward oligarchic consolidation when wealth and coercive authority converge. In the contemporary United States, increasing CEO-to-worker compensation ratios, intensified common ownership and concentration in essential sectors, and the proliferation of money in politics generate reinforcing pathways for elite power.

## How Positive Feedback Works

The compound advantage is that capital income and capital gains grow faster than wages, especially when tax policies favor capital.

Market power: platform economies and intellectual property create longer-lasting monopoly and monopsony rents; concentration makes it harder to negotiate wages.

Policy capture: lobbying and campaign money change the laws to help those already in office, while politicized philanthropy makes it harder to change policy.

Belief dynamics: tales of meritocracy and "just deserts" diminish support for redistribution, even amid declining mobility.

## Effects on Democratic Stability

When inequality rises, representation gets skewed, funding for public goods decreases, and distrust between groups grows. Polarization and economic instability work together to make illiberal inclinations more likely. In terms of CAS, the democracy equilibrium is less stable since it takes more corrective forces to bounce back from shocks. To arrest the drift, you need to change the system's rules, such as giving more power to the negotiators, strengthening antitrust laws, and giving the government more money to spend.

## Making the System a Fairer Attractor

Rebuild countervailing power: support for labor organizing, sectoral bargaining, and co-determination to raise the wage floor.

Change the rules on competition and antitrust: don't let people act in ways that keep others out, keep an eye on the most powerful platforms, and limit the benefits of shared ownership.

Tax design that targets rents: minimum corporate taxes that apply to everyone, progressive taxes on capital income, and taxes on wealth transfers.

To reduce capture and information gaps, make political funding and the media more available to everyone.

Put money into initiatives that make a major difference, such as early childhood education, basic research, and infrastructure to reduce carbon emissions. This will make "g" go up for growth that includes everyone.

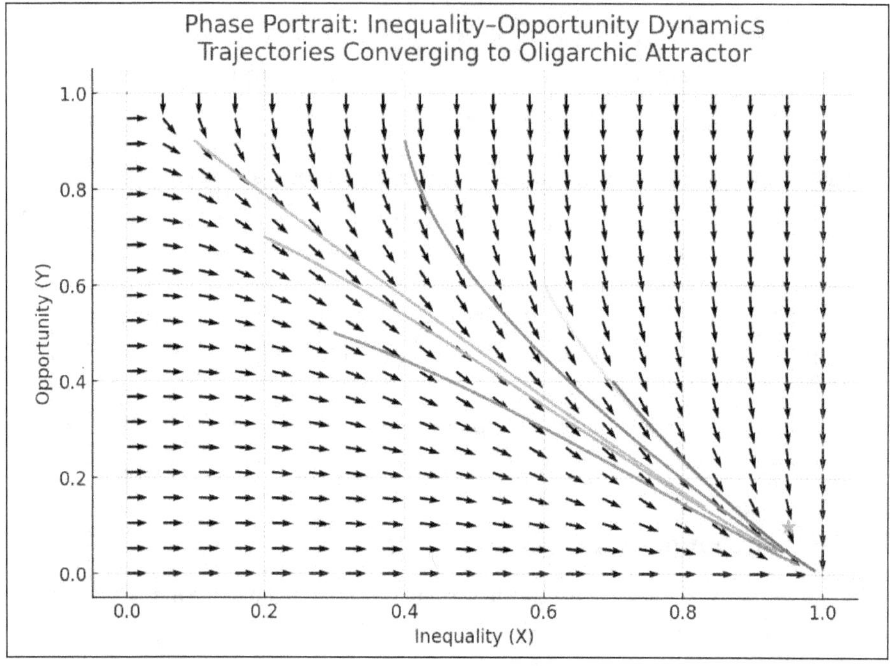


Figure X. A phase portrait
Inequality (x) and Opportunity (y), with a stylized oligarchic attractor (high x, low y).

# Strange Things That Happen in Economic Evolution: From Market Volatility to Institutional Collapse

## Abstract

This essay examines the metaphor and mechanism of strange attractors, which are important to chaos theory, in the context of how complex economic systems change over time. By examining how feedback loops, nonlinear adaptation, and institutional decay interact, this analysis shows that market volatility and systemic instability are not random events but natural features of self-organizing dynamics in capitalist systems. It argues that when unusual attractors in economic systems align with social and political resonance points—like growing debt, inequality, and loss of trust—economies can experience phase transitions that lead to institutional collapse.

## I. An Introduction to The Chaotic Heart of Capitalism

In the past, classical economics thought that stability was the natural balance of rational markets. But the late 20th and early 21st centuries have shown a different reality: economic systems work less like linear equilibria and more like chaotic weather systems. Prices, trust, and new ideas all work together to make things more unstable and provide order to chaos. In chaos theory, economies follow strange attractors, regions in a turbulent phase space where things remain stable. Their actions change when they are near certain regions.

## II. The Economic Phase Space and Strange Attractors

A weird attractor is the hidden shape that regulates how a nonlinear system changes over time in chaos theory. In economics, these kinds of attractors can be seen as multidimensional spaces defined by factors such as productivity, capital concentration, inequality, and institutional legitimacy. The system wanders through its phase space in intricate ways as various variables interact. It seldom repeats itself, but it never leaves the shape of its attractor.

## III. Evolutionary Economics and the Sources of Instability

Two evolutionary economists, Joseph Schumpeter and Brian Arthur, realized that capitalism doesn't grow steadily. Instead, it passes through cycles of creative destruction. When a new technology emerges, such as steam, electricity, computers, or AI, it affects the overall economy by creating a new attractor basin. But evolutionary adaptation also has certain flaws. When the system is too effective or too focused, it loses diversity and becomes less strong.

## IV. Market Volatility as a New Signal

People generally think of volatility as a sign of uncertainty, but it can also signal an unusual attractor that is changing the economy. The system tests the limits of its stability domain by changing prices, jobs, or capital flows. Information technologies speed up feedback cycles, which means markets are now very close to the brink of chaos, where order and disorder dwell together.

## V. The Breakdown of Institutions and the Loss of Coherence

Governments, central banks, and legal systems used to be stable institutions that could handle shocks and restore normalcy. But as things get more intricate, they have less power to influence how feedback loops work. When inequality, debt, and distrust reach a certain point, the institutional attractor loses its cohesion.

## VI. For a Moral Ecology of Economic Order

If weird attractors reveal how instability operates, then ethical and institutional design should be used to shape their edges in economic governance. Policies that encourage variety, openness, and equitable involvement make the stability basin bigger and push back the split. A moral ecology of markets wouldn't stop chaos; instead, it would guide it toward constructive change instead of destruction.

## VII. Conclusion

The weird attractor is a model and a metaphor for how modern economies fluctuate in ways that aren't always straight, like when markets go up and down or institutions fall apart. It indicates that instability is a normal element of complex systems, not an exception. So, the job of economic design is to sustain cooperation, justice, and adaptive resilience even when history is characterized by dysfunction and power asymmetries.

# Meta-Stable Democracies: Mapping the Chasm between Pluralism and Authoritarianism

## Abstract

Many people think of democracy as a stable political system; however, this is not true, as democracy is highly unstable. Democracies are meta-stable systems that only last when they are supported by cultural norms, faith in institutions, economic inclusiveness, and a shared sense of civic identity. This essay examines the blurry line between pluralism and authoritarianism, drawing on ideas from complexity theory, political science, and social psychology. It asserts that democracies do not disintegrate merely because of sudden coups or revolutions; instead, they decline through gradual feedback loops that erode norms, intensify polarization, reduce institutional autonomy, and delegitimize political opposition. Democratic systems are particularly vulnerable during periods of economic disparity and information fragmentation, as phase transitions may propel them towards authoritarian attractor states. You need to grasp this meta-stability to develop methods to strengthen democracy again.

## I. Introduction: Democracy as a System That Stays Stable

Political theory has long viewed democracy as a stable state: if a country accepts democratic government, it is thought to remain that way unless something terrible happens. Empirical evidence from the last century, from interwar Europe to present-day South and Central America, suggests a different narrative. Democracies frequently get worse over time, but they don't always fall apart completely. There are still elections, courts, and legislatures that assemble. People are starting to feel like the public realm is growing worse, though.

The concept of meta-stability derives from thermodynamics and complexity research. It describes systems that remain stable only when actively maintained. A meta-stable equilibrium is near the margin of a basin of attraction. It is sturdy on the outside, yet it doesn't like changes. Even a little force can shift the balance of a democracy, making it more like an oligarchy, authoritarian populism, or one-party domination. This is like a ball that is stuck in a narrow valley. In other words, democracy can't work on its own. It needs to be made again and again through activities that follow common rules, build trust amongst people, and make things seem real. When these things break down, democracy starts to transform from the inside out.

## II. The Nonlinear Dynamics of Political Systems and the Theory of Complexity

Democracy doesn't stay stable just because of formal rules. It's the way feedback loops work in politics, the economy, and culture that does so. Complexity theory posits that modest inputs can yield substantial systemic effects as a system approaches a critical threshold.

Some of the most important feedback loops are:

- Democratic Feedback Loop (Stabilizing): People are more likely to follow democratic rules if they trust institutions. Pluralistic competition makes people want to work together. It's okay to disagree politically with someone if you share a civic identity.

- Breaking the cycle of authoritarian feedback: Less trust means less involvement and greater doubt. Polarization makes people more likely to hold strong ideas and use language that doesn't back down. Factional identification sees disagreement as betrayal.

As these loops shift, democratic systems can undergo phase transitions, meaning the underlying assumptions about how things should work can change rapidly. When a political society views competition as a matter of life and death rather than a matter of procedure, the political system becomes increasingly authoritarian.

## III. Economic Inequality and the Loss of Shared Interests

Democratic government is based on the idea that the system gives everyone a fair chance and power. When the gap between rich and poor gets bigger:

1. The wealthy wield excessive influence over political financing, policy formulation, and legislation.

2. People are less sure that competition is fair because the middle class's security is getting worse.

3. People who are left behind are more likely to believe stories about betrayal, scapegoating, and conspiracy theories.

Thomas Piketty has shown that market economies without redistributive mechanisms that counteract wealth concentration naturally move toward greater wealth concentration. Daron Acemoglu and James Robinson argue that when economic power is concentrated, it often leads to political institutions that favor oligarchy over democracy. Inequality is a structural stressor that undermines democracy's legitimacy and makes people more receptive to authoritarian promises.

## IV. Identity Polarization and the Decline of Democratic Values

The idea of mutual recognition is what makes pluralistic democracy operate. People accept that their opponents are valid members of the government. But when political and cultural identities clash, party competition becomes a conflict without victors. Henri Tajfel's social identity theory exemplifies the human inclination towards in-group identification and out-group distinction. Populist movements now use this to imply that they speak for the "real people" against foes within.

When political differences become moral and existential, betrayal becomes compromise, institutions become battlefields, and violence becomes possible. This is the psychological center of the fall of democracy.

## V. Information Environments and the Fragmentation of Collective Reality

A shared set of facts is necessary for democracy. But current media ecosystems make it harder to know things. Cass Sunstein shows that algorithmic systems encourage anger, speed up radicalization, and keep people in echo chambers.

When different groups live in different worlds: Facts can't end arguments. Emotion replaces thought and reason. The prize of political struggle is who gets to tell the story.

Authoritarians don't have to convince people; they just have to wear them out. Confusion becomes a political tool.

## VI. The Purpose of Authoritarian Drift

When losing isn't an option, a democracy turns into an authoritarian system.

If political groupings believe that: If you lose power, you lose culture. You can't take away someone's economic power, or opponents are inherently illegitimate,

At that point, democratic processes stop being ways to maintain stability. Elections don't settle competition anymore; they make it worse.

## VII. Re-Stabilizing Democracies That Aren't Stable

To make democracy strong again, interventions need to focus on the system's feedback loops:

1. To rebuild a common economic stake, we need to reduce severe inequality.

2. To stop opportunistic capture, give institutions more freedom.

3. Rebuild a civic identity that encompasses everyone to resist tribalism within factions.

4. Rebuild the public epistemic infrastructure to bring back a common reality.

Democracy doesn't last because people don't like it. It persists because the conditions make pluralism reasonable, stable, and beneficial for most people.

## Conclusion

Democracies can only last if they work hard to sustain the systems of trust, legitimacy, identity, and inclusiveness that sustain them. When these underpinnings deteriorate, democratic systems do not collapse; rather, they gradually and subtly transform into authoritarian regimes that appear democratic but lack the essence of plurality.

This curve depicts how polarization may turn a political system from pluralism to authoritarianism as polarization increases.

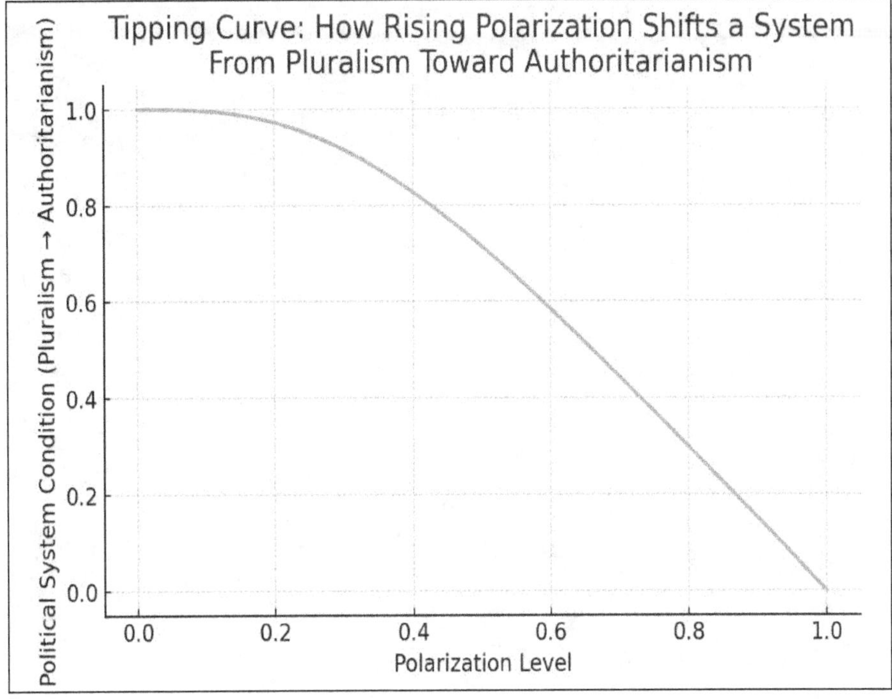

## Chapter 2

# Chaos Theory and Social Dynamics

## Chaos Theory and the Dynamics of Democratic Instability: Political Polarization and Income Inequality

### Abstract

This essay employs the principles of chaos theory to analyze the behavior of democratic societies experiencing profound political polarization and considerable income inequality. Chaos theory examines the dynamics of nonlinear, sensitive systems within complex systems, offering insights into how these conditions induce instability, diminish predictability, and increase the likelihood of systemic tipping points. This essay posits that polarization and inequality generate mutually reinforcing cycles that drive democratic societies toward imminent chaotic collapse, employing ideas such as sensitive dependence on initial conditions, feedback loops, strange attractors, and phase transitions. Policy implications require structural reforms that reduce feedback loops and restore systemic stability. There is also a chaos theory phase-space depiction showing how rising political polarization and income disparity, together with a decline in democratic stability, lead to a steady state in the phase space, which causes society to fall apart.

### Introduction

People often think of democratic countries as self-regulating systems in which public opinion, institutional checks and balances, and regular elections work together to keep the government stable. However, when societies are severely divided and have significant income inequality, their dynamics become less stable and more unpredictable. Chaos theory, which was first employed in math and science to investigate nonlinear dynamical systems, can help us understand why democracies like this one become increasingly fragile and subject to unexpected change over time.

## Sensitive Dependence on Initial Conditions

According to chaos theory, the "butterfly effect" states that slight changes in initial conditions can have a significant impact. In an unjust and divided democracy, even minor things like a fiery speech, a popular social media post, or a narrow court verdict can cause significant political problems. People respond more strongly when they don't trust one another, when they see things through a negative lens, and when they are more divided by identity.

## Feedback Loops That Don't Go Straight

The connection between income inequality and political polarization is a good example of a feedback loop that doesn't follow a straight line. Economic inequality breeds discontent and populist movements, widening ideological gaps. In turn, polarization causes policy paralysis and leads elites to take over institutions, worsening inequality. These forces act together to move the system away from equilibrium, making it harder to return to stability with small perturbations.

## Strange Attractors and Path Dependence

"Strange attractors" are patterns that a chaotic system moves toward, but they never happen the same way twice. Democracies marked by entrenched polarization and inequality often experience repeating cycles of political crises, encompassing mobilization, reaction, legislative gridlock, and fresh discontent. Path dependence, the propensity for historical trajectories to constrain future opportunities, renders these cycles difficult to transcend without altering the institutional incentives and material conditions that sustain them.

## Changes in Phase and Tipping Points

Chaos theory also discusses phase transitions, in which small disturbances can lead to large changes in quality. In a split democracy, this might mean that democratic norms suddenly break down, large protests quickly emerge, or democratic backsliding begins. These changes can happen without much notice and be driven by factors that wouldn't matter in a more stable system, because the system is already in a high-energy, unstable state.

## Loss of Predictability

Even if chaotic systems are deterministic, it's challenging to predict what will happen over a long period, as small errors accumulate and grow. Likewise, while the demise of democracy in a divided and inequitable society is not pre-determined, forecasting the exact date and characteristics of such a demise is difficult. Because things are less predictable, it is harder to govern; reactionary techniques are now the norm rather than preventive ones.

## Conclusion

When you use chaos theory to look at polarized, unequal democracies, you can see that these kinds of systems are always about to break down. They are sensitive to little things, have nonlinear feedback loops, go through the same crisis patterns over and over, and are likely to reach tipping points. To restore systemic stability, policymakers need to address polarization and economic inequality and reestablish networks of trust that bridge lines of difference. If these steps aren't taken, democracy could become a chaotic system where the outcomes are always unclear, and stability is always out of reach.

# A Chaos Theory Perspective on Monopolies, Market Concentration, and Income Inequality in American Society

## Abstract

This article examines the impact of monopolies and market concentration on income and wealth inequality in the United States from 1980 to 2024. We analyze the relationship between concentrated market power and inequality using chaos theory, uncovering non-linear processes that destabilize democratic and economic systems. We employ annual empirical data to construct a phase-space diagram that contrasts the Herfindahl–Hirschman Index (HHI) of market concentration with the Gini coefficient of income inequality. The results reveal how inequality and concentration work together to keep inequality running in a loop. This trend began in the early Reagan Administration, when enforcing antitrust laws was less important, and deregulation was favored.

## Theoretical Framework

Classical economic theory often asserts that markets naturally attain equilibrium through competition. But this balance of competition is disrupted when too many companies work together. Chaos theory provides a useful framework for understanding the unpredictable but structured dynamics that emerge from these feedback loops. Positive feedback loops, in which greater concentration worsens inequity and then reinforces it, are like attractors in dynamic systems. Over time, this renders political and economic systems less stable.

There are many links between concentration and inequality:

1. Wage suppression is due to monopsony power in labor markets.

2. Monopoly pricing that allows capital owners to extract rent from others.

3. Digital platforms and network effects made winner-take-all dynamics even stronger.

4. Barriers to entry that make it hard to establish a business and advance in life.

5. Political capture is when big firms use their position to modify rules to stay ahead of the game.

6. Wealth and opportunity are concentrated in specific regions.

## Example from 1980 to 2024

To empirically examine the relationship, we compare the Herfindahl–Hirschman Index (HHI), which measures market concentration, with the Gini coefficient, a standard measure of income inequality, from 1980 to 2024. The chaos-theory phase diagram below depicts a looping path, indicating a cycle that gets stronger rather than a straight line.

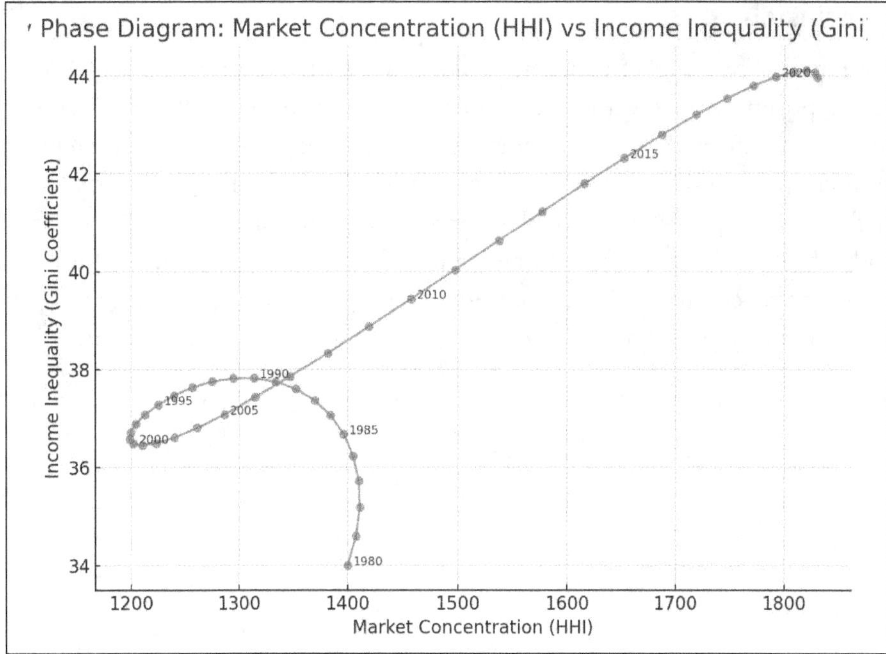


The phase diagram indicates that as market concentration (HHI) increased, so did income disparity (Gini). But the path isn't straight; it includes hills and what look like loops. This shows how shocks in politics, technology, and the law temporarily transformed the relationship. For example, the way the system changed in the early 1980s was due to antitrust enforcement, and the way it changed in the 1990s was due to deregulation. The emergence of digital platforms after 2008 produced a new draw that made the economy more concentrated and unequal.

## Examples of Cases

These dynamics can be seen in action in a number of industries:

- Technology: Companies like Amazon, Google, and Meta used network effects to take over markets, making shareholders and CEOs very rich, but making it harder for workers to negotiate.

- Healthcare/Pharmaceuticals: The concentration of the pharmaceutical market has led to higher drug prices, worsening rent extraction, and increasing inequality.

- Finance: Merging banks and investing services has increased systemic risk and concentrated wealth among the rich.

## Conclusion

Monopolies and market concentration are not merely economic events; they are deeply intertwined with the structural framework of inequality in American society. The chaos-theory view indicates that inequality and concentration have complicated, non-linear effects on each other that can't be fixed with easy fixes. If these trends persist, they could undermine both the fairness of the economy and the strength of American democracy. We need strong antitrust enforcement, improved safeguards for workers, and programs that shift money around to break the cycle and restore economic fairness.

# The Political Economy of Cognitive Capture

## Abstract

In modern political economy, the most consequential conflicts rarely involve only the direct ownership of productive resources. They are more interested in changing how others view things, what they think is "common sense," and how they see their own interests. Cognitive capture occurs when powerful economic and institutional groups systematically shape how people think, believe, and interpret. This leads people to believe stories that are good for those in power, even though these stories are bad for their own material well-being. Cognitive capture is more than just propaganda; it's not just about misleading information. It is a structural condition in which certain interpretations become so established that alternatives appear unthinkable, unreasonable, or illegitimate.

The Political Economy of Cognitive Capture looks at how the concentration of economic power in material things is supported and validated by cultural, psychological, and semiotic frameworks. The goal of this essay is to examine how cognitive capture came to be, how it persists, and how it affects political behavior, economic policy, and the limits of collective action.

In classical political economy, power was primarily derived from ownership of capital and productive goods. But as markets and governments have become more intricate, the ways people can change them have shifted from direct force to indirect methods that shape people's expectations, norms, and ways of looking at things. Cognitive capture occurs when organizations unite to establish a stable, self-reinforcing narrative alignment.

Psychological Anchors and the Internalization of Power. Cognitive capture relies on stable psychological mechanisms that influence individuals' comprehension and formulation of their political identities. Availability heuristics, status quo bias, identity signaling, and learned helplessness all help keep the popular stories going. Cognitive capture is most effective when individuals believe they are engaging in free thought, even though their interpretive frameworks are influenced by external factors.

The Market for Attention and the Rise of Narrative Platforms. In today's digital economy, attention is the most precious resource. Facebook, TikTok, X, and YouTube don't need to deliberately push beliefs. Their goal of getting as many people as possible to interact with their content leads to polarization, tribalism, and content that makes people feel strongly. On the same hand, having a few companies own much of the media limits the kinds of public discussion that are acceptable.

Policy Design Amid Cognitive Capture. In democratic democracies, economic policy depends on public opinion. When cognitive capture affects beliefs, policies end up serving the interests of the elite. Setting the agenda takes the public's attention away from structural inequity. It is moral to cut spending and loosen regulations. Policy fields are specialized areas that the general public cannot access.

Cognitive capture keeps power in place for now, but it makes the system weaker in the long run. It delays necessary reforms until the circumstances for collapse arise by keeping people from recognizing structural risks such as inequality, monopolistic power, and the ecological crisis. Systems that don't know when they're wrong can't correct them.

Toward Freedom of Thought. To be free from cognitive captivity, we need to change the way things are set up, not only make people smarter. We need a media system that is democratic, civic education that focuses on analyzing ideas, and a return to working together. These do not impose consensus; instead, they expand the domain of understanding essential for genuine democratic discourse.

## Conclusion

Cognitive capture is a systematic phenomenon that connects popular belief with concentrated authority by altering the boundaries of political imagination. It makes political economies more stable, but less able to change, which is needed for long-term resilience. To fight cognitive capture, a community needs to be able to see, picture, and act on other futures again.

# Inequality as a Unique Attractor: A Chaos-Theoretic Framework for Wealth Concentration

## Abstract

Wealth disparity has historically been a defining trait of capitalist societies, often revealed through capital accumulation, preferential returns, and network effects. Complexity economics, conversely, provides a more nuanced and pessimistic perspective: it posits that inequality may not signal a break from equilibrium but rather a peculiar attractor within the socioeconomic system. Wealth concentration, political capture, and social stability may generate a non-linear attractor that keeps inequality going even when reforms are tried. This is similar to chaos theory, in which deterministic laws lead to unpredictable yet bounded paths.

## The Complexity Perspective

Positive feedback loops strengthen this attraction. First, the idea that $r > g$, which Thomas Piketty saw in the way capital accumulates, makes the impacts of wealth stronger. Second, political feedback shapes legislation to safeguard the positions of the rich and powerful, ensuring that wealth leads to power. Third, network effects and monopolistic market arrangements yield returns that are too high for top corporations and their corporate hierarchies. Finally, strong cultural beliefs in meritocracy make discrepancies seem natural, thereby reducing the likelihood of calls for redistribution. After each disturbance, these feedbacks work together to bring the system's trajectories back into focus.

## Conclusion

People should talk about the economy differently if they think of inequality as a peculiar attractor. Redistribution may temporarily alter the paths of things, but the system will always return to concentration until fundamental feedback loops are broken. So, policymakers need to do more than just make things fairer. They also need to modify the shape of the phase space itself by creating a new attractor aligned with broad-based prosperity, economic justice, and social stability. Without this kind of change in the system, societies will remain stuck in the fractal cycle of wealth, oscillating between short-term reforms and long-term inequalities.

# Self-Organized Criticality in Capitalist Economies

## Abstract

This essay discusses self-organized criticality (SOC) as a framework for examining the built-in instability, adaptive resilience, and moral problems in modern capitalist economies. Drawing on complexity theory, network dynamics, and empirical political economy, it argues that capitalism approaches critical thresholds at which slight disruptions can trigger systemic transformation. Crises are not external disruptions; instead, they represent internal reorganizations of the system's complexity. The analysis links SOC dynamics to inequality, financial contagion, and institutional fragility, helping us understand how capitalism cycles through growth and decline.

## 1. Introduction

In capitalist economies, growth, crisis, adaptation, and renewal work together in complex ways. These repeating patterns show that capitalism is not a stable equilibrium system, but rather a complex adaptive structure that organizes itself. Self-organized criticality (SOC) is a useful framework for understanding and studying this phenomenon. It was thought of by physicist Per Bak. SOC refers to systems that naturally gravitate toward a critical state in which even minor changes can have significant effects. In economic systems, these processes manifest in business cycles, speculative bubbles, technological disruptions, and institutional resets.

In this view, capitalist economies are like heaps of money, people, and technology, with each grain representing a small investment, a new idea, or a bet. The pile grows larger, but the inside becomes more unstable and dependent. A single grain, like a poor loan, a regulatory failure, or a geopolitical catastrophe, can start an avalanche. The crisis that follows is not unusual; it is a necessary means for the system to get back on track. Capitalism constantly works on the border of chaos, when things are both in order and out of order.

## 2. Where Self-Organized Criticality Comes From

The concept of self-organized criticality was initially introduced by Bak, Tang, and Wiesenfeld in 1987 to elucidate the natural organization of complex systems toward a critical threshold. In their sandpile model, the way the pile is built determines whether grains of sand falling on it trigger minor slides or massive avalanches. The system gradually settles into a steady state in which the sizes of avalanches follow a power-law distribution, with many minor events and only a few large ones. The same mathematical patterns can be found in earthquakes, forest fires, neural networks, and, most crucially, in macroeconomic cycles and financial markets.

Bak's idea was that systems get critical when they get too complicated. In economies, fresh ideas, competition, and financial leverage all work together to create feedback loops that operate like self-tuning mechanisms. Capitalism doesn't need an outside factor to become unstable; it naturally moves in that direction. This perspective redefines crises as inherent to the system's evolution rather than as exogenous disruptions.

## 3. Capitalism on the Edge of Chaos

The edge-of-chaos paradigm posits that adaptive systems achieve maximal creativity and reactivity at the juncture of order and disorder. This is a terrific environment for capitalism to grow. Too many regulations stop new ideas from emerging, yet too much freedom can cause things to break apart. Capitalist systems self-regulate around this limit by going through cycles of boom and collapse. This creates dynamic equilibria that causes both social unrest and technological development.

This is what happens in the money markets. People feel more confident when asset prices rise, leverage increases, and things are more interconnected. These feedback loops make the system increasingly sensitive until it gets to a point where it can't handle it anymore. The next collapse, which may be the dot-com disaster of 2000 or the financial crisis of 2008, resets the system's complexity. So, every crisis is a chance to learn and make some connections stronger and others weaker. It hurts, but it helps.

## 4. Wealth Inequality and Legal Frameworks

Empirical studies of income and wealth distribution regularly reveal power-law connections, suggesting that a small fraction of the population holds a disproportionate share of resources. This is like how self-organized critical systems work, with a few huge avalanches and a lot of little ones. In economics, the concentration of wealth is both a cause and an effect of criticality. As capital accumulates, feedback mechanisms such as returns on capital, network benefits, and political influence exacerbate inequality.

The system is fragile because it scales like this. When too much money and power are concentrated in one place, the whole system can't respond as well to changing conditions. In these cases, a breakdown that arises only in one place might swiftly spread across the whole network. The 2008 crisis highlighted how concentrating risk in a few banks can affect people around the world. From the perspective of SOC, inequality is not only a social injustice but also an indication of systemic over-centralization approaching a critical limit.

## 5. Cascading Failure and Financial Contagion

Financial networks are like other complex adaptive systems in many ways. Banks, investors, and markets all depend on each other because they share information and money. In these kinds of systems, tiny changes in one location, such as defaults, rumors, or policy changes, can have tremendous effects worldwide. SOC illustrates why we can't know when some disasters will strike, even when they will. Avalanches occur at specified times and with certain amounts of force. This depends on how well the system is connected inside, not on shocks from outside.

The effects on policy are quite important. Interventions to reduce volatility may prevent minor corrective actions, potentially leading to the accumulation of systemic stress. The damage is devastating when the tension finally goes away. A system can only be genuinely robust if it can handle modest failures and fix itself without breaking down. Antifragility, a concept developed by Nassim Nicholas Taleb, posits that systems become more robust by embracing change rather than evading it. This thought goes along with the idea.

## 6. Adaptation of Institutions and Ethical Ecology

If capitalism inherently moves toward criticality, then moral and institutional evolution must focus on managing its border circumstances. Institutions help disperse surplus energy through taxes, social insurance, and public investment. When these buffers wear down, like when rules are relaxed, spending is cut, or corruption happens, the system can't keep instability in check. A moral economy is one that allows things to change while aiming to make them less harmful to people.

The concept of moral ecology expands the scope of SOC to encompass ethics alongside physics and economics. This view says that prosperity comes from keeping a dynamic balance; too much rigidity leads to stagnation, and too much volatility leads to collapse. Policies that encourage inclusiveness, education, and equal opportunity create feedback loops that keep things stable while allowing them to change over time.

## 7. Policy Implications and Complexity in Governance

Conventional macroeconomic policy aims for stability, assuming equilibrium as the norm. Complexity economics, informed by SOC, asserts that persistent disequilibrium is the standard. So, instead of trying to impose an order that never changes, governments and central banks need to keep systems on the edge of chaos under control.

You must be okay with not knowing everything in order to handle complexity properly. Regulatory frameworks should prioritize network transparency, diverse feedback, and redundancy. This implies letting people try things out in their own areas while keeping an eye on the whole planet. This way, creative destruction can happen without the whole system breaking down. This type of governance views the economy as an ecosystem to be nurtured, not a machine to be controlled.

## 8. Conclusion: Education on the Edge of Failure

Self-organized criticality redefines capitalism as a self-regulating system that learns from crises. Economic collapses do not signify failures of rationality; rather, they represent the system's evolutionary logic. By acknowledging this, politicians and communities can transition from the fallacy of control to stewardship—creating adaptive boundaries rather than suppressing instability. The ethical goal of the twenty-first century is not to remove volatility but to humanize it. Capitalism will persist at the precipice of chaos; it is our duty to ensure that its inventive energies are directed towards universal prosperity rather than systemic failure.

# Political Polarization as a Chaotic Divergence in Democratic Systems

## Abstract

This essay defines political polarization as a disorderly split in democratic institutions. This happens when institutional, social, and informational ecosystems lose their stabilizing feedback loops. Drawing on complexity economics, chaos theory, network science, game theory, and social psychology, the research outlines the progression of democracies from stable pluralism to unstable polarization, ultimately leading to authoritarian attractors. The bifurcation metaphor clarifies how incremental changes in parameter conditions, such as economic disparity, institutional deterioration, elite signaling, media fragmentation, identity-group sorting, and algorithmic manipulation, can trigger abrupt qualitative shifts in political behavior. The result is a system that swings back and forth in ways that are hard to foresee, makes things worse at both ends, breaks down trust, inhibits people from talking about things, and is more likely to be taken over by an autocrat.

## Introduction: Democracy on the Edge of Chaos.

Democracy is a system that changes constantly. It's a pluralistic equilibrium held together not by fixed institutions but by processes of negotiation, contestation, and information sharing that occur all the time. In typical situations, these mechanisms make things stable by making them different. This is because diverse interests and identities interact within defined bounds, making political developments easier to forecast. But when the system's basic rules change too much, political rivalry stops being cyclical and becomes chaotic. The system does not stabilize; rather, it disintegrates, becoming polarized and bifurcating, resulting in unpredictable fluctuations, radicalization, and the emergence of anti-democratic forces. This essay employs the concept of chaotic bifurcation to analyze contemporary polarization, particularly in the United States, and is applicable to other democracies experiencing similar structural challenges. By framing polarization as an emergent phenomenon within a nonlinear system, we can clarify the factors contributing to its apparent exponential growth, the unexpected collapse of institutional safeguards, and the abrupt shift of societies from pluralistic equilibrium to democratic disintegration.

## Bifurcation Theory and Democratic Dynamics

1. What does it mean to bifurcate? A bifurcation in nonlinear dynamics occurs when a slight change in a system parameter alters its long-term behavior. A system that used to have only one stable attractor now has two or more competing attractors. Each of these reflects a conceivable long-term state. In politics, a bifurcation means the democratic system is no longer advancing toward a moderate balance or consensus; instead, it is being dragged toward two attractors that are growing farther apart and increasingly hostile.

2. Splitting in a chaotic way. A regular bifurcation is better than a chaotic bifurcation since the system doesn't settle into a pattern that can be predicted. Instead, it indicates that it is sensitive to initial conditions, amplifies nonlinearly, is path-dependent, loses stability in equilibrium, and exhibits oscillations that grow over time. Democracies don't have normal politics anymore. Their politics are unstable because tales, identities, and institutions clash in ways that don't always make sense.

3. The political system is a space that changes over time. We might think of a political system as a phase space with axes representing how far apart people are in their beliefs, how emotionally divided they are, how much they trust institutions, how much knowledge is lost, how unevenly money and wealth are distributed, and how well elites work together. Political actors band together into distinct interest groups when stabilizing factors lose strength. Information goes into silos, complaints build up, and polarization rises, all of which push the system toward a phase change.

4. The Factors Behind Democratic Bifurcation: Economic Inequality as a Cause of Instability. Inequality increases disorder, decreases coherence, and destabilizes equilibria. Diverse life experiences, elite capture, and status anxiety engender political preferences that differ significantly. This causes ideological distributions to be bimodal, undermining the political center.

The disintegration of a shared reality, the chaos of information, and the growth of conspiracy theories, echo chambers, misleading information, and algorithmic amplification. When individuals stop sharing reality, the mechanisms that prevent things from getting too extreme break down, and then polarization can go crazy. Sorting identities and the growth of tribal pull factors. When people sort themselves by demographics, location, and culture, they become more similar within their groups and more hostile toward outsiders. A political dispute becomes existential, leading to heightened emotional intensity and a reduced readiness to compromise.

5. The decline of institutions and the weakening of feedback control. When institutions like courts, legislatures, electoral systems, and the media are weaker, they can't maintain stability. Political actors take advantage of these weaknesses to employ zero-sum tactics, which make matters worse and upset the balance. The elite are becoming more divided, and their strategies are becoming more radical. Elites make division worse by disregarding the rules, employing extreme rhetoric, and making tribal identity stronger. Elite polarization increases mass polarization through signaling processes.

6. Algorithmic Acceleration and the Dynamics of Attention. Algorithms on social media amplify rage, moral extremism, and identity conflict. These systems increase the Lyapunov exponent of democratic discourse, meaning that even tiny adjustments can swiftly escalate into major problems.

## The Systemic Mechanism: From Polarization to Chaotic Bifurcation

There are four things that cause chaotic bifurcation: stopping negative feedback, starting positive feedback loops, losing the center, and breaking apart transitional zones. The system splits into two attractors. It goes from a pluralistic equilibrium to macro-states that are hostile to each other and change in ways that can't be predicted.

## Polarization as a Precursor to Democratic Collapse

The authoritarian pull. As things get worse, authoritarian leaders declare they can provide order. People who are tired of disorder may put order ahead of democratic values. Strategic actors exploit instability. Political entrepreneurs weaponize polarization by portraying themselves as protectors of identity and adversaries of perceived dangers, mirroring historical instances of democratic erosion.

Stopping Chaotic Bifurcation: Restoring Systemic Stability. Two crucial things to do are to rebuild the middle class and close the gap between the rich and the poor. Strengthening democratic institutions. Improving the health of the information environment. Democracies can still end polarization by making the system more stable, lessening the structural factors that destabilize it.

## Conclusion

Democracy is at a crossroads. Modern democracies are at a highly pivotal stage in their history, where even little changes can have big effects. Polarization is structural and nonlinear, yet it can be undone with purposeful intervention. Understanding chaotic bifurcation shows that the only way to restore democracy is to restore the economic, institutional, and informational components that make pluralism viable.

# The Edge of Chaos: Innovation, Instability, and the Collapse of Shared Reality

## Abstract

Human societies have always evolved at the boundary between order and disorder. Too much rigidity suffocates creativity, too much chaos dissolves coherence. Complexity science refers to this critical threshold as the edge of chaos, a dynamic regime in which systems are maximally adaptive, innovative, and responsive to change. At this boundary, new patterns emerge, old structures dissolve, and transformative innovation becomes possible.

Yet the edge of chaos is not inherently benign. While it enables learning and creativity, it also carries the risk of fragmentation, instability, and collapse. In contemporary societies, particularly advanced democracies, the acceleration of technological innovation, economic complexity, and information flows has pushed social systems perilously close to this threshold. What once fostered pluralism and experimentation now increasingly undermines shared meaning, institutional legitimacy, and epistemic trust. This essay explores the paradox of the edge of chaos in modern societies: how the same forces that generate innovation also destabilize shared reality. Drawing on complexity theory, political economy, social psychology, and media studies, it argues that contemporary societies have crossed from productive complexity into epistemic fragmentation, where competing narratives no longer interact constructively but instead form self-reinforcing cognitive silos. The result is not merely polarization, but a deeper collapse of shared reality—an erosion of the common frameworks that make democratic coordination, collective problem-solving, and social trust possible.

## I. The Edge of Chaos in Complexity Theory

The concept of the edge of chaos originated in the study of complex adaptive systems, networks composed of interacting agents whose collective behavior cannot be reduced to the behavior of their individual components. Systems ranging from ecosystems to neural networks to economies exhibit a critical zone between equilibrium and randomness where adaptability peaks.

In highly ordered systems, behavior is predictable but brittle. Small shocks can propagate catastrophically because rigid structures cannot absorb disturbance. In highly chaotic systems, behavior is unpredictable and incoherent; signals dissolve into noise, preventing coordination. At the edge of chaos, however, systems display structured unpredictability—enough order to sustain coherence, enough disorder to allow experimentation and learning.

Biological evolution, for example, operates near this threshold. Genetic variation introduces disorder; selection pressures impose structure. Similarly, healthy economies rely on a balance between institutional stability and entrepreneurial disruption. Democracies depend on stable rules combined with open contestation of ideas.

Crucially, the edge of chaos is not a fixed point but a dynamic region. Systems can drift toward rigidity or collapse depending on feedback loops, external shocks, and internal incentives. The challenge for complex societies is not merely reaching this edge but remaining within its viable bounds.

## II. Innovation as a Destabilizing Force

Innovation is often celebrated as an unambiguous good—an engine of progress, efficiency, and human flourishing. Yet from a systems perspective, innovation is inherently destabilizing. Each technological or institutional breakthrough rewires incentive structures, redistributes power, and alters patterns of coordination.

Historically, societies absorbed innovation through relatively slow diffusion. Cultural norms, legal frameworks, and educational institutions adapted incrementally. Today, however, innovation cycles have compressed dramatically. Digital technologies, algorithmic systems, and globalized markets propagate change faster than social institutions can metabolize it.

Three interrelated domains illustrate this destabilization:

1.  Economic Innovation
    Financialization, platform economies, and automation have increased productivity while eroding traditional labor structures. Wealth concentrates through network effects, while precarity spreads across the workforce. This asymmetry generates both economic instability and moral dissonance—systems reward abstract capital flows more than socially embedded labor, weakening the perceived fairness of institutions.

2.  Technological Innovation
    Information technologies have radically lowered the cost of producing and disseminating narratives. Authority once mediated by expertise

and institutions is now flattened into algorithmically amplified attention markets. Truth competes with virality, and coherence competes with engagement.

3. Cultural Innovation
   Identity itself has become modular and performative. While this expands expressive freedom, it also fragments collective narratives. Shared symbols lose their integrative function, replaced by fluid micro-identities that resist common interpretation.

Innovation, in short, increases systemic degrees of freedom. Without compensatory mechanisms of integration, these freedoms push societies beyond the edge of productive complexity into disorder.

## III. From Pluralism to Epistemic Fragmentation

Pluralism, the coexistence of diverse perspectives within a shared framework, has long been a strength of democratic societies. It presupposes disagreement within a common epistemic space: shared facts, shared rules of evidence, and shared institutional arbiters.

Epistemic fragmentation occurs when this common space disintegrates. Competing narratives no longer contest interpretations of reality; they contest reality itself. Facts become tribal signals. Expertise becomes partisan. Institutions once trusted to adjudicate disputes are reframed as captured or illegitimate.

This shift reflects a deeper transformation in information ecology. Social media platforms and algorithmic curation systems optimize engagement rather than coherence. Content that provokes outrage, fear, or identity affirmation spreads more effectively than content that fosters understanding. Over time, individuals are nudged into self-reinforcing informational niches—echo chambers that amplify belief certainty while suppressing disconfirming evidence.

From a complexity perspective, these niches function as local attractors in cognitive phase space. Once individuals enter them, feedback loops stabilize belief systems regardless of external contradiction. The system loses its capacity for global coordination, even as local coherence intensifies. The result is not chaos in the sense of randomness, but pathological order, multiple internally consistent realities that cannot communicate meaningfully with one another.

## IV. The Psychological Dimension: Cognitive Load and Defensive Simplification

The collapse of shared reality is not merely technological or institutional; it is profoundly psychological. Human cognition evolved for small-group coordination, not for processing the relentless complexity of global systems.

As informational complexity increases, cognitive load rises. In the face of uncertainty, ambiguity, and rapid change, individuals seek psychological closure. Social psychology shows that under such conditions, people gravitate toward simplified narratives that reduce anxiety and restore a sense of control.

These narratives often exhibit common features:

- Moral dualism (good vs. evil)
- Personalization of systemic problems
- Scapegoating of out-groups
- Resistance to nuance or probabilistic reasoning

At the edge of chaos, such simplifications serve an adaptive function—reducing cognitive overload. But when widely adopted, they degrade collective intelligence. Societies trade epistemic humility for emotional certainty, sacrificing accuracy for coherence. Moreover, defensive simplification interacts with identity. Beliefs become entangled with self-concept and a sense of group belonging. To question a narrative is to threaten social bonds. This dynamic transforms disagreement into existential conflict, accelerating polarization and distrust.

## V. Institutions Under Strain: When Stabilizers Fail

Complex societies rely on institutions to dampen volatility and coordinate behavior across scales. Courts, scientific bodies, electoral systems, and media organizations historically functioned as stabilizing feedback mechanisms, absorbing shocks and translating complexity into manageable forms.

At the edge of chaos, these institutions face twin pressures:

1. External Acceleration
   The pace of social and technological change outstrips institutional adaptation. Rules designed for slower dynamics appear obsolete or arbitrary.

2.  Internal De-legitimation

> As narratives fragment, institutions are reinterpreted through partisan lenses. Neutral arbiters are reframed as adversaries. Procedural outcomes are rejected not because they fail, but because they contradict group identity.

Once institutional trust erodes, societies lose their primary tools for re-establishing shared reality. Disputes that once ended in acceptance now spiral into recursive conflict. Each institutional decision becomes another data point, reinforcing pre-existing beliefs.

This is a hallmark of systems that have crossed from the edge of chaos into structural instability: feedback loops amplify disturbances rather than dampen them.

## VI. Innovation Without Integration: A Systems Failure

The central failure of contemporary societies is not innovation itself, but innovation without integration. Complexity theory emphasizes that adaptive systems require both variation and selection, as well as exploration and constraint. When novelty proliferates faster than meaning-making structures can evolve, coherence dissolves.

Historically, shared rituals, narratives, and educational systems provided integrative capacity. Today, these functions are weakened by market incentives that reward fragmentation and novelty over synthesis and continuity. The result is a society rich in information but poor in wisdom, abundant in choice but starved of shared purpose. Innovation accelerates, but collective direction dissipates.

From a systems perspective, this represents a misalignment between micro-level incentives (attention, profit, identity signaling) and macro-level stability (social trust, democratic legitimacy, epistemic coherence). Left unchecked, such misalignment drives societies toward bifurcation—either authoritarian consolidation or chronic dysfunction.

## VII. Re-Stabilizing at the Edge: Conditions for Renewal

The edge of chaos need not culminate in collapse. Properly managed, it can become a site of renewal. The question is not how to eliminate complexity, but how to rebuild integrative capacity commensurate with systemic scale.

Several principles emerge:

1.  Epistemic Institutions Must Be Reinforced
    Societies require trust mechanisms for truth-seeking that are insulated from attention markets and partisan capture. Transparency alone is insufficient; legitimacy must be actively cultivated.

2.  Narrative Integration Matters
    Shared reality is sustained not only by facts, but by meaning. Societies need inclusive narratives that can accommodate diversity without dissolving coherence.

3.  Complexity Literacy Is Essential
    Education systems must equip citizens to reason probabilistically, tolerate ambiguity, and understand systemic causation. Without such literacy, complexity breeds fear rather than insight.

4.  Technological Incentives Must Be Realigned
    Platforms that shape collective cognition cannot be neutral about outcomes. Design choices influence epistemic health. Governance must reflect this reality.

Stability at the edge of chaos is an achievement, not a default. It requires deliberate design, ethical restraint, and institutional courage.

## Conclusion: The Choice at the Threshold

Modern societies stand at a critical threshold. The forces of innovation have propelled humanity into unprecedented complexity, expanding creative potential while eroding shared reality. At the edge of chaos, systems can either reorganize at a higher level of coherence or fragment into mutually unintelligible parts. The collapse of shared reality is not inevitable, but neither is renewal guaranteed. The outcome depends on whether societies can recognize complexity not as an enemy to be simplified away, but as a condition to be responsibly governed.

The edge of chaos is where futures are decided. It is a place of danger and possibility alike, where innovation can either deepen fragmentation or catalyze a more integrated, resilient, and humane social order.

# The Power–Capital Feedback Loop: A Lorenz Model of Oligarchy Formation

## Abstract

This essay models oligarchy formation as a nonlinear dynamical system governed by reinforcing feedback loops between capital concentration, political capture, and institutional decay. Drawing on chaos theory and Lorenz attractor dynamics, it demonstrates that modern economies evolve toward oligarchic dominance not as moral failure but as a mathematically stable phase-space attractor. The "Power–Capital Feedback Loop" explains why inequality persists, why reforms decay, and why democratic institutions collapse into plutocratic control even under repeated reform attempts. Oligarchy emerges not through conspiracy, but through deterministic systemic convergence.

## Introduction: Oligarchy as a Dynamical Attractor

Modern political economies are not drifting toward oligarchy. They are converging.

Classical political theory treats oligarchy as a form of corruption. Complexity economics reveals it as a *stable attractor*. This discussion introduces the **Power–Capital Feedback Loop (PCFL)**—a nonlinear dynamical model that explains why political power and capital concentration self-amplify, generating a Lorenz-like strange attractor in which democratic equilibria become metastable, and inequality becomes structurally locked in.

## The Three-State Lorenz Model of Political Economy

Let the system be defined by three interacting state variables:

| Variable | Symbol | Description |
| --- | --- | --- |
| Capital Concentration | C | Wealth and market power concentration |
| Political Capture | P | Degree of institutional control by elites |
| Social Mobility / Trust | T | Democratic legitimacy and mobility |

Where feedback coefficients represent regulatory strength, lobbying power, media influence, and legitimacy decay. The system exhibits chaotic but bounded trajectories that converge to oligarchic strange attractors.

## The Power–Capital Feedback Loop

The PCFL operates as follows:

1. Capital buys political influence
2. Political influence rewrites market rules
3. Market rules concentrate more capital
4. Legitimacy erodes
5. Reform capacity collapses
6. Capture accelerates

Each loop increases system entropy while strengthening elite dominance.

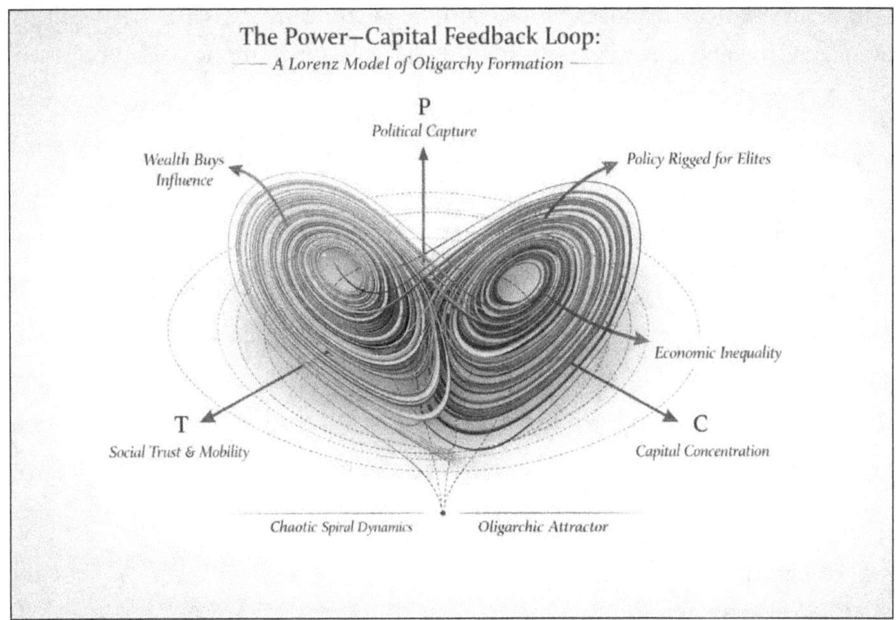


## Inequality as a Strange Attractor

Phase-space modeling reveals:

- Temporary egalitarian reforms are transient orbits
- Long-run trajectories spiral back to high-C/high-P states
- Inequality is not deviation—it is equilibrium

Oligarchy is the basin of attraction.

## Why Reform Fails: Meta-stability and Elastic Capture

Reforms reduce C or P temporarily, but feedback elasticities restore dominance:

- Regulatory capture
- Revolving-door governance
- Narrative manipulation
- Financialization feedbacks

Reform becomes noise around a stable attractor.

## Empirical Resonance (1980–Present)

Data from antitrust rollback, financial deregulation, tax cuts for the wealthy, campaign finance liberalization, and digital platform monopolization map cleanly onto PCFL dynamics:

- Concentration rises
- Inequality rises
- Democratic trust falls
- Policy responsiveness collapses

The system shifts permanently into a high-inequality attractor.

## Institutional Entropy and Democratic Collapse

As T declines:

- Polarization rises
- Civic trust collapses
- Collective action fails
- Governance legitimacy decays

Democracy has become a ceremonial shell.

## Breaking the Attractor: Structural Escape Conditions

Escape requires altering coefficients—not rhetoric:

- Antitrust as entropy reduction
- Campaign finance firewalling
- Public banking
- Algorithmic commons governance
- Institutional redundancy

Only the coefficient redesign alters the attractor topology.

## Conclusion: Oligarchy as System Destiny Without Redesign

Oligarchy is not chosen. It is computed.

Without systemic redesign, democracy collapses into a mathematically inevitable attractor.

## Chapter 3

# Game Theory and Collective Dynamics

## The Planetary Prisoner's Dilemma: Coordinating Climate and Energy Policy on a Global Scale

## Abstract

Humanity confronts an unprecedented paradox: the ability to undermine global stability via carbon-intensive expansion has surpassed the international system's capacity to facilitate collective restraint. Climate change, energy insecurity, and the geopolitical shifts of the 21st century have created a structural trap—a global version of the classic Prisoner's Dilemma—in which reasonable choices by individual governments lead to collectively irrational results. The international arena is becoming more like a series of defection equilibria, where short-term national advantages take precedence over the long-term need for the planet to survive.

The Planetary Prisoner's Dilemma (PPD) is not a metaphor; it is a structural explanation of the incentive structure that governs global energy and climate policy. States have a lot to gain right away from continuing to extract fossil fuels and expand industries. On the other hand, the long-term, dispersed benefits of decarbonization don't have a clear way to be enforced or rewarded. The outcome is a global coordination dilemma with stakes encompassing comprehensive climate stability, economic resilience, geopolitical order, and intergenerational equity.

This essay investigates the systemic underpinnings of the PPD, analyzes the reasons for the inadequacy of current institutions to transcend their inherent logic, and suggests avenues for sustainable collaboration grounded in complexity economics, game theory, and systems humanism. The world can only move from competitive defection to mutual preservation by changing how incentives work, not just by appealing to people's sense of right and wrong.

## II. The Framework of the Planetary Prisoner's Dilemma

In the classic Prisoner's Dilemma, the best move for each person is to betray the other, even though working together would provide them both a better payoff. The reasoning applies directly to global climate governance:

Defection is using as much fossil fuel as possible, keeping energy dominance, and passing on environmental costs to others.

Working together means lowering emissions, investing in clean technology, and being okay with short-term economic changes.

The PPD has four structural problems that make the problem worse:

1.  Uneven Distribution of Benefits and Costs
    Some countries gain more than their fair share from carbon-intensive development, while others suffer more than their fair share from its effects. This imbalance leads to different political incentives and timing preferences.

2.  Long Feedback Loops
    The benefits of climate change unfold over decades, while the costs of making the switch happen right away are immediate. Democracies and autocracies tend to value short-term stability over long-term rewards, thereby increasing the likelihood of desertion.

3.  No Way to Enforce It
    There is no one in charge of the international system who can coerce cooperation. Naming and shaming, voluntary promises, and soft law tools don't have the power to compel people to act.

4.  Energy as a Source of Power in World Politics
    Being in charge of energy means having military, commercial, and political power. Emerging multipolar powers face the risk of diminished strategic autonomy as they reduce reliance on fossil fuels.

These traits work together to create a self-reinforcing balance in which states make choices that, in the long run, make it harder for them to survive.

# III. Why Traditional Climate Governance Has Not Worked

## A. The Paradox of Collective Action

Global climate agreements don't work because the way they're structured doesn't align with the interests of sovereign governments. The outcome is a system characterized by ambition, credibility, and equity deficits.

## B. The Green Technology Race is a game that doesn't add up to anything.

Geopolitical competition is making the energy transition increasingly like a race to control supply chains, rare-earth minerals, battery production, and green hydrogen. This turns decarbonization into a competition, which runs counter to collaboration.

## C. Political Fragmentation at Home

Climate politics recreate the PPD within the country, as domestic groups such as fossil fuel lobbyists, industrial sectors, and populist movements push for defection.

# IV. The Economics of Complexity and the Dynamics of Global Climate Coordination

## 1. Lock-In and Growing Returns

Fossil-fuel infrastructure exhibits increasing returns, leading to carbon lock-in and making it expensive for one country to work with another.

## 2. Effects at the Threshold and Tipping Points

The climate system has nonlinear thresholds, just as political thresholds for working together do.

## 3. Amplifying Risk Through Networks

Climate effects spread through agricultural systems, migratory movements, and financial markets, creating systemic risk far greater than individual assessments.

## 4. Concentration of Emerging Power

State-owned oil enterprises, global energy conglomerates, and petro-states have too much power, which keeps the balance off-kilter.

## V. The Energy Transition as a Game with Many Levels

The easiest way to think about global climate policy is as a game with many levels:

> Level 1: A game of politics at home

> Level 2: A game about geopolitics

> Level 3: An ecological game on a planetary scale

The incentives at each level don't match up: incentives for internal issues reward defection, incentives for geopolitical issues reward dominance, and incentives for ecological issues require cooperation.

## VI. Getting out of the Planetary Prisoner's Dilemma

### A. Climate Clubs That Can Be Enforced

Climate clubs can use border carbon adjustments and trade incentives to make it hard to leave and smart to work together.

### B. Carbon Pricing as a Worldwide Standard

A unified carbon pricing offers the same incentives in all economies.

### C. Technology-Sharing Agreements

Sharing renewable technologies, green hydrogen systems, carbon capture, and storage lowers the costs of making the switch and opens up more ways for people to work together.

### D. Money transfers and climate reparations

Countries that are still developing need money to reduce carbon emissions. Grants, low-interest loans, and debt swaps bring together global equity and global sustainability.

### E. A worldwide framework for clean energy security

A new government might be based on renewable corridors, battery storage networks, hydrogen systems, and the management of important minerals.

### F. Putting Long-Termism into Domestic Politics

Independent climate councils, carbon budgets, long-term planning organizations, and public ownership of important infrastructure can help keep climate policy stable from one election to the next.

## VII. The Moral Framework of Cooperation and Systems Humanism

Systems humanism stresses the importance of being dependent on others, taking responsibility for future generations, and making ethical decisions about risk. It changes the way we think about climate policy from a technological issue to a moral and civilizational one.

## VIII. Conclusion: Moving Toward a Planetary Civilization That Works Together

The PPD reveals a deep contradiction: the way modern geopolitics works doesn't align with how the earth actually works. To solve the problem, we need to change the way global incentives work, strengthen cooperative institutions, ensure that technology and finance align with the planet's limits, and embed long-termism into political systems.

The way forward is clear: working together is the smart decision. The only thing that matters is whether people will work together in time.

# A Game Theory Perspective on United States Foreign Aid

## Abstract

Foreign aid has often been debated as either an altruistic distribution of resources or a strategic tool of geopolitical maneuvering. From a game-theoretic perspective, it functions more as a strategic maneuver in a dynamic, multi-player game than as benevolent financial assistance. States participate in ongoing cycles of cooperation, competition, and signaling, employing aid as a strategic tool to maximize long-term advantages. This essay examines the benefits of U.S. foreign aid to developing and poor countries using game-theoretic analysis.

## Foreign Aid as a Game of Strategy

Game theory shows that states operate in an environment where their decisions influence others' outcomes. The United States' offering of help can be viewed as a two-stage game: 1. Step 1: The U.S. decides if it will aid. Stage Two: The country that receives help decides whether to support the U.S. or switch sides and align with other powers. In this system, offering aid is a way to signal that you want to work together and shift the balance of power.

## The Payoff Matrix in Dynamic Game Theory

The following payoff matrix depicts how the U.S. decided whether or not to grant aid and how the person who got it responded strategically:

- If the U.S. sends aid and the other side accepts, both parties obtain a dividend that is excellent for both sides (+3, +3). The U.S. loses money (−2) if it sends aid, but the recipient doesn't approve. However, the recipient still benefits (+2).

- If the U.S. doesn't send aid and the other side agrees, both sides only earn a tiny reward (+1, +1).

- If the U.S. doesn't send aid and the recipient doesn't agree, the U.S. loses a lot of money (−3), but the recipient still gains (+2). The matrix shows that the U.S.'s best course is to send aid. This is because it increases the likelihood of good outcomes and decreases the likelihood of bad outcomes.

## Benefits of Game Theory

Stabilization of Cooperation (Repeated Games): Aid helps create a long-term balance of give-and-take, which makes it more likely that countries will work together again in trade, diplomacy, and security.

Influence and Signaling (Costly Signals): Aid serves as a credible symbol of U.S. leadership, helping the country build allies and improve its reputation world-wide.

Market Expansion (Positive-Sum Games): When people in other nations get wealthy, they want to buy more American goods and services.

Reducing the Impact of Rivals (Competitive Games): Aid makes it less advantageous to side with U.S. rivals such as China or Russia.

Global Public Goods (Commons Dilemmas): Investing in health, climate, and stability prevents negative outcomes that could affect U.S. interests and people.

## Conclusion

From a game-theoretic standpoint, U.S. foreign aid is not an altruistic endeavor but a strategic investment in global cooperation, influence, and stability. The dynamic reward matrix indicates that providing aid is advantageous for both the giver and the receiver, as it leads to higher predicted payoffs. On the other hand, not giving aid makes it more likely that enemies will work together and cause problems. So, giving money to other countries helps the U.S. by making it more likely that conflicts will resolve peacefully. Even rich countries have a moral duty to help poorer ones, especially when the help is only a small fraction of what the federal government spends each year.

# A Fair Social Contract and Rawls' Veil of Ignorance

## Abstract

John Rawls's "veil of ignorance" is one of the most fundamental notions in modern political philosophy. The veil of ignorance, introduced in "A Theory of Justice" (1971), redefines the social contract tradition by encouraging individuals to evaluate principles of justice from a hypothetical perspective, devoid of knowledge regarding their personal characteristics, social status, or inherent capabilities. This epistemic tool changes the way people think about politics and puts decision-makers in a condition of symmetrical ambiguity. This sets the stage for justice, reciprocity, and institutional legitimacy. This essay examines Rawls' veil of ignorance as a philosophical instrument and a practical framework for constructing a just social compact in contemporary cultures.

## I. The Original Position: An Epistemic Reconfiguration of the Social Contract

Rawls' "original position" is a hypothetical scenario that illustrates the fairness of selecting political principles. People who are beneath the curtain of ignorance don't know what color, gender, financial level, abilities, family status, or general ideas they have. This great lack of self-awareness makes moral randomness impossible and forces people to choose rules they can agree with, no matter what happens in the future. The initial position converts the social compact from a game of bargaining to a moral choice. People who don't know who they are must choose values that everyone can agree on.

## II. Justice as Fairness: The Normative Framework

"Justice as fairness" requires that chosen principles exhibit widespread acceptability and impartiality. Rawls argues that no person behind the veil of ignorance would support maximizing overall welfare at the expense of minorities, unlike utilitarianism. The veil establishes regulations that protect people's basic rights and ensure that everyone has a fair shot and gets a fair share.

Institutions must meet two conditions to be legitimate: they must defend basic rights and make sure that everyone understands why there are differences.

## III. The Two Fairness Principles

Rawls asserts that sensible individuals would endorse two principles from the original viewpoint.

### 1. The Principle of Freedom

Everyone has the same right to a full set of basic freedoms that don't infringe on others' liberties.

### 2. The Difference Principle and Fair Equality of Opportunity

There are only valid reasons for social and economic differences if:

a. Everyone has a fair shot at getting a job.

b. The Difference Principle suggests that differences aid those who are the least well-off.

People might be okay with inequities that make the whole system more productive, but only if there are stringent restrictions in place.

## IV. Rawls, Utilitarianism, Libertarianism, and the Capabilities Approach

Rawls' framework is different from the main alternatives:

- Utilitarianism may sacrifice the rights of minorities for the benefit of the majority.

- Libertarianism (Nozick) emphasizes property rights, but individuals cannot assume any particular claim behind the curtain.

The Capabilities Approach (Sen, Nussbaum) focuses on what people can achieve and become, whereas Rawls gives a reason for protecting such talents.

## V. Employing the Veil of Ignorance to Comprehend Inequality in the 21st Century

Rawls' ideas are still highly significant in today's world of escalating inequality, automation, and division. People would desire the following behind the veil:

- Everyone should have access to health care
- A fair public education
- Rules that help close the gap between the rich and the poor

- Protections for democratic participation
- Fairly dividing the risks and profits of AI and automation

These instances demonstrate the continued relevance of Rawlsian justice.

## VI. A Fair Social Contract for Democracies That Are Complicated and Diverse

A Rawlsian social contract includes:

- Strong civil rights
- Equal rights in politics
- Redistribution that makes things better
- Equal access to health care and education
- Economic systems that keep power from getting too concentrated
- Making choices in a democracy based on public reason

The veil of ignorance stabilizes moral reasoning in complex societies by emphasizing fairness and equal moral consideration.

## Conclusion

The veil of ignorance proposed by Rawls remains one of the most valuable concepts in contemporary political philosophy. Rawls rethinks the social contract using epistemic symmetry. This gives us a morally good and effective approach to creating fair institutions at a time when inequality is high and democracy is weak.

# A Game Theory Examination of Competitive Authoritarianism: Strategic Threats to American Society, the Economy, and Democratic Institutions

## Abstract

This study applies game theory to investigate the formation and risks of competitive authoritarianism within democratic institutions, particularly in the United States. Competitive authoritarianism is a hybrid system characterized by democratic institutions that are undermined by those in authority, who use electoral, judicial, and informational mechanisms to maintain their power. This brief explores the conduct of political leaders, opposition figures, and the voters using strategic models, sketching scenarios in which democratic regression may materialize.

## Introduction: What is Competitive Authoritarianism?

Competitive authoritarian regimes preserve the illusion of democracy through elections, political parties, and judicial systems, while in practice contravening democratic principles. Opposition parties are allowed, but the people in power utilize legal tricks, control of the media, gerrymandering, voter suppression, and making institutions political to make things unfair.

Some instances are Hungary under Viktor Orbán, Russia in the 2000s, Turkey under Erdoğan, and, to some extent, recent developments in India and Israel.

## A Framework for Game Theory

We use non-cooperative game theory to model interactions between three main players:

1. People who already have authority (I)
2. Opposition/Challengers (O)
3. Public/Electorate (P)

Every player has their own plans, payoffs, and perceptions about what other players are doing.

## Setting Up the Game:

Players: I, O, and P

Plans:

> I: (D) Respect democratic standards, (M) Manipulate institutions
> O: {Fight decently (C), Get people to fight back (R)}
> P: {Vote (V), Protest (P), Leave (N)}

Things we think are true:

- The person who currently holds the position cares more about power than legitimacy.

- The opposition seeks to gain political power and legitimacy.

- The public's utility rests on rights, stability, and perceived equity.

## 3. Dynamics and Equilibria in Strategy

Stage Game 1: Decision by the Incumbent

Situation

> I's Choice
> O's Response
> P's Answer

1. Result: D, C, V
A democracy that works

2. M, C, V, or N
Dictatorship of elections

3. M, R, P, or N
A hybrid government that isn't stable

4. D, R, V, or N
Crisis in democracy

When the cost of protest is high and institutions are weak, the Nash Equilibrium frequently favors M, C, and N.

## Consequences of Repeated Games

Incumbents realize that little manipulation yields electoral benefits at minimal cost.

Voter weariness and disillusionment cause people to lose interest in politics (P→N).

Over time, the repeated manipulation approach becomes a subgame, which eventually destroys democracy.

## Risk Scenarios in the U.S.

Judicial Capture and Institutional Decline

A game-theoretic study suggests that long-term utility-maximizing incumbents will prefer acquiring non-elected institutions to overt repression.

Example: Appointing judges strategically to retain power in the hands of one party.

Changing the outcome of elections by gerrymandering or discouraging people from voting

Gerrymandering makes the contest unfair by changing the balance from a fair one (D, C, V) to a skewed one (M, C, N).

People who use suppression measures have to pay more to vote, which makes P less likely to vote (→N).

## Media Capture and Misinformation

If voters can't distinguish between manipulation and true governance, P acts as if I selected D, which gives I more power.

## Interfering with Free Markets

If the government utilizes regulation, antitrust enforcement, and limits R&D and innovation to get in the way of the free market.

## Policy Interventions as Strategic Disruption

Game theory asserts that particular institutional reinforcements and social factors can modify the equilibrium: Intervention

## Impact on Game Theory

- Commissions for redistricting that aren't linked to a single party
- Cut down on the benefits of cheating
- Making voting easier
- Increases the expense of stopping people from voting
- Learning about civic life
- It makes it easier for P to find M.
- Laws concerning understanding the media
- Reduces the power of erroneous information

## Coalitions against

- Increasing the price of regime manipulation

In conclusion, democracy is in danger.

In game theory, democracy does not sustain itself. When rational individuals put power first, and the public stops caring, competitive authoritarianism finds a stable balance. The American system can still be divided, and it's easier to trick people when the rules are weaker and false information spreads. They are also less likely to fight back. To halt competitive authoritarianism, we need to adjust the benefits for everyone. This means getting voters involved again and strengthening independent institutions, such as the Federal Reserve's independence.

# Moral Signaling Games and the Erosion of Trust in Post-Truth Societies

## Abstract

In an era characterized by algorithmic echo chambers and performative virtue, moral signaling has evolved from a nuanced social indicator to a significant strategic activity influencing politics, economics, and culture. This essay examines the game-theoretic foundations of moral signaling, scrutinizing the strategies individuals and institutions employ to leverage symbolic gestures for reputational advantage in "post-truth" societies, contexts marked by the fragmentation of shared epistemic standards and the erosion of collective trust. We analyze the emergent dynamics of signaling equilibria and their adverse effects on social cohesion, governance, and democratic legitimacy using the lenses of behavioral game theory, complexity economics, and moral psychology.

## Beginning: The Time of Performative

Jean Baudrillard called this the "simulacrum of meaning," in which symbols take the place of substance, and moral identity is acted out rather than felt. In this context, exhibiting moral integrity has become a key type of social capital. Companies use "virtue branding," while political groups use moral posturing to keep people loyal rather than sticking to their beliefs. It's not about being honest or sticking to your morals in the game; it's about being seen and fitting in with other moral groups.

This development illustrates that information settings change when individuals doubt the truth; signaling becomes the way people work together rather than honesty. This leads to a form of moral inflation, where people need increasingly extreme signals to maintain a high reputation. This causes cycles of distrust, division, and moral fatigue.

## The Game-Theoretic Basis of Moral Signaling

Moral signaling can be understood as a strategic game defined by inadequate knowledge. Each agent determines whether and to what extent to convey their virtue, cognizant that others will interpret these signals as indicators of moral integrity or allegiance to the collective. In equilibrium, signaling strength is determined not by inherent morality but by perceived reputational advantages.

- Strong Signal (S)
- Weak Signal (W)
- Mutual validation (+2, +2) / High reputational cost (-1, -1)
- S grows more believable (+3), and W loses credibility (-2).
- Weak Signal (W)
- W obtains a good name (+2), but S perceives hypocrisy (-2).
- Stable but not very easy to see (+1, +1)

In this dynamic, prevailing methods often gravitate towards exaggerated signaling, since the social incentives for public moral behavior outweigh the private motivations for ethical integrity. The result is a dividing equilibrium in which people who don't signal are seen as immoral or disloyal, leading to an arms race of moral expression.

Behavioral aberrations occur when messaging is disconnected from concrete ethical repercussions. People don't do things for the good of the collective; they do things to protect their reputation among their peers. Timur Kuran coined the term "preference falsification," which means people publicly endorse opinions they don't privately agree with. This makes systemic hypocrisy worse.

## Complexity Dynamics and the Breakdown of Trust

From a complexity-economic perspective, moral signaling operates as a feedback loop linking network connections, information entropy, and reputational incentives. As social networks grow, moral rules stop holding things stable and start spreading like a disease. Likes, retweets, and endorsements are examples of recursive amplification that help each signal spread. This leads to moral cascades that can quickly split public opinion. Trust, an emergent attribute of stable equilibria, diminishes when actors do not distinguish between genuine and performative goodness. When epistemic coherence is absent, moral coherence is likewise absent. According to complexity theorists, the system reaches a high-entropy state when moral information degrades due to noise introduced by reproduction. People are quite cynical because of this.

The result is moral entropy, which is when the signal-to-noise ratio of ethical communication falls below a certain level. People don't trust each other, and institutions don't trust people. Each actor keeps signaling louder and louder, not because they believe it, but because they know that quiet indicates guilt.

## Post-Truth and Why You Should Be Skeptical

Post-truth cultures are not marked by ignorance; rather, they are defined by the weaponization of information. In the public domain, there are so many stories competing with one another that the truth becomes a game of getting others to see things your way. It's hard to trust people in these kinds of systems; being skeptical is a good approach to deal with them. The rational agent learns that signaling is more important than honesty; honesty becomes irrelevant.

People curate their online profiles to garner moral approbation rather than genuine discourse, companies engage in "greenwashing" and "social justice branding," and politicians deploy faux anger rather than real policy skills. The end result is institutional entropy, which means no one can really claim moral authority because everyone is using the same signaling logic.

The system is becoming more intricate, which is splitting it into two. One branch leads to performative authoritarianism, which is when moral purity is enforced by violence. The other leads to nihilistic relativism, where all statements are equally questionable. Both results show that trust has been broken.

## To a Restorative Balance

If moral signaling erodes trust, restoring trust requires re-establishing moral conduct through shared authenticity. From a game-theoretic standpoint, this necessitates reconfiguring payoff structures to ensure that honesty and integrity yield more favorable long-term outcomes than performative alignment. There are several approaches to help society develop toward a cooperative equilibrium, such as open discussions, reputation systems that promote consistency over intensity, and institutions that punish hypocrisy.

The issue is systemic; moral exhortation alone cannot restore truth; it requires structural feedback loops that incentivize honesty, humility, and epistemic discipline. Complexity theory asserts that when trust networks decline below a critical threshold, restoration requires the deliberate introduction of new attractors—dialogic areas insulated from performative incentives.

The moral advancement of post-truth societies depends on transforming signaling from an instrument of tyranny into a medium for genuine ethical dialogue.

## Conclusion

The moral signaling game shows the contradiction of a post-truth society: the more we say we are good, the less we trust each other. What began as a means for collaboration has devolved into a competitive performance arena that undermines the trust it was intended to foster. Game theory, moral psychology, and complexity dynamics converge on a frightening insight: without recalibrating the incentive structures of signaling, civilizations risk sliding into self-referential distrust.

To restore moral order in a time of show, we need more than merely confirming facts or showing virtue; we need to think about authenticity as a communal balance in a new way. The future of trust doesn't depend on bigger signals; it depends on softer realities.

# Behavioral Game Theory and the Fallacies of Equity in Income and Wealth Disparity

## Abstract

Behavioral game theory started to develop in the 1950s, thanks in large part to the work of Maurice Allais (1953) and Daniel Ellsberg (1961). Their recognition of the Allais and Ellsberg paradoxes illustrated that human decision-making often deviates from the forecasts of traditional (mathematical) game theory. Experimental studies conducted in the 1950s and 1960s contributed to the discipline's elucidation. The development of choice theories, particularly prospect theory, by Tversky and Kahneman in the 1970s further institutionalized it.

In 1944, Von Neumann and Morgenstern formally established the field of game theory. Behavioral game theory, on the other hand, distinguishes itself by systematically incorporating psychological ideas and experimental data on how people behave into game-theoretic frameworks.

Income and wealth inequality are persistent features of modern, industrialized economies; nevertheless, public views of these discrepancies are not only shaped by material self-interest. Classical economic theory assumes individuals are rational utility maximizers; in contrast, behavioral game theory incorporates psychological realism by integrating social preferences, bounded rationality, and fairness rules into strategic decision-making. Examining income and wealth inequality through the lens of behavioral game theory helps explain why certain forms of inequality are accepted or endorsed, while others provoke resistance and demands for redistribution.

## Behavioral Game Theory versus Classical Game Theory

People will accept any outcome that raises their total payoff, even if it isn't fair, according to classic game theory. In the traditional Ultimatum Game, the rational choice for a responder is to accept any offer greater than zero. However, empirical evidence demonstrates that most people reject low offers, even at a personal detriment, to sanction perceived unfairness. Cooperative games often have altruistic players. Consequently, behavioral game theory emphasizes the impact of social preferences, such as inequity aversion, reciprocity, and loss aversion, on decision-making, so challenging the idea that the acceptance of inequality is exclusively a result of self-interested rationality.

## Social Preferences and Aversion to Inequity

The Fehr–Schmidt model of inequity aversion explains how people feel bad when they are either less off than others or better off than others. In this theory, utility decreases with inequality, determined by two parameters: aversion to detrimental inequality ($\alpha$) and aversion to beneficial inequality ($\beta$). This framework clarifies the reasons for the intense resistance to inequality among individuals in the middle or lower income brackets ($\alpha$ is high), while simultaneously addressing the tendency of certain wealthy individuals to engage in philanthropy or corporate social responsibility ($\beta$ is non-zero).

Bolton and Ockenfels' ERC (Equity, Reciprocity, and Competition) model extends this theory by showing how reciprocity shapes people's perceptions of fairness.[3] People are more inclined to accept inequality when it is portrayed as merit-based, meaning it is based on effort, risk-taking, or productivity. Conversely, inequality stemming from rent-seeking or corruption engenders punitive preferences, such as support for wealth taxes or regulatory changes.

## Experimental Evidence: Ultimatum and Dictator Games

Laboratory tests provide empirical evidence concerning the impact of fairness rules on the acceptability of inequality. In the Ultimatum Game, proposers frequently offer 30–50 percent of the total pie, while offers below 20 percent are often turned down. In the Dictator Game, on the other hand, proposers nevertheless gladly give up a part of their endowment, showing that they care about fairness. These results suggest that people worry about more than just how much money they make; they also care about the distribution's equity.

This clarifies the reasoning behind the diminished controversy surrounding wage disparities or executive bonuses when associated with concrete contributions—such as job creation or philanthropy—while analogous disparities provoke public outrage when linked to financial manipulation or tax evasion.

## Reference Points, Loss Aversion, and System Justification

Prospect theory improves the study of accepting inequality by showing how important reference points and loss aversion are. People look at their economic results and compare them to a baseline they consider fair, such as their past income or their peers' income. People feel much more unfairly when inequality rises while salaries remain the same. This is because they regard the gap as a loss. Conversely, in periods of robust economic expansion, significant disparity may not incite as much anger, as the majority of individuals are experiencing increased wealth.

System justification theory provides an extra psychological paradigm that explains why excluded groups may accept inequality. Individuals alleviate cognitive dissonance by justifying uneven outcomes as acceptable, inevitable, or temporary, thereby promoting social stability despite actual differences in income and wealth.

## The Dynamics of Game Theory in Society

Behavioral game theory clarifies how fairness norms are translated into social equilibria. You can use different game structures to represent how individuals feel about unfairness:

- Kind of Game
- How Behavior Works

What happens because there is inequality:

A. Ultimatum Game
- Saying no to deals that aren't fair
- Support for redistribution

B. Dictators' Game
- Choose to be fair
- Giving money to charity and raising pay

C. The Game of Public Goods
- Working together with conditions
- Progressive taxation if people follow the rules

D. Trust Game
- Reputation and giving back
- Being okay with wealthy "benefactors."

E. Games that Need Coordination
- Making sure that social norms are followed
- The societal acceptance or rejection of inequality

These dynamics demonstrate that inequality is not universally accepted; it fluctuates according to social norms, perceptions of legitimacy, and the behavior of affluent individuals.

## Effects of Policy

Comprehending the behavioral foundations of inequality acceptance has significant policy implications. When framed as upholding justice, such as closing tax loopholes, redistribution programs are more likely to function politically than when framed as punitive wealth transfers. Similarly, voluntary acts of fairness by elites, such as wage raises or charitable donations, might reduce the desire for forced redistribution by reinforcing norms of social reciprocity. Lastly, redistribution tactics that work in egalitarian societies may not function as well in countries that value individual mobility and meritocracy because different cultures have different ideas of what is fair and what is not.

## Conclusion

Behavioral game theory demonstrates that individuals' perceptions of justice, rather than solely their self-interest, influence their acceptance or rejection of income and wealth inequality. People make strategic decisions that are heavily influenced by social norms and psychological heuristics, such as loss aversion, inequity aversion, reciprocity, and reference dependency. Policymakers and scholars can deepen their understanding of the enduring nature of inequality by incorporating these behavioral insights, thereby facilitating the development of policies that harmonize economic policy with existing ethical and fairness considerations.

# The Dynamics of Multipolarity: Game Theory in a Post-American World System

## Abstract

The global system is experiencing a structural realignment marked by the decline of unipolar American hegemony and the emergence of competitive regional powers. This transition, commonly called the move toward "multipolarity," is not merely a change in geopolitics; it is also a fundamental shift in the game-theoretic structure of international order. From the standpoint of complexity economics and strategic interaction, multipolarity creates new equilibria, increases systemic uncertainty, and sets up nonlinear feedback loops that can lead to both stability and disastrous failures. To comprehend the post-American world, it is essential to integrate classical game theory, network analysis, and evolutionary dynamics. This essay formulates a game-theoretic framework for analyzing multipolarity as a dynamic system defined by fluctuating payoffs, unstable alliances, and strategic ambiguity. It shows how rising powers such as China and India, the EU, regional blocs, and non-state actors interact in a decentralized system where no single group has full control. It does this by using ideas from repeated games, signaling theory, coalition formation, and deterrence theory. As a result, the world becomes a place where working together is harder, leaving is more appealing, and mistakes in the system are more likely.

## THE FALL OF UNIPOLARITY AS A GAME-THEORETIC

The world was in a unique historical balance after 1991, when the US was the most powerful country. The US developed and implemented rules that affected markets, security alliances, and international conventions worldwide. In game theory, this was an example of a "hegemonic-stability equilibrium," in which a strong player pays the price of maintaining order because they gain enormous returns. The U.S. is losing power in the economy, the military, and institutions to other countries that are getting stronger. This is making the world's structure more resemble a "decentralized coordination game" with multiple centers of power. In this kind of game, no one can make the rules on their own. • The rewards fluctuate depending on the area, the domain, and the alliance structure. • Cooperative equilibria operate because of weak norms, not robust enforcement. This transition is like moving from a stable Nash equilibrium to a landscape with many distinct equilibria. Systems with multiple equilibria are usually path-dependent, can be shocked, and are likely to exhibit cascades. The decline of unipolarity fundamentally increases uncertainty rather than merely incrementally.

## RATIONALITY IN MULTIPOLAR CONTEXTS

A post-American system reveals the inherent paradoxes in rational-choice models that presuppose stable preferences and foreseeable incentives.

1. In a world with numerous poles, actors shift what they want based on how they think about their power paths.

2. Changes in technology, sanctions, or the quantity of individuals living in a region can swiftly modify how payoffs are set up.

3. It's harder to guess what people will do because everyone is trying to figure out what everyone else will do. This creates a "higher-order uncertainty" framework. In these situations, classical rational-actor game theory doesn't work, but evolutionary game theory, which models strategies that change over time, does. In other words, multipolarity is an evolutionary tournament, not a static game.

## STRATEGIC INTERDEPENDENCE AND THE EXPANSION OF THE REGION

In a world with multiple powers, the global system becomes a web of interconnected regional games. In a hegemonic system with rules that are the same all over the world, multipolarity creates different semi-autonomous areas:

- East Asia: deterrence, economic statecraft, and competition at sea
- Europe: stable institutions, unified defense, and energy security
- Middle East: proxy relationships and resource leverage
- Africa: diplomacy for development, the politics of debt, and the race for resources

Each region becomes a strategic subgame with its own rewards, but these subgames are linked to each other. An externality that affects more than one region occurs when something happens in one region that modifies the incentives in another. China's naval maneuvers in the South China Sea could influence how India utilizes its military. This could then change how the U.S. and Russia respond. So, multipolarity is like a multiplex network with several levels of strategic interactions.

# MULTIPOLARITY AS A COALITION GAME

In traditional bipolar systems, such as the Cold War between the U.S. and the Soviet Union, permanent alliances can form because each side encourages loyalty and punishes defection. On the other hand, multipolarity makes coalitions less stable. In a coalition game involving three or more prominent participants, no alliance is stable for good:

1. Actors are continuously weighing the advantages and cons of switching sides.

2. Smaller governments can have more authority to negotiate by pitting major countries against each other. This thing, called "strategic triangulation," makes it harder for systems to communicate with each other. It also makes it less likely that large, stable alliances will form. There will be short-term alliances based on specific topics, such as commerce, technology, energy, arms procurement, climate change, or infrastructure.

3. Problems with security in a world with many poles. Security problems become more serious when there are more influential people. In a unipolar system, it's straightforward to see what the main state intends to do. But under a multipolar system:

It's not clear what people desire. People view capabilities from a competitive perspective.

The perception of threats becomes increasingly subjective. This creates a deterrence game with signals that could go in many different directions. According to signaling theory, these types of events are more likely to lead to misconceptions, increasing the likelihood of a crisis. Also, multipolar deterrence is inherently less reliable because actors must keep more than one enemy from attacking simultaneously. This sets off a chain reaction: each state receives more weaponry to deal with the unknown, which in turn triggers more responses across the network. The next arms race is not straight and could cause an explosion.

# MULTIPOLAR INTERDEPENDENCE AND ECONOMIC COMPLEXITY

Globalization has rendered the world's greatest nations increasingly dependent on one another, especially in energy systems, supply lines, and digital infrastructure. These interdependencies are both a strength and a weakness in a world with numerous poles. Interdependence complicates the "iterated prisoner's dilemma" from a game-theoretic perspective. Everyone gains from collaboration; yet the allure of violating regulations through fines, protectionism, or geoeconomic coercion intensifies. More people are interested in economic statecraft. It employs trade, money, and technology as weapons. This shows that people are leaning toward methods that combine cooperation and defection. This dynamic creates what complexity economists call a "fragile equilibrium." The system remains stable until something pushes it past a tipping point, at which point it starts to break up. The post-American system is therefore on the verge of economic phase changes.

## THE NEW STRATEGIC LANDSCAPE OF TECHNOLOGY, DATA, AND COMPETITION

Technology makes a new form of strategy that isn't dependent on territory or concepts like competition. Artificial intelligence, quantum computing, semiconductor capacity, cyber offense, and space infrastructure are all part of a new high-stakes event with uneven rewards. In this case:

- Small technological advantages can turn into significant strategic advantages.

- Cyber conflict makes it easier for smaller countries to join the engagement.

- People are more prone to get things wrong when they don't have all the facts.

Replicator dynamics show us how this tech game works best: strategies evolve based on how well they function, not on what they think. It's better to be powerful, flexible, and innovative than to rely on a strict military structure like the US's.

## MULTIPOLARITY AND THE DANGER OF A SYSTEMIC CASCADE FAILURE

One of the most worrisome aspects of multipolarity is that it can trigger a chain of failures. The global system is like a network that is virtually critical, as it includes multiple feedback loops that affect one another, such as military, technological, economic, and ideological ones. In critical situations, even small changes can have a tremendous effect. Game theory says that these things are more likely to happen: Crisis spirals, Mistakes in alliances, Feedback loops that make things worse, Belief cascades that are zero-sum, Institutions falling apart,

Local conflicts that make people around the world react. Multipolarity does not guarantee instability; instead, it enhances variability, increasing the likelihood of extreme outcomes, both positive and negative.

## POSSIBLE FUTURES: BALANCES IN A WORLD SYSTEM POST-AMERICA

Using evolutionary game theory, we can uncover four alternative long-term balances.

1. Managed Multipolarity. A system that is not centralized but functions together, where institutions alter, and new rules are formed. Needs to be able to trust commitments and talk to people well.

2. Competitive Multipolarity. States aim to get ahead of one another, which makes coalitions weaker. A lot of violence, a lot of difficulties, and an economy that is breaking apart.

3. Bipolar Regression. If two actors have too much influence, multipolarity shifts into a new form of bipolarity, likely between the U.S. and China or China and India.

4. Systemic Breakdown. The worst thing that could happen is that conflicts will keep happening, institutions will fail, the economy will break apart, and the world will stay unstable. The path depends on how well powers can adapt, how well they can embed cooperation into their institutions, and how well feedback loops function.

## Conclusion

The dynamics of multipolarity are driving substantial changes in how countries interact strategically. The post-American world is characterized not only by the diminishment of the United States but also by the concurrent emergence of various power centers engaged in intricate, nonlinear, and frequently surprising relationships. To better grasp this environment, we need to stop using static models and start using more dynamic, evolving ones. This paradigm should be aware of how fragile global equilibria are and how powerful strategic adaptation can be. A universe with several poles doesn't have to be chaotic; it might make the system richer and more diverse. But the system might not work if people can't be honest, work together, and keep their word. In the 21st century, the goal is to build institutions that can manage complexity rather than trying to eliminate it. In a world where no single individual is in command, it's also necessary to establish goals that strengthen everyone.

# How Game Theory Destroys Collective Illusions

## Abstract

Game theory studies strategic interactions among rational or limitedly rational decision-makers seeking to optimize outcomes under specific circumstances or initial conditions. A game-theoretic method can be a powerful way to break down collective illusions, which are erroneous ideas or assumptions that a community holds even when there is evidence to the contrary. This is because games can be competitive or cooperative.

I got the inspiration for this essay from a fun and interesting book called "Collective Illusions: Conformity, Complicity, and the Science of Why We Make Bad Decisions" by Todd Rose. Hachette Book Group, Inc. (New York) put it out in 2022.

This is how game theory addresses communal delusions and exposes the distinction between social myths and truth.

## Turning the Illusion into a Game of Coordination

Many collective illusions arise when people do or believe something because they think others want them to. For example, "pluralistic ignorance" happens when people privately reject a rule yet outwardly follow it, even if there are no consequences for not following it.

In game theory, this can be seen as a "coordination game with multiple equilibria," where one possible outcome is that everyone pretends to believe in the illusion, and another is that everyone rejects it.

The goal is to get the group to go from the "illusion equilibrium" to the "truthful equilibrium."

## Finding Ways to End the Delusion

People typically continue to believe in group illusions because they are terrified of what their peers will do to them if they don't follow a social or community norm. For example, they might be left out of a group. Societal punishment could be real or just something that people think about. People will follow the rules if they fear punishment.

Game theory can identify "critical players," such as leaders or influencers, who wield significant social power or reputation. Their actions can alter the reward structure, making it safer for others to abandon the illusion. The illusion might not go away completely until other kinds of social reinforcement are utilized, and the "first-mover" problem will make it take longer for people to adapt.

If a leader openly rejects the illusion, it makes it simpler for others to do the same. This is a "tipping point" tactic that will be supported by the "cascade effect."

## Cheap Talk and Signaling

People might not say what they actually think because they don't get good signals from society, the community, or the organization they want to be a part of. People won't take the risk of openly following the rules if they don't have reliable indications. This is especially true when it comes to religion and politics.

Game theory suggests mechanisms such as "costly signaling" (e.g., public pledges) or "cheap talk" (e.g., repeated interactions that build trust) to help people signal what they really want.

One technique to show that most people don't agree with the illusion in private is to undertake anonymous surveys (where individuals are paid or not). This fractures the false consensus.

## Herding and Information Cascades

"Information cascades" can make people believe things that aren't true, such as when they ignore their own signals and do what everyone else is doing. People do this kind of thing a lot on social media and in the financial market. It's simpler to disregard your own signals when you're with a group.

Game theory shows that "contrarian incentives" (such as rewarding dissent) or "transparency" (such as making aggregated private signals public) can stop cascades.

In business, for instance, having "devil's advocates" helps stop groupthink, as long as people don't get in trouble for disagreeing.

## Designing Mechanisms to Encourage Honesty

"Mechanism design" in game theory can create systems in which being honest is the best strategy. Some illusions persist because individuals find themselves in a "Prisoner's Dilemma," in which everyone detests a policy yet no one protests alone.

For instance, prediction markets and Bayesian truth serum systems get people to speak the truth by ensuring their payoffs are based on reliable, accurate sources.

Some solutions are "repeated interactions," which help people trust each other, and "external enforcement," in which a mediator ensures that those who disagree are safe.

## The Effects of Networks and Contagion

Social networks help disseminate false beliefs among groups. Game theory can help us pinpoint crucial points in "network games" where we can step in and cause problems. People who are highly connected, also known as "superspreaders" of truth, can help end the illusion faster.

Here are some good examples:

- Social Media: Algorithms could be designed to surface different points of view, breaking up echo chambers.

- Corporate Culture: Encouraging "psychological safety" changes the payoff matrix, making it less expensive to disagree.

- Political Reform: Institutions might be created to incentivize honesty rather than conformity to party doctrine.

## Conclusion

To keep a dynamic political system running smoothly, it's important to break up collective illusions. These are false beliefs or assumptions that a group, community, or society holds onto even when there is evidence to the contrary. Collective illusions can lead to chaos and a loss of freedom when most people unknowingly follow wrong minority norms. Game theory studies the strategic interactions among rational, well-informed decision-makers who seek to achieve the best possible outcomes. In contrast, systematic reliance on reliable scientific evidence that sustains true norms erodes and destroys communal illusions. Collective illusions often appear as "Nash equilibria," stable situations in which no one has a reason to act alone. Game theory helps create plans for moving the group toward a better equilibrium where the truth prevails.

# An Interdisciplinary Analysis of Game Theory and Complexity Economics

## Abstract

The combination of game theory and complexity economics gives a fundamental paradigm for appreciating the strategic interactions and emergent behaviors within intricate economic systems. Researchers can gain deeper insights into the functioning of real-world economic systems by integrating the analytical precision of game theory with the dynamic, systems-oriented methodology of complexity economics.

## Agent-Based Modeling and the Establishment of Norms and Institutions

Game Theory investigates the creation of norms, traditions, and institutions from repeated interactions and strategic behavior, such as in repeated games and evolutionary game theory. Complexity Economics explores the evolution of structures in complex systems, including social norms, institutions, and market behaviors. Intersection: Both subjects help us understand how agents can construct order and institutions through decentralized interactions, without central coordination. They also help us appreciate how crucial information loops are.

## Network Theory

Game Theory studies games played on networks, where how people interact (who interacts with whom) affects the outcomes. Complexity Economics studies economic systems as networks of actors that interact with one another, and the network's structure shapes how the system operates. Intersection: The analysis of network games and the influence of network structure on economic systems is a shared domain with consequences for financial markets, trade networks, and social interactions.

## Changes Over Time in Evolution

Evolutionary game theory examines the temporal evolution of strategies through mechanisms such as imitation, learning, and natural selection. Complexity Economics: Focuses on the adaptive behavior of actors and the temporal evolution of economic systems.

Both fields employ evolutionary dynamics to analyze the temporal changes in tactics, behaviors, and economic structures in response to initial conditions, evolving environments, and interactions.

## Dynamics that Are Not in Equilibrium

Game Theory has historically focused on equilibrium concepts, notably the Nash equilibrium in cooperative games, and on the dynamics that lead to or depart from equilibrium. Complexity Economics often investigates systems that exhibit substantial deviations from equilibrium, making traditional equilibrium analysis ineffective. Intersection: Both studies examine non-equilibrium dynamics in economic systems, where agents constantly adapt and the system evolves over time.

## Behavioral Factors

Behavioral game-playing is part of game theory. It examines phenomena such as limited rationality, cognitive biases, and other psychological factors, including collective illusions and economic altruism. Complexity Economics: Stresses the necessity of limited rationality and flexible behavior in complicated systems. Intersection: Both fields accept that agents are not usually perfectly rational and that their conduct is constrained by cognitive limitations and social influences, leading to more accurate models of economic interactions.

## Making Policies and Mechanisms

Game Theory gives you the tools you need to create policies and processes that function in strategic circumstances. What it means to be the best and how to act. Complexity Economics: It shows how policies can alter complex systems in unexpected ways. Combining game-theoretic mechanism design with complexity economics can yield policy recommendations that are more robust and account for the complex, unpredictable, and adaptive nature of economic systems.

## Competition and Changes in the Market

Game Theory examines the behavior of enterprises and consumers within various market systems, focusing on strategies for competitiveness, market equilibria, and initial conditions. Complexity Economics: Looks at how markets change over time, including how market structures change, how prices change, and how technology and new ideas affect markets. The relationship between strategic conduct and market evolution is an important area of overlap. It may be used to analyze competitiveness, innovation, and market stability.

## Knowledge and Learning

Game Theory examines the mechanisms by which agents acquire knowledge and adapt their strategies in response to available information, including Bayesian updating and learning processes within games. Complexity Economics examines the distribution of information within networks and the processes by which agents obtain knowledge from their environment and from each other. The examination of information dissemination, acquisition, and adaptation within economic systems is a common area of interest, bearing significance for comprehending financial markets, technology integration, and social learning.

## Risk of a Crisis and a System

Game Theory examines how people make strategic decisions when things go wrong, including during bank runs, financial panics, and market failures. Complexity Economics examines systemic risk and how shocks propagate across interconnected economic systems, both in the US and around the world. Both fields help us understand how strategic interactions and network structures can lead to systemic risks and failures that spread through economic systems.

## Conclusion

The integration of game theory and complexity economics provides a robust framework for clarifying strategic interactions and emergent behaviors in complex economic systems. By integrating the analytical rigor of game theory with the dynamic, systems-oriented approach of complexity economics, researchers can better understand how real-world economic systems operate. The transdisciplinary nature of complexity economics greatly enhances our understanding of complex dynamic economic processes.

# A Game-Theoretic Model of Significance and Restraint in Asceticism and Affluence

## I. Introduction: The Contradiction of "More"

There are many underlying contradictions in the modern economy. Billions of people have more money, yet their feelings of happiness and fulfillment have not changed or may even have gotten worse. The same things that make people happy and give them a lot of stuff also make them desire more, compare themselves to others, and find new ways to fight for status. As people get more, their expectations change, and it becomes harder to find a happy medium. Philosophy and religion's ascetic traditions recognized this contradiction. These traditions did not repudiate riches; rather, they sought to understand the proliferation of want and the distortion of meaning in the absence of regulation. Asceticism, in its advanced form, represents discernment rather than rejection. It's knowing when you have enough and not going for things you don't need. This essay formalizes ascetic moderation as an economically viable technique that stabilizes well-being and protects social cohesion.

## II. Prosperity as a Competition

Economic life is not only about acquiring absolute resources; it also involves positional rivalry. People judge how well they are doing by how well others are doing. These kinds of comparisons produce status dynamics that make consumers buy more to keep or better their social standing. The reward matrix shows this competition. Each person's choice to eat more or less affects both their personal well-being and society's well-being. When both sides get worse, they spend a lot of money and get very little in return. When both are reasonable, they enjoy a good amount without too much effort.

## III. Asceticism and Collaboration in Iterated Games

Strategies do not operate autonomously in recurrent interactions. People's values and goals change throughout time, which changes what everyone else expects. Ascetic self-limitation serves as a cooperative signal, indicating that a person is not worsening the competition and instead encouraging others to do the same. When moderation is viewed as a consistent approach, it can guide the system towards a cooperative equilibrium. The repeated-game format demonstrates that once trust is established, the cooperative equilibrium of mutual moderation becomes self-sustaining. People only breach it when they bring back status escalation, which makes the system more competitive.

## IV. Meaning as a Valuable Thing

Meaning is a rare and useful economic good. You can't produce, buy, or store meaning like you can with things. To figure out who you are and what you want to do with your life, you need to spend time, think about things, and be in relationships. Moderation in asceticism helps you focus on improving these areas. People have more room in their minds and emotions for creative, intellectual, civic, and spiritual activities when they aren't locked in cycles of consumerism and status anxiety.

## V. Cultural Practices of Moderation

Many societies have declared moderation a moral duty. For instance, Stoicism advised people to be clear-headed and not get overly connected to what they want. Buddhism teaches people not to get too connected to things. Monastic Christianity teaches people how to live simply with others. Many Indigenous cultures encouraged individuals to value their connections more than their possessions. These customs helped keep culture stable by staying important over time.

## VI. Modern Ethics of Sufficiency

To bring back the stabilizing role of ascetic moderation, modern cultures need to change how they think about wealth. Instead of seeing it as the constant rise in spending, they should see it as the ability to live by ideals that you set for yourself. Prosperity becomes meaningful when individuals have autonomy over their goals and the capacity to determine how they allocate their time, attention, and care.

## Conclusion

Asceticism and wealth are not opposites; they work together. We need prosperity to be free and asceticism to find meaning in life. They all work together to help people and communities build ways of living that are rich, stable, and enduring.

# Payoff Asymmetry and the Ethics of Inequality: The Evolution of Fairness into a Non-Equilibrium State

## Abstract

Traditional ethical frameworks often view disparity as a static condition, reflecting only an unjust distribution that can be rectified by principles of fairness, desert, or necessity. This essay argues that a static analysis is inherently inadequate for understanding the most pernicious forms of inequality in modern capitalist, information-centric societies. The concept of payoff asymmetry—where the rewards for success are significantly higher than the sanctions for failure—allows us to see systemic inequality not as a fixed, though unfair, balance, but as a process that continues and worsens. This essay will analyze how reward asymmetries, particularly in finance, technology, and social mobility, create a systemic bias that promotes the accumulation of advantage. We will examine how these dynamics change and weaken established ethical frameworks, such as utilitarianism, Rawlsian justice, and theories of desert. When there are big differences in payoffs, we say that the ethical ideal of a "fair" or "just" society changes into a non-equilibrium state that is inherently unstable and likely to devolve into more entrenched hierarchies unless strong, proactive institutions work to break these self-reinforcing feedback loops.

## Introduction: The Dynamics of Unfairness

The ethical debate over inequality has historically focused on the search for an appropriate distribution principle. Should utilitarians' idea of distributing commodities based on their usefulness be followed? John Rawls suggested that a social contract should help those who are not doing well. Or based on what people deserve based on how hard they work and what they give? A fundamental presumption in these talks is that the economic and social game transpires on a level playing field, where results, while potentially uneven, arise via a process that can be assessed as fair or unfair independently.

This essay proposes a shift in our perspective. The main moral problem of the 21st century may not be the shape of the distribution curve at any one time, but the mechanism that produces that distribution. Payoff asymmetry is a major factor in how these things work. In a symmetric system, the risks and investments are roughly equal to the gains and losses. This proportionality doesn't function when the system isn't even. A little bit of luck, a modest advantage, or one fresh idea can lead to big, compounding rewards. On the other hand, a similar mistake or bad luck can only lead to a loss that is easy to handle. This is how the market works when the winner takes all or most of the money.

When these kinds of discrepancies are built into the system, they become quite biased. It ceases to be a fair place to compete and becomes a way to make things unfair. The moral effect is big: "fairness," or the idea that results should be approximately in line with merit, effort, or need, is no longer a stable draw. It is not stable; rather, it is a fragile state like a pencil balanced on its tip. A minor alteration, such as a modest bequest, an opportunity for networking, or becoming the initial entrant into a new market, might initiate a feedback loop that propels the system indefinitely towards pronounced and entrenched inequality. Ethics must go beyond defining a just end-state to establishing institutions that can stabilize a just process in the face of these inherent centrifugal tendencies.

## I. How Payoff Asymmetry Works: From Matthew Effects to Feedback Loops That Go Out of Control

Before we can appreciate the moral issue, we need to figure out how payoff asymmetry works. These are not typical market failures; instead, they often define extremely efficient, network-centric systems.

### A. The Matthew Principle and the Cumulative Advantage

Robert K. Merton, a sociologist, coined the term "Matthew Effect" to describe the phenomenon in which prominent scientists receive greater recognition for their contributions than lesser-known scholars. This is based on Matthew 25:29, which says, "For to everyone who has will more be given, and he will have an abundance." This concept pertains to other domains beyond science. In finance, an initial capital endowment lets you invest in different assets and take on risk, which increases the capital base further. In the employment market, having a prestigious early career credential, like a degree from a top university, can help you connect with people and find possibilities that will help you later, no matter how well you do.

This is a good feedback loop. Advantage offers you an edge. The prize for winning the first round is not only the win, but also a better probability of winning the next round. On the other hand, losing typically implies losing future opportunities, which puts people and enterprises in a vicious cycle of disadvantage.

## B. The Economics of Platforms and Network Effects

The digital economy has changed the way people make money in ways never seen before. The value of a platform, such as Facebook or Uber, depends on the size of its network. The advantages of being the best platform are considerable, so "the number two player is the first loser." It doesn't cost much to develop an app or a social media profile, and everyone who wants to join pays the same amount. But the way the money is split is really unjust. A small number of apps or influencers get most of the attention and money, while most don't get much at all. The winners aren't always thousands of times more skilled or hard-working; it's just that the system favors big names and big stars.

## C. Risk that Isn't the Same for Everyone

Modern financial tools create big differences in payoffs. The "privatized gains and socialized losses" strategy adopted during the 2008 financial crisis is a good illustration. People who work in finance could assume big, systemic risks. A trader or business could make as much money as they wanted, but they could only lose as much as they could go bankrupt. The government would then have to pay for its mistakes, which would cost the public a lot of money. This sets up a bizarre system of incentives: the easiest way to make money is to take on more risks, which is incorrect in the first place. The moral failing here is not simply the outcome, but also the fact that the way the choice was made was altered before it happened.

# II. The Breakdown of Ethical Frameworks

These ever-changing inequalities make traditional ethical frameworks untenable, since the system's built-in bias takes over or cancels out their fundamental concepts.

## A. The Utilitarian Calculus in a World Where One Person Wins Everything

Utilitarianism, which seeks to optimize collective welfare, encounters considerable difficulties due to payoff asymmetry. It can appear like a system that lets one person make $100 billion is really useful at first glance. But this formula doesn't show how that wealth was made over time. The network effects and monopoly power that make people so rich often hurt total welfare by limiting competition, exploiting user data, and producing deadweight loss. A billionaire's dollar doesn't help them, but if the same amount of money were divided among many people, they could avoid many difficulties. The idea that "a rising tide lifts all boats" is useful, but it doesn't work when a few people control the tide and leave others stuck. The static assessment of total wealth fails to account for the systemic loss of utility arising from persistent inequality of opportunity.

## B. The Rawlsian Veil and the Bias of the Starting Gate

Many individuals believe that John Rawls's theory of justice, which includes the Difference Principle (that social and economic inequalities should be to the greatest benefit of the least-advantaged members of society), is a strong strategy for addressing inequality. Payoff asymmetry, on the other hand, attacks the theory at its core: the fairness of the "starting gate." Rawls thinks that rational actors would choose principles that protect them from ending up at the bottom if they were behind a "veil of ignorance." But in a world where cumulative advantage is strong, the position of the least-advantaged is not a fixed fate but a trap that changes over time. Rich individuals don't just give their kids money; they also provide them with a better chance of a good life by offering better education, healthcare, and social connections.

When the Difference Principle is employed in a static way through redistributive taxation, it becomes a work that never ends. It addresses the symptoms (wealth inequality) but not the underlying cause (the unequal dynamics that sustain it). A truly Rawlsian society would need to design its basic structure not only to redistribute outcomes but also to prevent payoff asymmetries from arising in the first place. For example, it could do this by breaking monopolies, imposing strict inheritance taxes, and ensuring that everyone has access to high-quality public goods. This would ensure that competition for positions is truly fair. If you redistribute once in a system with significant asymmetric feedback, it's like pouring water into a bucket that leaks. The system's dynamics will swiftly bring back the old gradient.

## C. The Desert Paradigm and the Distinction of Reward from Effort

The concept of desert—that individuals ought to receive what they merit for their efforts and contributions—may represent the most culturally influential ethical framework. This connection is broken by differences in payoffs. When a fund manager gets a billion-dollar bonus for making hazardous bets with hidden government guarantees, their award has nothing to do with how much they serve society or how well they did their job. When a tech founder's success is primarily because they were the first to enter a market expected to generate network effects, their big payoff is more a sign of being in the right place at the right time than of being a nice person.

This disconnect is terrible for people's spirits and the economy as a whole. It creates a world where the idea of meritocracy remains the same, but the reality is one of "lottery," where a few big prizes make it seem like there are chances, while the median outcome stays the same. The ethical concept of desert devolves into a hollow justification for outcomes primarily driven by systematic luck and cumulative advantage, undermining the moral framework that liberal nations utilize to justify inequality.

## III. Stabilizing Fairness: Ethics for an Unbalanced World

If fairness is a non-equilibrium condition, the ethical pursuit must shift from defining a just distribution to developing a system defined by suitable dynamics. This requires a shift from ex-post redistribution to ex-ante pre-distribution, as well as the deliberate monitoring of feedback loops.

1. Dampening Positive Feedback Loops: The goal is to minimize the returns on current advantages. This could mean anything, like these rules:

   Strong antitrust enforcement: putting an end to market concentration and the monopoly power that makes it so that only one person can win.

   Progressive wealth and inheritance taxes: These taxes directly reduce the capacity of the rich to generate additional wealth over time, functioning as a "leakage" in the feedback loop of dynastic accumulation.

   Public Financing of Elections: Making the connection between economic and political power weaker, which is utilized to get even more economic power.

2. Making negative feedback loops stronger for the wrong reasons: the goal is to stop early failures from becoming permanent traps. This is what a strong social safety net should do, but in a way that changes with time:

   Universal Basic Services: Making sure that everyone can get excellent housing, health care, education, and childcare. This gives people strength by ensuring that being sick or unemployed doesn't permanently reduce their human capital.

   Programs for lifelong learning and retraining: Understanding that careers don't always follow a straight line in a changing economy. These programs give folks an opportunity to start again and get their careers back on track.

3. Structural Systems of Payoffs: This implies modifying the laws of the game such that everyone has a fair chance of winning and losing.

   Financial Regulation: Making corporations take on more risk by requiring them to have more capital and making it illegal for executives to get compensation if their risky choices lead to failure.

   Giving workers more power to negotiate: Unions and codetermination ensure that productivity gains are shared more fairly between capital and labor, so that capital owners don't get all the benefits.

## Conclusion

The pervasive and intensifying inequality of our time is not merely a result of the erroneous application of ethical principles. The widespread presence of payoff asymmetries that make a fair society unstable is a sign of a bigger problem with the system. Ethical theories that focus solely on the final distributional outcome are like putting a cold compress on a fever to make it go away, without treating the infection that caused it. The realization that fairness forms a non-equilibrium situation is simultaneously a frightening and liberating discovery. It is depressing because it illustrates that justice is not a natural endpoint in the formation of society, but rather a fragile objective that must be worked on continually. It is empowering because it gives you a new way to look at challenges and a new set of skills. We can start to establish institutions that make fairness a strong and stable state by looking at how our economic and social systems operate together, identifying the feedback loops, asymmetries, and attractor states. The ethical imperative of the 21st century necessitates a transition from a static theory of justice to a dynamic practice of justice: the ongoing, institutionalized effort to mitigate the intrinsic tendencies of complex, asymmetric systems to devolve into inequality, while guiding our collective existence towards a more stable and authentically humane equilibrium.

# A Game-Theoretic Basis of Solidarity

## Abstract

Solidarity is frequently regarded as a moral objective, an ethical obligation to mutual assistance, shared destiny, and collective accountability. But solidarity is not just a moral ideal imposed on social systems from above. It is also an emergent characteristic of strategic interaction within particular institutional, informational, and temporal contexts. Game theory, often linked to rational self-interest and competitive equilibria, offers a surprisingly strong analytical framework for comprehending the emergence and frequent collapse of solidarity. This essay posits that solidarity is not opposed to rationality; rather, it signifies a superior equilibrium in repeated, interdependent games marked by uncertainty, incomplete information, and collective vulnerability. When framed correctly, solidarity can be seen as a stable strategy in situations with long time horizons, reliable commitment mechanisms, and environments rich in feedback. On the other hand, when these conditions break down, strategic behavior gives way to defection, mistrust, and social fragmentation. In addition, this essay analyzes classic and modern game-theoretic models, such as the Prisoner's Dilemma, coordination games, public goods games, evolutionary dynamics, and networked games, to illustrate that solidarity is not merely a sentimental anomaly but a structurally rooted phenomenon. Furthermore, it illustrates how contemporary political and economic frameworks systematically erode the prerequisites for solidaristic equilibria, resulting in what can be described as strategic atomization: a rational yet socially detrimental equilibrium trap.

## I. Solidarity as a Strategic Notion

In traditional political and moral philosophy, solidarity is conceptualized in terms of ethical dimensions such as fraternity, altruism, and collective moral responsibility. Game theory redefines solidarity as a strategic approach, a behavioral pattern adopted in expectation of others' actions within specified payoff frameworks.

In terms of game theory, solidarity can be defined as:

> A consistent trend of collaboration among agents who acknowledge their enduring interdependence and modify their strategies accordingly.

This definition brings out three main parts:

- Interdependence: Means that the actions of others affect the results.

- Temporal extension: The benefits accumulate over time as you interact with the same person repeatedly.

- Expectation formation: What you think about how others will act in the future affects what you do now.

Solidarity arises not from irrationality or self-sacrifice among agents, but rather because cooperation optimizes expected utility within specific structural parameters. When these conditions vanish, solidarity becomes strategically tenuous, despite the persistence of strong moral commitments.

## II. The Prisoner's Dilemma and the Fallacy of Inevitable Defection

The Prisoner's Dilemma (PD) has historically functioned as the principal argument against collaboration. In its one-time form, defection is the best move for both players, leading to a Pareto-inferior outcome. Many people have wrongly thought that this means that rational agents can't stay together.

But this conclusion is based on very strict assumptions: only one interaction, no future effects, no effects on reputation, and no enforcement by institutions. Once these assumptions are relaxed, the logic changes completely.

### Prisoner's Dilemma Again and Again

In repeated PD games, cooperation can become a stable equilibrium if players place enough value on future payoffs (i.e., have a high discount factor). Tit-for-Tat, Grim Trigger, and Win-Stay, Lose-Shift are all examples of strategies that show that working together can be both logical and stable over time.

In this case, solidarity is a conditional strategy: work together as long as others do. This is not naive altruism; rather, it is a response to demonstrated reciprocity. In this framework, solidarity is earned and strengthened, not given without thought.

## III. Public Goods, Free Riding, and Cooperation with Conditions

In games with more than one player, like public goods games, solidarity becomes harder to understand. These games simulate scenarios in which individuals invest in a communal resource at personal expense, while the benefits are distributed.

The common prediction is that many people will take advantage of free riding. But real-world evidence consistently contradicts this result. Instead, most players show conditional cooperation: they are willing to help if others do too, but they stop helping when they think they are being taken advantage of.

This behavior shows that solidarity is very sensitive to how fair and reciprocal people perceive it to be. So, game theory explains not only why solidarity can form, but also why it breaks down when inequality or asymmetry becomes apparent. When agents see that profits are privatized and costs are shared, it makes sense for them not to work together.

## IV. Coordination Games and the Strength of Common Expectations

Coordination games have more than one equilibrium, some of which are helpful and some of which are harmful. The problem isn't resisting the urge to defect; it's getting everyone on the same page.

Some examples are:

- Picking which side of the road to drive on
- Adopting shared standards or rules
- Keeping democratic institutions in place

In these types of games, solidarity happens when agents agree on expectations that help each other. Once they are set up, solidaristic equilibria can become self-stabilizing, which is important. Deviations are expensive, not because they are wrong, but because they don't make sense considering what other people expect.

But narrative disruption can break up coordination equilibria. When faith in shared norms diminishes due to polarization, misinformation, or institutional deterioration, systems may abruptly transition into suboptimal equilibria. So, game theory gives a formal reason for social breakdowns that seem irrational in hindsight.

## V. Evolutionary Game Theory and the Rise of Working Together

Evolutionary game theory broadens analysis from rational computation to dynamics at the population level. Strategies that perform well proliferate over time, regardless of agents' conscious intentions.

In these models, cooperative strategies can dominate under conditions of:

- Interacting repeatedly
- Assortative matching (cooperators work with other cooperators)
- Punishment of those who leave
- Reputation effects

When social settings reward cooperation and punish exploitation, solidarity becomes an evolutionarily stable strategy. On the other hand, when institutions don't enforce reciprocity, exploitative strategies have an evolutionary edge.

This insight underscores a central theme: solidarity is not merely a cultural value, but a product of systemic selection pressures. When societies reward cooperation, they tend to create norms that encourage solidarity. When they reward predation, they tend to create norms that encourage distrust.

## VI. Networks, Inequality, and the Vulnerability of Solidarity

Networked interactions are becoming increasingly important in modern game theory. In real societies, agents don't all interact in the same way. They have different levels of power, information, and influence.

What networked games show us is that:

- Centralized actors can leave at a lower immediate cost.
- Peripheral actors face excessive risks.
- Inequality changes the way incentives work.

As inequality increases, solidarity becomes strategically precarious. Actors with high status have less reason to work together, while actors with low status lose faith in reciprocity. The system moves toward asymmetric equilibria based on extraction rather than mutuality. This dynamic helps explain why social fragmentation and economic inequality grow together. The decline of solidarity is not solely a moral failing; it is a logical reaction to skewed incentive structures.

## VII. Institutions as Tools for Making Promises

If solidarity is strategically contingent, institutions are crucial for maintaining it. Laws, norms, and enforcement mechanisms serve as commitment devices that sustain cooperative equilibria.

Some examples are:

- Progressive taxation as a way to provide public goods
- Labor protections as tools for coordination and power sharing
- Social insurance as games that pools risks

Institutions diminish uncertainty, synchronize expectations, and modify payoff matrices to render cooperation rational from a game-theoretic standpoint. When institutions are dismantled or seized, solidaristic strategies become ineffective, even among well-meaning individuals. Instead of seeing political conflict as a fight between selfishness and virtue, this sees it as a fight over the rules of the game itself.

## VIII. The End of Solidarity as a Change in Balance

When solidarity breaks down, it often looks like moral decay or cultural division. Game theory provides a more accurate diagnosis: a transition from cooperative to non-cooperative equilibria induced by evolving incentives. When trust fades, inequality grows, and the future looks less bright, it makes sense to leave. People go into defensive mode not because they don't believe in solidarity, but because the system no longer supports it.

This realization is sobering: Calls for solidarity without structural change are strategically useless. You can't keep solidarity going just by telling people to do it. It needs institutional structures that make cooperation sensible, clear, and long-lasting.

In conclusion, reclaiming solidarity as a rational strategy

Game theory doesn't hurt solidarity; it helps us understand it. Strategic analysis does not show that cooperation is naive or irrational; rather, it shows that solidarity is a complex balancing act that depends on time horizons, reciprocity, fairness, and institutional design. The tragedy of modern political economy is not the rise of selfishness among individuals, but the growing incentives for defection within systems. So, rebuilding solidarity needs more than just moral appeals. It necessitates reconfiguring the games we engage in—modifying incentives, rebuilding trust, and broadening collective time horizons.

In this way, solidarity is not a dream but a smart way to deal with shared weakness. When the rules of the game reflect this truth, working together is not only possible, but also necessary.

# The Game-Theoretic Foundations of the Importance of Collective Solidarity

## Abstract

Solidarity is often treated as a moral aspiration—an ethical commitment to mutual aid, shared fate, and collective responsibility. Yet solidarity is not merely a normative ideal imposed upon social systems from above. It is also an emergent property of strategic interaction under specific institutional, informational, and temporal conditions. Game theory, typically associated with rational self-interest and competitive equilibria, provides a surprisingly robust analytical foundation for understanding when and why solidarity emerges—and why it so often collapses.

This essay argues that solidarity is not antithetical to rationality but instead represents a higher-order equilibrium in repeated, interdependent games characterized by uncertainty, imperfect information, and shared vulnerability. When properly framed, solidarity can be understood as a stable strategy under conditions of long time horizons, credible commitment mechanisms, and feedback-rich environments. Conversely, when these conditions erode, strategic behavior devolves toward defection, mistrust, and social fragmentation.

By examining classic and contemporary game-theoretic models, including the Prisoner's Dilemma, coordination games, public goods games, evolutionary dynamics, and networked games, this essay demonstrates that solidarity is not a sentimental anomaly but a structurally grounded outcome. Moreover, it shows how modern political and economic systems systematically undermine the conditions necessary for solidaristic equilibria, producing what may be termed strategic atomization: a rational yet socially destructive equilibrium trap.

## I. Solidarity as a Strategic Concept

In conventional political and moral philosophy, solidarity is framed in ethical terms: fraternity, altruism, or shared moral obligation. Game theory reframes solidarity as a strategy pattern of behavior adopted in anticipation of others' actions under defined payoff structures.

From a game-theoretic perspective, solidarity can be defined as:

> A sustained pattern of cooperative behavior among agents who recognize their long-term interdependence and adjust their strategies accordingly.

This definition highlights three core elements:

1. Interdependence – Outcomes depend on others' actions.

2. Temporal extension – Payoffs accrue over repeated interactions.

3. Expectation formation – Beliefs about others' future behavior shape present decisions.

Solidarity emerges not because agents are irrational or self-sacrificing, but because cooperation maximizes expected utility under certain structural conditions. When these conditions disappear, solidarity becomes strategically fragile—even if moral commitments remain rhetorically strong.

## II. The Prisoner's Dilemma and the Myth of Inevitable Defection

The Prisoner's Dilemma (PD) has long served as the canonical argument against cooperation. In its one-shot form, defection is the dominant strategy for both players, leading to a Pareto-inferior outcome. This has often been misinterpreted as proof that rational agents cannot sustain solidarity. However, this conclusion rests on highly restrictive assumptions: single interaction, no future consequences, no reputation effects, and no institutional enforcement. Once these assumptions are relaxed, the logic changes fundamentally.

### Repeated Prisoner's Dilemma

In repeated PD games, cooperation can emerge as a stable equilibrium when players value future payoffs sufficiently (i.e., have a high discount factor). Strategies such as Tit-for-Tat, Grim Trigger, and Win-Stay, Lose-Shift demonstrate that cooperation can be both rational and evolutionarily stable.

Here, solidarity functions as a conditional strategy: cooperate so long as others do. Importantly, this is not naïve altruism but a contingent response to demonstrated reciprocity. Solidarity, in this framework, is earned and reinforced, not blindly bestowed.

## III. Public Goods, Free Riding, and Conditional Cooperation

Solidarity becomes more complex in multiplayer settings, particularly in public goods games. These games model situations in which individuals contribute to a collective resource at personal cost, while the benefits are shared.

The standard prediction is widespread free riding. Yet empirical evidence consistently contradicts this outcome. Instead, most players exhibit conditional cooperation: they are willing to contribute if others do, but withdraw support when they perceive exploitation.

This behavior reveals a crucial insight: Solidarity is highly sensitive to perceived fairness and reciprocity.

Game theory thus explains not only why solidarity can emerge, but why it collapses when inequality or asymmetry becomes visible. When agents observe that gains are privatized while costs are socialized, cooperation rationally unravels.

## IV. Coordination Games and the Power of Shared Expectations

Unlike the Prisoner's Dilemma, coordination games feature multiple equilibria—some cooperative, others destructive. The challenge is not overcoming temptation to defect but aligning expectations.

Examples include:

- Choosing which side of the road to drive on
- Adopting common standards or norms
- Maintaining democratic institutions

In such games, solidarity emerges when agents converge on mutually reinforcing expectations. Importantly, once established, solidaristic equilibria can become self-stabilizing. Deviations are costly not because they are immoral, but because they are strategically irrational given others' expectations.

However, coordination equilibria are vulnerable to narrative disruption. When trust in shared norms erodes—through polarization, misinformation, or institutional decay—systems can tip abruptly into inferior equilibria. Game theory thus provides a formal explanation for sudden social breakdowns that appear irrational in hindsight.

## V. Evolutionary Game Theory and the Emergence of Cooperation

Evolutionary game theory extends analysis beyond rational calculation to population-level dynamics. Strategies that perform well proliferate over time, regardless of agents' conscious intentions.

In these models, cooperative strategies can dominate under conditions of:

- Repeated interaction
- Assortative matching (cooperators interact with cooperators)
- Punishment of defectors
- Reputation effects

Solidarity emerges here as an evolutionarily stable strategy when social environments reward cooperation and penalize exploitation. Conversely, when institutions fail to enforce reciprocity, exploitative strategies gain evolutionary advantage.

This insight underscores a central theme: solidarity is not merely a cultural value, but a product of systemic selection pressures. Societies that structurally reward cooperation will tend to produce solidaristic norms; those that reward predation will normalize distrust.

## VI. Networks, Inequality, and the Fragility of Solidarity

Modern game theory increasingly emphasizes the importance of networked interactions. In real societies, agents do not interact uniformly; they occupy positions of unequal power, information, and influence.

Networked games reveal that:

- Centralized actors can defect with lower immediate cost.
- Peripheral actors bear disproportionate risks.
- Inequality distorts incentive structures.

As inequality rises, solidarity becomes strategically unstable. High-status actors face weaker incentives to cooperate, while low-status actors lose faith in reciprocity. The system drifts toward asymmetric equilibria characterized by extraction rather than mutuality.

This dynamic helps explain why economic inequality and social fragmentation co-evolve. The erosion of solidarity is not a moral failure alone—it is a rational response to distorted payoff landscapes.

## VII. Institutions as Commitment Devices

If solidarity is strategically contingent, institutions play a decisive role in sustaining it. Laws, norms, and enforcement mechanisms function as commitment devices that stabilize cooperative equilibria.

Examples include:

- Progressive taxation as a public goods mechanism
- Labor protections as coordination devices
- Social insurance as risk-pooling games

From a game-theoretic perspective, institutions reduce uncertainty, align expectations, and alter payoff matrices to make cooperation rational. When institutions are dismantled or captured, solidaristic strategies lose viability—even among well-intentioned actors.

This reframes political conflict not as a clash between selfishness and virtue, but as a struggle over the rules of the game itself.

## VIII. The Collapse of Solidarity as an Equilibrium Shift

The breakdown of solidarity often appears as moral decay or cultural polarization. Game theory suggests a more precise diagnosis: a shift from cooperative to non-cooperative equilibria driven by changing incentives.

When trust erodes, inequality rises, and future horizons shorten, defection becomes rational. Individuals withdraw into defensive strategies—not because they reject solidarity in principle, but because the system no longer supports it.

This insight carries a sobering implication: Appeals to solidarity without structural reform are strategically impotent. Solidarity cannot be sustained by exhortation alone. It requires institutional architectures that make cooperation rational, visible, and durable.

## Conclusion: Reclaiming Solidarity as a Rational Strategy

Game theory does not undermine solidarity; it explains it. Far from revealing cooperation as naïve or irrational, strategic analysis shows that solidarity is a sophisticated equilibrium, one that depends on time horizons, reciprocity, fairness, and institutional design. The tragedy of contemporary political economy is not that people have become selfish, but that systems increasingly reward defection. Rebuilding solidarity, therefore, requires more than moral appeals. It requires reconstructing the games we play, reshaping incentives, restoring trust, and extending collective time horizons. In this sense, solidarity is not a utopian ideal but a rational response to shared vulnerability. When the rules of the game reflect this reality, cooperation is not only possible but also inevitable.

# Chapter 4

# Economic Systems and Political Dynamics

## Envisioning a Post-Capitalistic Economy for the United States: Achieving Economic Justice, Income Equality, and Social Mobility

## Abstract

The twenty-first century has revealed the shortcomings of American capitalism. It doesn't look good. People have less faith in democratic institutions because income and wealth inequality is growing, social mobility is decreasing, and political polarization is rising. These trends indicate the necessity for an alternative economic system that does not rely on capitalism. The core of this new system should be fairness, justice, ethical outcomes, and democratic accountability, while also protecting innovation and individual freedom. This is a humanistic vision that requires collaboration between both parties in politics.

## The Concepts Underlying a Post-Capitalist Economy

A new system would be based on four main principles: fairness in the economy, equal pay, social mobility, and a stable democracy. Economic justice means that resources and opportunities are shared fairly. Equal pay doesn't mean that everyone gets the same amount of money. It means closing large pay gaps so that everyone gets a fair and lasting wage. Social mobility means that anyone can improve their life, no matter where they come from. For democracy to work, there needs to be institutions that are not controlled by a small group of powerful people and that listen to the people. We can all work together to make these things happen.

## Making Institutions

### 1. Ownership Models That Include Everyone
Tax breaks and other incentives would make businesses more likely to adopt employee-ownership models such as cooperatives, ESOPs, and multi-stakeholder enterprises. This gives everyone access to capital and links pay increases to productivity gains, which closes the pay gap between CEOs and workers.

### 2. Innovation and Public Venture Capital in Society
Publicly funded venture funds would help new businesses in health care, green technology, and infrastructure development. Intellectual property resulting from government-funded research and development should either remain in the public domain or be licensed at fair rates. This method ensures that new ideas benefit everyone, not just a small group. This is especially true for DARPA, which uses taxpayer money to fund technological advances that improve national security, yet the profits go only to defense contractors' shareholders, not to taxpayers.

### 3. Basic Services for All
Along with cash transfers, the system would also provide high-quality universal services in health care, education (including lifelong learning), public transportation, and access to digital technology. These make life less expensive and give everyone a chance to improve their situation.

### 4. Taxation that is Both Progressive and Automated
Wealth taxes, financial transaction levies, and a new income tax system would all be automatically collected at the source using digital technologies. This would make it harder for people to avoid paying them. Tax money would pay for universal services and a sovereign wealth fund that gives money to everyone.

### 5. Democratically Planning the Economy
Instead of top-down central planning, the system would use participatory budgeting at the local and regional levels and algorithmic coordination for large-scale resource allocation, such as real-time carbon pricing and supply-chain management. Using both human judgment and AI-assisted forecasting, citizens' assemblies would set broad priorities. In practice, equal income and social mobility.

This model reduces income inequality through shared ownership, universal services, and automatic dividends rather than stringent wage controls. Kids from poor families get the same health care and education as kids from rich families. This stops the cycle of inherited disadvantages. Mobility metrics, like measuring intergenerational income elasticity, neighborhood opportunity indices, and access to capital, would help policymakers make changes.

## Keeping Democracy Stable

In a post-capitalist America, there would be rules to stop plutocracy. For example, there would be strict limits on how much money people can give to campaigns, rules against the "revolving door" between business and government, and clear digital platforms for political donations. The system spreads wealth, making it harder for the rich to control policy. This makes people trust the government more. Participatory mechanisms, including citizens' juries, deliberative polling, and digital plebiscites, would improve representative democracy without replacing it.

## Finding a Good Balance Between Planning and Markets

There would still be markets for most goods and services, but strict rules would be in place to curb monopolistic behavior, data abuse, and environmental damage. Core digital infrastructure, energy, health, housing finance, and other important areas would be treated like public utilities or heavily regulated public spaces. This mixed setup allows entrepreneurship to evolve while ensuring that social needs are met and the environment is safe.

## How to Make the Change

The move to post-capitalism would happen gradually, starting with pilot programs at the state and municipal levels. These would include cooperative business incubators, trials of universal basic services, and participatory budgeting projects. Then the federal government would ensure that successful experiments worked in every state. A modern three-way approach to social dialogue among workers, employers, and the government would help prevent problems and facilitate agreement.

## Conclusion

In the United States, a post-capitalist system does not necessitate the elimination of markets or the inhibition of individual initiative. Instead, it is a way to make the economy work better while still following democratic principles and lasting for a long time. By making economic justice, income equality, and social mobility part of its institutional DNA, a system like this would make American democracy stronger, not weaker. This would guarantee that everyone has access to freedom and wealth. This is not a political vision; it is a moral and humanistic one.

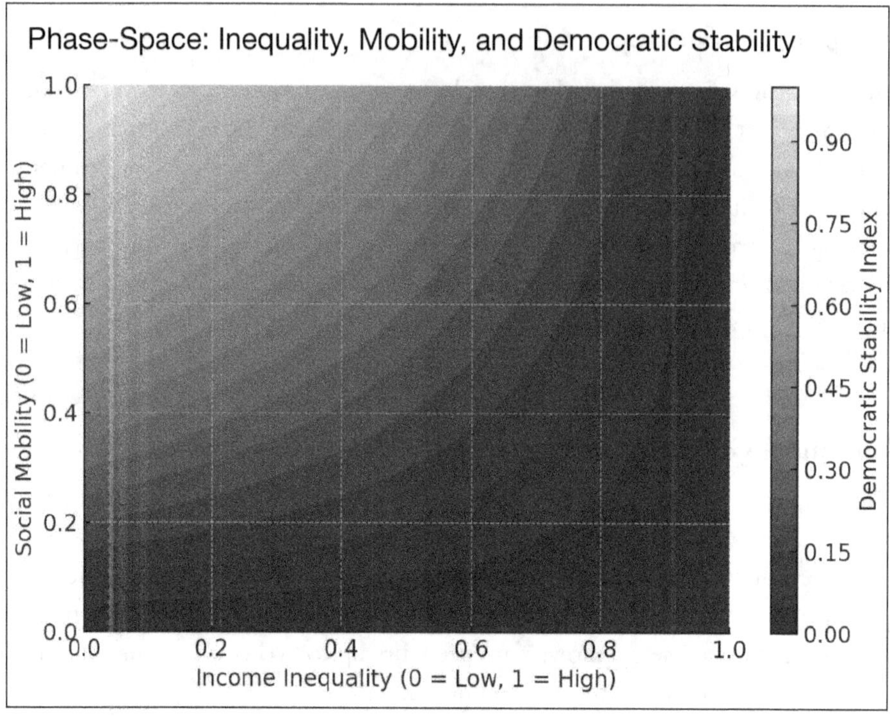


The above phase-space model demonstrates the interrelation of inequality, social mobility, and democratic stability. The yellow shading shows the optimal location, which is in the Northwest quadrant.

# The Military-Industrial Complex and Its Influence on American Geopolitics

## Abstract

President Dwight D. Eisenhower first used the term "military-industrial complex" (MIC) in 1961. It has since become one of the most powerful and long-lasting systems that shape how the US acts in the world. The structural interdependence of defense contractors, political institutions, and military bureaucracy ensures the persistence of high defense spending, a global military presence, and an interventionist foreign policy. This essay analyzes the Military-Industrial Complex (MIC) utilizing complexity economics and systems theory, clarifying its function as a self-reinforcing feedback loop that transforms national security requirements into economic incentives, leading to persistent distortions in domestic fiscal policy, democratic accountability, and international stability.

## Introduction

The American military-industrial complex is a unique group that brings together political and economic power. President Eisenhower's warning that this network could "endanger our liberties or democratic processes" (Eisenhower 1961) has come true. Today, the MIC is a big system that includes defense contractors, congressional committees, lobbying groups, and research centers. It has changed how the U.S. interacts with other countries and has made the world always ready for war, growing since World War II.

## The Historical Roots of the Military-Industrial Complex

World War II brought American businesses together in a way never before seen, leading to the modern MIC. The Cold War made this alignment official by integrating military spending and new weapons development into the economy (Melman 1970). The containment doctrine and nuclear deterrence framework ensured the continued political necessity of a substantial peacetime defense establishment. The Vietnam War, rearmament during Reagan's presidency, and interventions after 9/11 all made this relationship stronger, making the MIC a permanent part of American political economy (Bacevich 2005).

Politics and Economics are Getting Worse.

Some of the defense contractors that make up the MIC's economic core are Lockheed Martin, Boeing, Northrop Grumman, and Raytheon. These companies use advanced lobbying, spreading contracts across different areas, and the "revolving door" between military service and corporate leadership (Stanger 2020) to get Congress to help them. Complexity economists use the term "positive feedback loop" to describe this. More money is given to the military when politicians support defense spending. The MIC is a self-organizing system that works best for making money and keeping the bureaucracy alive, not for making things run more smoothly.

## Geopolitical Expressions

The MIC has a lot of say in how the U.S. deals with other countries. Its structural bias toward militarized solutions reinforces interventionism, as seen in the Persian Gulf, Iraq, and Afghanistan (Johnson 2004). The notion of perpetual readiness for war has extended to cyber, space, and artificial intelligence warfare, actualizing what Bacevich (2016) terms "perpetual war." Arms exports serve both as a means for the U.S. to gain geopolitical power and as a way to support its own industry. They keep arms races going worldwide and keep allies in U.S.-led security networks.

## Effects at Home: Unequal Treatment and Fiscal Distortion

The MIC takes a lot of money away from social programs in the US. The U.S. defense budget for 2025 is over $900 billion, which is almost 40% of all spending that isn't required by law. Infrastructure, healthcare, and education are still not getting enough money, though (SIPRI 2024). This is an example of militarized Keynesianism, which uses defense spending to boost the economy rather than fair or productive investments (Galbraith 1998). The interaction between inequality, militarization, and political capture creates a new way for democracy to break down. This works as a socio-economic chaotic attractor that keeps the system stable around inequality and ongoing conflict.

## The Phase Space Representation of Military Power

The above phase-space model shows how defense spending (x-axis), intervention frequency (y-axis), and their effects—global instability (z-axis) and domestic inequality (color gradient)—all feed into each other. As defense spending and the number of interventions rise, instability increases nonlinearly. When the system goes too far, it enters a chaotic attractor where militarization is both the cause and the effect of geopolitical disorder. Cutting back on spending doesn't fix the system right away; it stays out of balance because of inertia and vested interests.

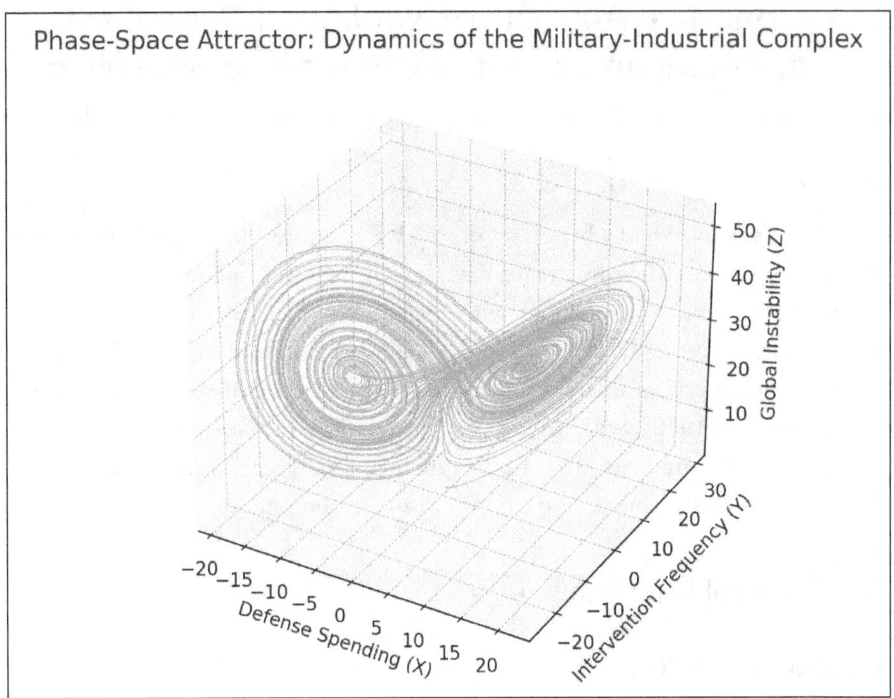


## Possibilities for Change

Reform requires structural realignment: increased transparency in procurement, restrictions on revolving-door employment, and a redefinition of national security to include climate, infrastructure, and health resilience (Stanger 2020). Redirecting defense R&D toward dual-use and civilian applications could shift technological innovation without compromising industrial capacity. But systemic change is still hard because the MIC has become what complexity theorists call a resilient adaptive system. This means that it can protect itself with stories, lobbying, and new technologies.

## Conclusion

The military-industrial complex persists not merely due to bureaucratic inertia or political corruption, but because it has transformed into an adaptive, self-sustaining system embedded within American capitalism and identity. Its effect on geopolitics shows a paradox: America's desire for security through dominance often makes the world less stable and hurts democracy. Using systems analysis and complexity to understand the MIC shows that it is not a conspiracy but a natural part of how power works today. It says it protects the republic, but its equilibrium puts it in danger.

# A Comparative Analysis of Neoliberal Capitalism and an American Variant of Democratic Socialism

## Abstract

Capitalist ideas have had a big effect on the US economy and politics for a long time. But in the last 40 years, wages have stayed the same, inequality has grown, and people have become unhappy with society. This has made arguments about other models, especially democratic socialism, even more heated. This essay compares neoliberal capitalism, which has been the dominant economic model since the late 1970s, with a type of democratic socialism that people often confuse with communism. It examines their philosophical foundations, policy objectives, societal impacts, and implications for democratic governance.

## The Philosophical Foundations

### Neoliberal Capitalism

In the 1970s, people thought Keynesian welfare capitalism wasn't working well enough, so neoliberalism came about. Some of its main ideas are free markets, less government control, privatization of public goods, fiscal austerity, and a small role for government in the economy. It is based on classical liberal ideas about personal freedom and the economy's ability to regulate itself. It says that competition and private business are the main drivers of growth.

### Democratic Socialism in the United States

Democratic socialism in the United States is based on progressive reform ideas like the New Deal and the Great Society. It doesn't back either laissez-faire capitalism or authoritarian socialism. It supports a mixed economy in which services like healthcare, education, infrastructure, and sometimes housing and energy are considered public goods. Private businesses, on the other hand, stay in places that aren't as important for the common good. This approach places significant weight on economic rights, collective bargaining, and allowing people to vote on important policy decisions. The goal is to find a middle ground between market fairness and social justice.

# Policy Priorities and Institutional Frameworks

## Neoliberalism in Capitalism

The main goals of neoliberalism are to lower taxes for people and businesses that make a lot of money, get rid of rules on financial markets, make free trade deals, and sell off public assets. Since Reagan became president, the U.S. has seen these changes: top tax rates have gone down, fewer people are joining unions, and the government has become less strict about issues like finance and telecommunications. The result has been greater freedom of capital to move and a focus on shareholder value rather than stakeholder interests.

## Democratic Socialism in the U.S.

If the United States had a version of democratic socialism, some of these priorities would change. It would likely expand universal healthcare, strengthen labor protections, invest heavily in public infrastructure and green technologies, and fund social programs through progressive taxation. Instead of getting rid of markets, it would make them more strictly controlled to stop monopolies, protect the environment, and narrow the gap between the rich and the poor. The model is similar to the Nordic social democracies, but it works better in the U.S. because the political culture is more decentralized and diverse, with strong civil society groups.

## Outcomes for Society and the Economy

Neoliberalism has driven significant economic growth and innovative ideas in certain domains; however, it has also led to pronounced disparities among groups. Since 1980, productivity in the U.S. has grown much faster than the average wage. This has made growth and widespread prosperity less connected. The pay gap between CEOs and workers has gotten bigger, and most of the money is in the hands of the top 1%. The cost of public goods like healthcare and education has gone up and become less fair. This makes it harder for people to move up in society and makes politics more divided. People who support democratic socialism say it would more evenly distribute wealth and income, allow people to move up in society, and strengthen social ties. Universal programs could help the middle and working classes have more stable finances, and public investment could help productivity grow over time. Some people say that social programs could lead to waste, higher taxes, and inaction by the government. However, data from Denmark and Sweden show that well-designed social programs can work even amid significant competition and new ideas.

## Effects on Democratic Governance

Neoliberal capitalism often results in the concentration of economic power, which can transform into political influence. The "revolving door" between government and business, corporate lobbying, and the way campaign finance works could all make it harder for democracy to hold people accountable. When the economy is unstable, populist backlash can worsen, and trust in institutions can decline.

## Democracy and Democratic Socialism

The goal of American democratic socialism is to strengthen democracy by ensuring that economic inequality doesn't undermine political equality. It stresses the importance of public input when making policies, giving workers better representation, and stopping corporations from taking over politics. But putting such a model into action means dealing with powerful groups that don't want to change and a constitution that makes it hard to quickly redistribute wealth.

## Conclusion

Neoliberal capitalism and American democratic socialism represent divergent frameworks concerning the relationship between markets and states. Neoliberalism prioritizes the freedom of the market and private businesses, while democratic socialism prioritizes economic rights, the common good, and democratic control over essential services. Both models have their pros and cons, but the comparison makes one thing clear: to have a stable democracy in the 21st century, we may need to change economic policy to make it fairer and restore widespread prosperity. One way to do this is to change democratic socialism to fit American institutions and culture.

# The Impact of Globalization on the American Middle Class

## Abstract

People have long believed that the American middle class is the basis for economic growth and political stability. But globalization has significantly changed the economy over the last 40 years, making this once-secure socioeconomic stratum less stable. This essay analyzes the impact of globalization on the middle class, highlighting the detrimental effects of offshoring, wage stagnation, and technological change, while simultaneously intensifying income inequality. It also examines how this process affects society, politics, and culture, and considers what policies could help restore widespread prosperity. This essay doesn't talk about how artificial intelligence will change society in the future, which is another thing that annoys me.

## The Rise and Fall of the American Middle Class

After World War II, the US economy grew quickly, and the middle class grew as well. People could move up in the world in ways never before possible, thanks to strong labor unions, a lot of manufacturing in the US, and government spending on infrastructure and education. From the 1940s to the 1970s, real wages steadily rose, the wealth gap narrowed, and homeownership increased rapidly. But by the end of the 1970s, globalization and the loss of factory jobs began to erode this income. Changes in technology and trade liberalization made it easier to relocate manufacturing jobs to lower-wage areas. In the 1990s and 2000s, free trade agreements like NAFTA and China's accession to the World Trade Organization accelerated these changes. This was a big deal for the US middle class.

## How to Hollow Out

There are a few things that explain how globalization hurt the middle class in the US:

First, moving manufacturing jobs abroad eliminated millions of stable, unionized jobs that were the backbone of middle-class life. Globalization has made things cheaper for people to buy, but it also hurt businesses in the US. The decline worsened because wages weren't rising, and the labor market was becoming more polarized. Even as competition around the world grew, wages for workers with mid-level skills remained unchanged. Instead, jobs grew in fields that required a lot of skill and paid well, like technology and finance, as well as fields that didn't require much skill and paid poorly, like retail and hospitality. This made the middle empty. Second, globalization and technological changes worked together to eliminate boring jobs. Automation made global trade even more important by taking away jobs in clerical work and manufacturing. The growth of the knowledge economy helped people with more education, but it made some people's jobs less secure. Lastly, the decline of labor unions made it harder for workers to negotiate. Unions used to be a stronghold for middle-class pay and benefits, but membership fell as employers used global competition to undermine collective bargaining.

## Effects on Society and the Economy

The loss of the middle class has changed American society in a big way. The top 1% of earners now take home more than 20% of the national income, up from about 9% in 1978. This shows that income inequality has increased significantly. The middle class's wealth hasn't changed, but the rich have made too much money from capital markets worldwide. Many people lost their jobs in the Rust Belt, and their populations shrank. Their social networks also fell apart. Finding work has become harder and harder because of the rise of the gig economy and service-sector jobs that often don't come with benefits, pensions, or job security.

## Effects on Culture and Politics

Besides economic changes, globalization has also changed politics and culture in significant ways. Both left- and right-wing populist movements have used people's anger over free trade and job insecurity to their advantage. Economic nationalism, skepticism regarding immigration, and critiques of elite narratives on globalization have gained prominence. The American Dream is fading, and this has made the political divide even worse. Families are having trouble paying for housing, health care, and school. Communities that used to be stable because of manufacturing jobs have lost not only jobs but also civic institutions and social ties.

## Responses and Discussions about Policy

Different policies have been put in place to deal with the loss of the middle class. Tariffs and renegotiating trade deals are two examples of protectionist policies that could bring back manufacturing to the US. However, they could also lead to trade wars with other countries. The CHIPS and Science Act and the Inflation Reduction Act are two recent examples of industrial policies that aim to bring production back to the U.S. in key areas such as clean energy and semiconductors. Policymakers have also often emphasized the importance of education and retraining programs, but they haven't always worked. Universal healthcare, child tax credits, and wage subsidies are examples of broader social policies intended to stabilize the economy and help the middle class.

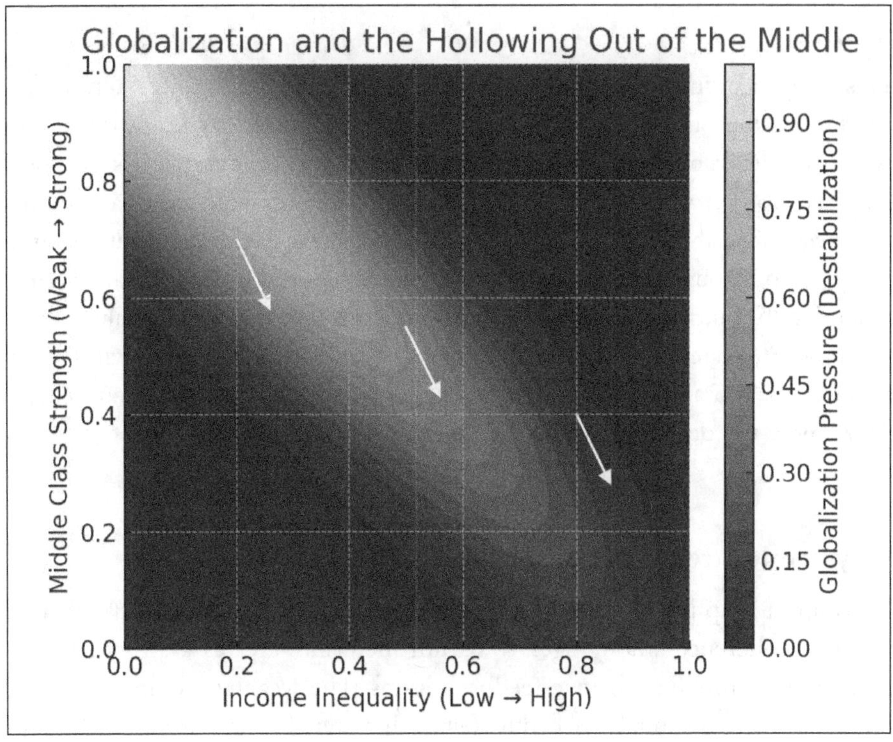


The above phase space diagram shows how globalization affects the middle class in the United States. The x-axis shows how income inequality is getting worse, the y-axis shows how strong the middle class is, and the lines show how globalization is making things less stable. As inequality grows and the middle class weakens, globalization increases the risks of destabilization, making the system less stable.

## Conclusion

Globalization has created a paradox for American society. It has improved efficiency, lowered prices for customers, and enabled new technologies, but it has also hurt the middle class. Policymakers need to find a way to preserve the benefits of global integration while rebuilding the social contract needed for a stable, prosperous middle class. If we don't work to fix inequality, unstable jobs, and regional decline, the middle class will keep getting smaller. This will put both the economy and democracy at risk.

# The Path to Anarchy: Economic Disparity and the Emergence of Authoritarian Influences

## Abstract

This essay examines the nonlinear interactions among wealth inequality, democratic erosion, and the rise of authoritarian tendencies within intricate socio-economic frameworks. It draws on chaos theory, network analysis, and political economy to argue that very unequal economies create feedback loops that destabilize the mechanisms of democratic balance. As inequality grows, societies go through a phase transition in which political order naturally forms around authoritarian attractors. These are regimes that promise stability while speeding up systemic entropy. The analysis places this transition within the overarching moral and informational disintegration of late capitalism, elucidating how the decline of trust and institutional legitimacy paves the way for chaos.

## I. Systemic Stressors: Complexity and Inequality

In complex adaptive systems, equilibrium relies on decentralized feedback and adaptive coherence among agents. Wealth inequality creates a structural imbalance that amplifies positive feedback loops. The wealthy acquire increased power, whereas the impoverished forfeit both material and informational agency. The system is moving toward critical points of instability, where democratic mechanisms that once kept things stable are now being distorted by the concentration of power. Thomas Piketty's "Capital in the Twenty-First Century" demonstrates that when the return on capital (r) consistently exceeds the growth rate (g), inequality escalates at an exponential rate. In terms of dynamics, this is a runaway process, a "strange attractor" of inequality, where differences grow over time, leading to self-reinforcing stratification and, eventually, a split between oligarchic elites and the dispossessed masses.

## II. The Political Phase Transition: Shifting from Democratic to Authoritarian Forces

Authoritarianism does not arise ex nihilo; it develops as a self-organizing attractor within a destabilized phase space of politics. When institutions can no longer control negative feedback (i.e., limits on concentrated power), the system begins to seek alternative organizational structures. As inequality grows, social frustration "heats up," which makes democratic norms less sticky. This makes it easy to switch to a more rigid but fragile structure—autocracy. This transition is similar to a thermodynamic phase change.

This pattern has been clear in the Weimar Republic, the late Roman Republic, and the current political situation in the United States. Economic polarization causes trust to break down, media ecosystems to become more divided, and moral tribalism to grow. People who are confused by uncertainty look for stability in strongman figures who promise to "restore order." These authoritarian attractors use the energy of chaos to turn general social anxiety into concentrated political power.

## III. Network Entropy and Losing Trust

A wide range of voices, institutions, and points of view make up the network entropy in a healthy democracy. This keeps the system flexible. As economic power becomes more centralized, network entropy decreases. The informational bandwidth democratic feedback relies on is shrinking due to media consolidation, financial oligopoly, and algorithmic echo chambers. The resulting information asymmetry leads to a feedback loop: people no longer share a common base of knowledge, making it impossible to discuss things. Legitimacy, which is based on how fair and open something appears to be, declines. The loss of informational coherence is like the loss of thermodynamic balance, which is the first step toward a system breaking down.

## IV. The Moral Vacuum: From Civic Virtue to Cynical Realism

Wealth inequality undermines the moral foundation of civic life. When prosperity is separated from contribution and success from virtue, society's moral economy falls apart, and people care only about their own interests. The public sphere becomes a game of signaling rather than substance. This is made worse by digital media, where performative outrage takes the place of group discussion. In these circumstances, moral signaling supplants moral action. Citizens and elites both go into echo chambers that reinforce their sense of self but weaken their sense of shared responsibility. This moral fragmentation accelerates the search for simple stories such as nationalism, conspiracy theories, or populism. All of these turn anger into obedience, which helps the authoritarian attractor.

## V. The Road to Anarchy: The Inability to Adapt

The system's ability to adapt and re-equilibrate breaks down when inequality and distrust reach a certain level. Complexity shifts from an asset to a liability. Democratic institutions, which are meant to encourage discussion and compromise, are not quick enough to deal with problems of legitimacy and distribution.

At this point, social unrest looks like anarchy, but not in the idealized anarchist sense of people working together; instead, it looks like the breakdown of shared rules. In this disordered area, the authoritarian attractor is the only thing that appears to be order. But this order is fake: authoritarian regimes make things more fragile and speed up their collapse by ignoring complexity instead of dealing with it. Ironically, the path to anarchy goes through the false idea of stability.

## VI. For a Moral Ecology of Wealth

Moral and systemic renewal, not technocratic reform, is the answer to authoritarian attractors. This means putting the idea of shared prosperity at the center of the complicated web of the economy and society. This necessitates reconfiguring economic institutions to optimize distributed agency rather than centralized power. Complexity economics provides tools for simulating adaptive systems: decentralized governance, participatory budgeting, and cooperative ownership frameworks serve as negative feedback mechanisms that restore systemic equilibrium.

People can only return to a creative order by rebuilding a moral ecology where freedom and responsibility go together, and prosperity and contribution go together.

## Conclusion

The emergence of authoritarian attractors in unequal societies is not an anomaly but a resultant characteristic of systemic imbalance. Wealth inequality breaks feedback loops, undermines legitimacy, and turns democracies into self-organizing hierarchies of control. Anarchy doesn't come from revolution; it comes from apathy. It's the slow moral decline of complexity without a conscience. To change this path, we need more than just redistributive policy. We need to rethink the social contract as a dynamic balance between freedom, fairness, and systemic coherence.

# An Examination of Gun Legislation Efficacy and Firearm-Related Violence via Phase Transition

## Abstract

I usually write about political economy and not pure politics. But the recent mass shooting in Minneapolis made me feel like I had to give an evidence-based answer to this horrible act of violence. A major point of contention in the ongoing debate over gun control in the US is whether stricter gun laws would reduce the number of gun deaths. There is growing evidence that this link really does exist. States with strong gun safety laws, like Massachusetts, California, and New York, tend to have many fewer gun deaths than states with weaker laws, like Mississippi, Louisiana, and Alaska. This difference resembles a non-linear pattern common to complex systems. Small changes don't have much effect until a certain point is reached, and then a sharp change occurs.

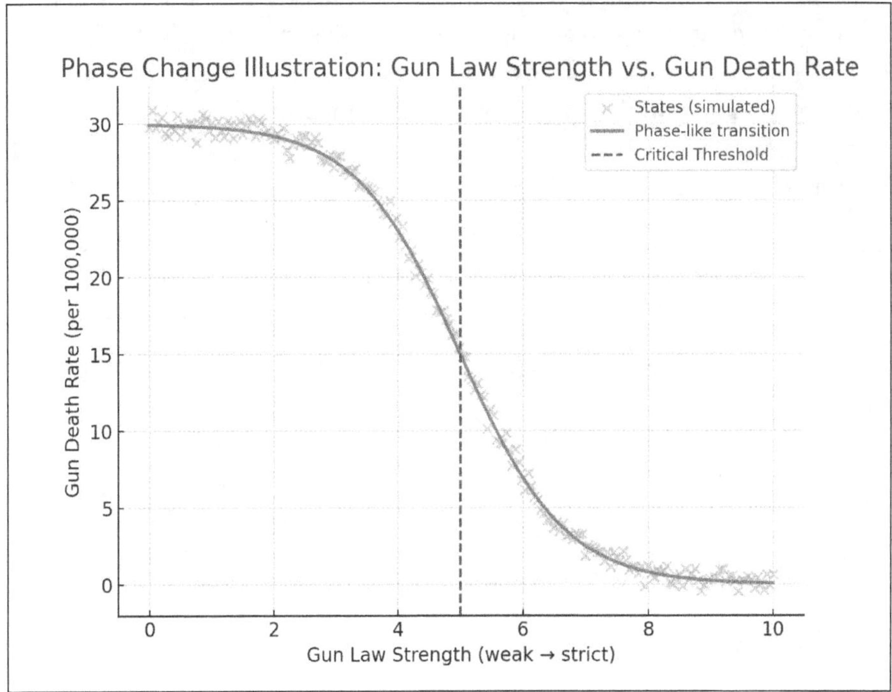


The illustration accompanying this shows how it works. The x-axis shows how strict or weak gun laws are, and the y-axis shows how many people die from guns for every 100,000 people. The data simulation shows a phase-like change: when there aren't many rules, the death rate stays high and stable, but once the rules become stronger, the death rate drops quickly. This phenomenon aligns with public health research indicating that policies like universal background checks, permit-to-purchase mandates, and limitations on high-capacity magazines can significantly decrease both homicides and suicides. For example, California. The gun death rate in the state fell by more than 55% from 1993 to 2017, which was faster than the national rate. Because of its strict rules about who can own guns and how they must be stored, Massachusetts also has one of the lowest gun death rates in the country right now. States that have weak or lenient gun laws, on the other hand, still have a lot more gun deaths than other states. The implication is that gun safety regulation does not merely shift outcomes incrementally but functions as a lever for systemic change—what complexity theorists would identify as a phase shift in social outcomes.

This phase change illustration shows how the strength of gun laws and the number of gun deaths are related. The data ultimately indicates that the correlation between law and violence is nonlinear rather than linear. Incremental regulation below the threshold yields minimal effects, whereas comprehensive frameworks result in swift and enduring reductions in gun fatalities. The policy implication is clear: to effectively reduce gun violence, both states and the federal government must pursue not only incremental reforms but also comprehensive and enforceable legislation that collectively exceeds the threshold for systemic change.

# Ayn Rand's Wrong Ideas About Economics and the Rise of Our Hunger Games Economy

## Abstract

Ayn Rand is one of the most important figures in American economic thought. Objectivism, her philosophy based on extreme self-interest, laissez-faire capitalism, and the moral rejection of altruism, has had a significant impact on modern neoliberal thought. Rand saw herself as a prophet of freedom and human flourishing. However, her ideas about the economy have led to one that is becoming more and more like a dystopia, with huge inequality, instability, and a social order that pits people against each other in a competition that has no winners. This essay critiques the core of Rand's philosophy, examines how her ideas became embedded in U.S. economic policy, and argues that the resulting system—our 'Hunger Games economy'—represents not a triumph of freedom but a betrayal of justice and democracy.

## Rand's Philosophy: The Goodness of Self-Interest

Rand's Objectivism values reason, individuality, and rational self-interest. In her books "Atlas Shrugged" and "The Fountainhead," heroic businesspeople and artists are better than the average person in a society where everyone works together. People who are altruistic are seen as weak, while people who are selfish are seen as the best. This means they have an unshakable faith in free markets and don't like taxes, regulations, or redistribution in the economy.

In the 1950s and 1960s, Alan Greenspan was a close friend of Rand's. He became Chairman of the Federal Reserve in 1987. It was clear that his policy decisions, especially the deregulation of financial markets, were based on Randian ideas of "rational" self-interest. After the 2008 financial crisis, Greenspan said that this way of thinking failed to account for the harmful effects of unchecked greed.

## From Philosophy to Policy: The Rise of Neoliberalism

Rand's ideas fit well with the rise of neoliberalism in the 1980s, when Ronald Reagan was president in the U.S. and Margaret Thatcher was prime minister in the U.K. Both leaders wanted to cut taxes for the rich, get rid of rules, and make it harder for workers to organize, which fit with Rand's dislike of social welfare and collective bargaining. The effects were huge:

- Financialization changed the economy from one based on making things to one based on speculative capital.

- CEO pay ratios are going through the roof. In 1980, the average CEO made 42 times what the average worker made. The ratio exceeded 350:1 by 2022.

- Wage stagnation: American workers' real wages have not changed since the 1970s, even as productivity has increased.

Rand's "virtue of selfishness" evolved into both a cultural ethos and a structural rationale for policies that facilitated the upward redistribution of wealth. Inequality was redefined as a sign of merit, and poverty was seen as a sign of moral failure.

## The Hunger Games Economy: Making Inequality a Show

Suzanne Collins' "The Hunger Games" is a powerful metaphor for Rand's legacy. In Collins' dystopia, the rich live in luxury in the Capitol while the poor work hard in the outer districts for the rich to enjoy. In the same way, in the U.S.:1. The top 1% of Americans now have more money than the bottom 90%.2. Insecurity as the norm: Many Americans are one emergency away from losing everything because of gig work, student debt, and not being able to get health care. Spectacle as distraction: Just as the Games keep districts from revolting, modern media spectacles like reality TV, consumer branding, and political theatrics hide systemic inequality. The Hunger Games metaphor shows not only material inequality but also psychological alienation: people are taught to see one another as competitors in a rigged contest rather than as members of a society.

## Why Rand Was Wrong

There are a few reasons why Rand's philosophy doesn't work: 1. Misunderstanding Human Nature: Behavioral economics and social psychology show that people are basically cooperative and want things to be fair. The Randian 'homo economicus' stereotype is inaccurate. System Fragility: Complexity economics emphasizes the interdependence of agents within a system. Too much inequality destabilizes feedback loops, which can lead to financial crises and political extremism. 2. Moral Bankruptcy: Rand's idea of greed as a virtue weakens civic duty and the legitimacy of democracy, making it easier for an oligarchy to take over. Joseph Stiglitz has said that inequality is not just an economic problem, but also a threat to democracy itself.

## Toward a Different Vision

The U.S. must reject Rand's praise of selfishness and instead build institutions grounded in fairness, solidarity, and shared prosperity to get out of the Hunger Games economy. Policy steps include: 1. Progressive taxation to move wealth from people who have too much of it to people who don't have enough. 2. Changes to make CEO pay more closely match worker pay. 3. Putting money into healthcare, education, and infrastructure to bring back public goods. 4. Better protections for workers will help level the playing field between workers and capital.

These changes aren't perfect, but they are needed to keep a complicated democratic economy stable.

## Conclusion

People used to think Ayn Rand's ideas about economics were too radical, but they have since become part of neoliberal capitalism. Its legacy is evident in the grotesque disparities of the contemporary Hunger Games economy, a society that venerates the few while sacrificing the many. We must reject Rand's perilous myth of virtuous greed and return to an economic perspective that prioritizes economic justice, solidarity, and widespread prosperity.

# The Commoditization of Privacy: A Menace to Democracy

## Abstract

People have always thought of privacy as more than just a personal choice; it is a basic human right that is necessary for freedom, dignity, and being a good citizen in a democracy. You need a safe place inside where you can think, talk, and connect with other people without anyone watching you or pressuring you to do so. Privacy is something that can be bought, sold, tracked, valued, and used in increasingly advanced ways to obtain information in the digital age. What used to be a normal part of being human is now something businesses, political groups, and algorithmic systems designed to change behavior can buy and sell. This essay contends that the commercialization of privacy represents a fundamental threat to democracy. People and organizations have more power over one another when privacy is treated as a product. This makes it easier to manipulate people, figure out what they'll do, get them to do something, and break up groups of friends. This change alters how democracy works, weakens public reason, and replaces the free exchange of ideas with algorithms that control how people think. Over time, democracy becomes less stable, not because people don't care, but because the information people use to make decisions has changed a lot.

## I. The Historical Significance of Privacy and Democratic Liberty

For a long time, the spread of democratic ideas and privacy have been closely linked. Enlightenment philosophers regarded the private sphere as the domain in which individuals constructed their identities, a domain essential to autonomous political participation. People needed time and space to think things through, learn to reason better, and do the right thing to become citizens. Alexis de Tocqueville said that democracies need people who can think for themselves and groups that people choose to join. Both of these things need privacy so that the state or society doesn't have too much power over them.

Liberal democracy recognized privacy as a legal right in the 1800s and 1900s by granting people constitutional rights, limiting government surveillance, and fostering cultural norms that value personal space. The private sphere kept the public sphere in check, preventing democratic power from becoming authoritarian centralization.

But the shift to digital networks, data-driven business models, and widespread surveillance technologies fundamentally altered this balance. Privacy protections used to work, but now that people can track and sell their identities, behaviors, and preferences on a large scale, they no longer do. If the contract doesn't say anything else, what was once private is now public. Businesses, not people, make the rules for the contract.

## II. The Economy of Surveillance Is Growing

When targeted advertising models became popular in the early 2000s, privacy became a commodity. For instance, Google and Facebook found they could use people's personal information, such as their search histories, social networks, browsing patterns, and location signals, to build profiles that predict how people will act. These profiles help companies understand what people want, how they buy things, and how they make decisions.

The surveillance economy makes sense from a business point of view: the more detailed the personal data, the better the prediction of behavior, and the more money it can make. So, privacy is slowly being taken away, not by direct threats, but by how easy it is to use, how often people do it, and how much they depend on networks. People share their personal information so they can use the internet, have fun, talk to others, and feel like they belong.

In this system, the user is not the one who buys; they are the one who sells. The main goal of the deal is not to give a service, but to get behavior. Every time we click, scroll, message, buy, or stop, we change a model of ourselves that is always changing. You can do more than just watch this system; you can also take action. Algorithms don't just guess what people will do; they also change what they do. Using the best persuasion techniques, cognitive psychology, and behavioral economics can help you get, hold, and guide people's attention. The end result is a digital space where people's choices are carefully and consistently guided.

## III. The Political Effects: The Decline of Public Reason

Democracy needs a public space where people can talk about facts and ideas. When privacy is treated like a product, this shared public space breaks down into separate information realities. Social media sites choose news, political messages, and cultural stories that will get the most people to interact with them, not because they are true or good for the public. When people are put in echo chambers of their own beliefs, their biases grow stronger, making it harder to find common ground. Micro-targeted political ads go even further. You can now make political messages that play on the weaknesses of some people's minds. People may hear very different things about the same election, policy, or public event, and each story is meant to make them feel differently rather than think about it.

This fragmentation is not just about knowledge; it's also about how things are put together. It changes democratic discourse from a group effort to change people's minds into a market for personalized campaigns. The public stops being a group of people who talk things over and becomes a set of demographic clusters that can be controlled. Social cohesion diminishes, polarization escalates, and the legitimacy of democratic institutions wanes.

## IV. Power Imbalance and Behavioral Control

The commercialization of privacy reallocates power in ways that erode democratic equality. Political groups and businesses that use big data analytics can see how people behave in ways no one else can. They can accurately predict how people will behave collectively, identify societal issues, and employ tactics to influence individuals to comply with their desires. This ability to collect information is superior to any other program the government used to spy on people in the past. It doesn't make direct threats; instead, it changes what people want, believe, and who they are in subtle ways. People believe they are making their own choices, even when others are influencing them. This is a type of "soft control," meaning running things through behavioral architecture rather than laws. There is a risk not only because this power exists, but also because it is not clear what it does. People don't know how their choices are being changed, how their identities are being tracked, or how their data is being used. Democracy can't work without openness. You can't see power, but it's everywhere.

## V. The Fall of Democracy

These things make democratic systems less stable overall. When privacy becomes a commodity, individuals forfeit their autonomy. They can't see the algorithmic forces that affect their beliefs and decisions. The reason for the group goes away. The shared public space becomes a set of separate information silos. Political identity is divided into factions. Instead of being logical, engagement becomes emotional, split, and flashy. People don't trust institutions anymore. People stop trusting each other when they see things differently. Power unites people. People who manage data infrastructures have too much power over everyone else.

Democracy is less about free people talking together and more about a market of influence run by platforms that profit from anger, division, and spying.

## Conclusion: Taking back privacy as a group asset

Technological progress does not have to lead to the commercialization of privacy. It is the result of political choices, like rules, business plans, and cultural norms, that put making money and being efficient ahead of freedom in a democracy. We need to stop thinking of privacy as a personal choice and start seeing it as good for democracy and the public. We need to improve the law to better protect people. The right to data must be a basic right. There should be a rule about how clear algorithms are. We need more than just laws and rules, though. We need to change how we think about privacy. It's not a luxury that can be given up for convenience; it's what makes freedom possible. Democracy cannot endure in a context where human identity is commodified, and personal experiences are susceptible to algorithmic exploitation. We need to rebuild the walls that protect people's freedom to keep democracy alive. Privacy shouldn't be thought of as a product; it should be protected as the most important part of democracy.

# Why Countries Choose Collapse Over Reform: The Main Reasons for Decline

## Abstract

Countries have had many chances to start over in the past, but they have always chosen to go down instead. These chances were possible to achieve in terms of structure, economy, and politics. This isn't just a story about empires that went too far, democracies that lost their meaning, or monarchies that didn't get how society worked. It is a more profound and systemic paradox: Why do nations consciously persist on trajectories that foreseeably culminate in collapse, despite the availability of viable alternatives? The pattern keeps coming back in strange ways, from the Late Roman Empire to the Qing Dynasty, from the French ancient régime to Weimar Germany, and from the Soviet Union to today's divided democracies and fragile autocracies. Societies that have the means to do so make choices that are bad for them rather than those that are good for them. They prioritize the safety of powerful groups over long-term stability. They let bureaucracies get stuck, institutions get stronger, inequalities grow, and public goods fall apart. They keep using systems that don't work until the cost of change exceeds the cost of failure. This essay argues that countries collapse because their internal incentive systems, along with the psychological, institutional, and geopolitical feedback loops they generate, make decline the best option for important players. Not knowing something is not what causes collapse; not having incentives, imagination, and working together as a group is. Even the smartest players choose strategies that lead to disaster when the game rewards self-preservation over shared prosperity.

## The Reason for Decline: Why Rational People Get Unreasonable Results

The main idea behind game theory and complexity economics is that systems fail not because people are crazy, but because they are stuck in incentive structures that make rational behavior bad for everyone. Mancur Olson's theory of "distributional coalitions" explains how societies build up interest groups that are hard to change over time because they want to keep their rents. These coalitions are small, strong, and highly motivated, while the benefits of reform are spread out and take a long time to materialize. This means that reform costs powerful groups money and power right away. • Decline lets those groups keep their power and privileges for a little while longer. Because of this, there is a collective-action trap where:

- The system rewards short-term extraction over long-term investment.

- No one person can start reform without having to pay unfair costs.

- Collapse is a stable state until the system fails. Decline happens naturally in systems where powerful people can stop changes to institutions.

## Why the Powerful Would Rather Things Get Worse Than Better: Leadership Incentives

It's easy to blame bad leaders for a country's fall, but even leaders who want to do the right thing often have to deal with systems that punish change and reward staying the same.

## Short Time Frames in Politics

Leaders, whether democratic or authoritarian, have a lot to do in a short amount of time. Reform requires enduring immediate political hardship for advantages that may not materialize for years. On the other hand, collapse is far off, not clear, and can be blamed on enemies from outside, past administrations, international forces, or people within the organization who want to sabotage it.

## Crisis as a Means of Control

Leaders often benefit from crises because they grant them emergency powers, weaken the opposition, rally loyalist groups, divert attention from bad management, and allow elites to change the rules of institutions. In these situations, national decline becomes a political advantage.

## Elite Protection and the Illusion of Safety

Elites believe they can endure the nation's decline due to their access to private healthcare, private education, gated communities, offshore accounts, and foreign passports. People think they are insulated from society's problems, which leads to deregulation, the privatization of public goods, and opposition to redistributive reforms.

## Cognitive Capture, Identity Politics, and the Psychology of Decline

Societies don't just fall apart because the elites do; the people themselves also make choices that hurt them.

1. Identity Over Material Gain. Political psychology shows that people often care more about their identity than their economic well-being. If policies help their group identity, voters will support them even if they hurt their financial interests. People see reform as a betrayal and decline as a way to protect culture.

2. Group Illusions and Epistemic Collapse. Societies that are getting worse have information ecosystems that don't work well together. When people stop believing in shared truths, false information spreads, and conspiracy theories fill in the gaps in what we know. You can't work together if you don't have the same information.

## Behavioral Biases

People are naturally attracted to stability. People are more afraid of losing than of gaining because they don't want to lose. People with status quo bias feel normal even when things get worse. Hyperbolic discounting values short-term comfort over long-term survival. People don't want change because it's scary, even when things keep getting worse.

## The Political Economy of Stagnation: How Inequality Stops Recovery

The structure of the economy is one of the most important factors shaping a country's future. Societies with a lot of inequality always show that they can't make changes as easily. When wealth is concentrated, so is power. When a small group of people has a lot of money, rules are made to protect their interests. Monopolies grow, infrastructure breaks down, and social mobility stalls. The end of public goods: When powerful people rely on private goods, public goods suffer. Private schools replace public schools, private policing replaces public safety, and private healthcare replaces public hospitals, for example. The worse public systems get, the harder it is to make changes. Money Traps: When inequality rises, tax bases shrink, debt grows, austerity gets worse, and polarization gets worse. The state ultimately relinquishes its fiscal capacity for reform, irrespective of the emergence of political will.

## Rigid Institutions and Structural Inertia

Institutions are like living things, becoming stiff as they age.

1. Bureaucratic Stagnation: Bureaucracies become stuck in their own rules, don't want to hear new ideas, are too strict, and are defensive. Reform becomes a threat to existence instead of a benefit.

2. Gridlock in the Constitution. Older republics tend to have too many veto points, too many disagreements between the two chambers, too many rules for a supermajority, and too much interference from the courts. These systems prevent tyranny, but they also prevent renewal.

3. Reliance on a Path and Lock-In. Institutional lock-in makes sure that early political deals set limits on what can happen in the future. Coordination failures keep old systems in place, which makes decline the easiest way to go.

Short-sightedness in geopolitics and overreaching in strategy driven by overinvestment in domestic military capabilities.

Countries also decide to break up on the world stage.

1. Arms races and rising tensions. Militarization and competition between countries waste resources and create cycles of aggression that feed on themselves.

2. The Empire Has Too Much Power. A great power will fall apart if it has more obligations to other countries than it has resources. But elites don't want to cut back on their commitments because of their status, the political costs, and the fact that bureaucrats don't want to do it.

3. The Curse of Resources. States with abundant resources fall apart because the rich extract rents, innovation stalls, corruption worsens, and institutions weaken.

## Nonlinear Dynamics: How Collapse Happens Faster

Things don't fall apart in a straight line; they fall apart in a nonlinear way.

1. Positive feedback loops. Corruption breeds distrust, which breeds populism, which breeds more corruption. Unequal treatment leads to division, which leads to gridlock, which leads to stagnation, which leads to more inequality.

2. Effects of the Threshold Systems stay stable until they reach a certain point: public trust breaks down, violence becomes normal, institutions lose their legitimacy, and the state's ability to do its job drops.

3. Changes in Phase: When inequality, polarization, debt, or corruption get too high, social systems change quickly.

## The Game Theory of National Self-Sabotage

The decline of a nation resembles a prisoner's dilemma involving multiple participants:

Cooperation fosters reform; Defection safeguards individual power; Mutual defection results in collapse. Everyone knows that it's better to work together. People don't think that others will help. So everyone goes alone. What happens when it falls apart?

## Historical Case Studies of Certain Declines

In late Rome, the rich didn't pay taxes, the army was too big, and politicians fought with each other. The Qing Dynasty didn't want to change because it was stuck in its old ways. Germany during the Weimar Republic: a lot of fighting and weak institutions. The Soviet Union was stuck and had many rules.

Inequality, division, and the capture of institutions in modern democracies were the result.

## Choosing Renewal: Building Systems That Don't Get Worse

Some nations transform. For renewal to work, there must be social trust, open economic institutions for everyone, bureaucracies that can change, elite sacrifices, long-term planning, and changes to the constitution. Countries don't break up because they must; they do it because their incentive systems make it seem like a good idea. The answer is to change how incentives work so that working together is the best choice, and to let politics change.

## Conclusion

A Possibility, Not a Certainty of Collapse. Countries break up because their structures make it the best choice for them to do so. Leaders put short-term power first, elites protect their rents, people put their identity above their interests, institutions become rigid, polarization destroys trust, geopolitical competition drains resources, and nonlinear feedback loops speed up the decline. We will not fail because of fate. It is a choice—distributed, emergent, path-dependent, and tragically rational for actors caught in dysfunctional equilibria. But it can be unchosen. When the system changes, the strategy changes too. If the plan changes, the result will change.

# Algorithmic Inequality: How Complexity Affects AI-Driven Economies

## Abstract

AI is no longer just a new technology; it is a force that is changing the way economies work, the job market, institutions, and social hierarchies. People often say that AI will change the way people work, but a closer look through the lens of complexity economics shows a more worrying trend: AI isn't just making things more efficient; it's also making new kinds of inequality by creating feedback loops that make advantages bigger, speed up concentration, and make traditional ways of moving up less stable. The result is a new level of stratification largely driven by algorithmic power, data asymmetries, and automated decision architectures, rather than by who owns the capital. In this essay, I examine algorithmic inequality as a nonlinear phenomenon resulting from complexity feedback mechanisms that create self-reinforcing advantages for firms, platforms, and individuals with preferential access to data, computational resources, and algorithmic infrastructure. I assert that AI-driven economies exhibit characteristics of complex adaptive systems, such as sensitivity to initial conditions, amplification of positive feedback, emergence of power-law distributions, and phase transitions in labor and capital dynamics. These traits create a new economic system in which inequality is caused not only by how the market works, but also by how algorithms are used to improve things. The main point is that AI exacerbates inequality in two ways: first, it speeds up market consolidation by centralizing data and computing power; second, it makes decisions based on algorithms, which reinforce historical biases and economic differences between groups. These loops make inequality more automatic, less clear, and harder to fix with normal policy tools. A complexity-economics perspective is essential for understanding the mechanisms and persistent systemic risks associated with AI-driven stratification.

## I. The Rise of Algorithmic Power as Economic Power

Data is the new capital, growing. In economies that use AI, data isn't just information; it's a valuable asset that grows in value as more of it is collected. The feedback loop strengthens on its own: more users mean more data, which leads to better models, which lead to better services, which lead to more users. This classic preferential-attachment loop generates power-law distributions, which are common in hard-to-understand networks. A small number of platforms capture most of the world's data, and it's getting harder and harder for competitors to enter effectively. Digital capitalism depends on informational capital, which makes more money than the initial investment.

## Set Compute Capacity as a New Limit

It's unfair in a new way now that you can train big AI models. Now, training runs at the frontier level cost hundreds of millions of dollars. Some groups, like big tech companies, state-funded labs, and institutions with sovereign wealth funds, have the money to run these tests. This creates a computational oligopoly, where only a few people make models, while many people use them.

## Algorithmic Control as a Structural Advantage

Companies that use advanced algorithms can improve their supply chains, pricing, logistics, advertising, and resource use in real time. Their algorithmic edge grows over time: optimization lowers costs, which increases market share, which gives them more data, which helps them train their models better, which makes their models more competitive. Over time, these rents change how the market operates by making optimization more important than product quality.

## II. Using Algorithmic Inequality to Get Feedback on Complexity

There are good feedback loops in the job market. AI systems are increasingly deciding who gets hired, how much they get paid, how they get promoted, and how they get credit. Algorithmic hiring platforms analyze resumes, skills, and other information to estimate how useful a worker will be. These systems often use correlation-based learning to maintain social and economic hierarchies. For example, workers who have had advantages in the past get higher scores, better chances, and stronger expectations from the algorithm. This dynamic means that past inequality shapes future choices, leading to path-dependent stratification.

## A Feedback Loop for Division and Automation

Automation divides the job market into two groups: skilled workers get more done, and unskilled workers need to find new jobs. Automation takes away jobs in the middle tier, meaning more people can work for less money. This means wages go down, and machines are more likely to take on additional work. A downward spiral starts, leading to a barbell-shaped job distribution: an elite tier improved by AI and a large base of service workers who could lose their jobs.

**How network effects make life harder for people who are already poor**
AI-powered platforms need network effects to work well. This means that the more people use a service, the better it gets. But network effects make things harder for people who are already poor. The most popular platforms collect the most data, which improves AI performance and attracts more users. This creates a concentration attractor, a systemic tendency toward oligopolistic equilibria.

## III. The Growth of Social Stratification in Algorithmic Societies

The Rise of the Algorithmic Overclass. A small group of AI engineers, data scientists, and entrepreneurs who work with algorithms gets paid too much money. Their skills are useful because they work well with AI systems. The new upper class changes how AI is developed and used, thereby strengthening its own benefits.

**The Lower Class That Gets the News**
AI models use data created by millions of people, but they don't get much in return. Platforms collect data on how people behave, process it, and then sell it to other businesses. In a colonial system, people produce raw materials that other groups turn into finished products for profit.

**Loss of freedom and rule by algorithms**
AI decides who can get medical care, welfare, credit, education, and legal help. When decisions are made automatically, people lose their freedom and control over their own lives. People who can read or have money can use these systems; everyone else is controlled by math. Politics is how power is shared, and inequality is what makes politics work.

## IV. AI and the Quickening of Capital Concentration

The winner-take-all dynamics of economies based on platforms. AI makes trends toward concentration in structures even stronger. Platforms run markets by bringing together all the different ways people can interact. AI makes things more personal and helps people make predictions, which adds value. It's harder to switch when prices are higher, and high switching costs reinforce dominance. These reinforcement loops use algorithms to maintain monopolies' stability.

### AI's Financialization and Unfair Chances

Investors put money into AI companies that are already doing well. Investors use algorithmic tools to amplify this convergence, turning perceived dominance into real dominance.

### The Fall of Small and Medium-Sized Businesses

SMEs are at a structural disadvantage because they can't access the latest models, don't have their own data, and have to compete with big companies that use AI. Entrepreneurs become less active, making it harder for middle-class people to get ahead in life.

## V. The New Picture of the Economy

Uneven Distribution of Productivity Gains. AI helps people get more done, but only businesses that own algorithms can really use it. Workers receive a smaller share of their pay, which speeds up the concentration of wealth. Finding Rent with Algorithms. Companies use algorithms to set prices that are just right, change how people act, make it harder for people to bargain, and keep an eye on people to keep them in line. Digital exploitation takes money from both workers and customers and gives it to companies.

### Risk that isn't linear and macro-instability

AI makes the system more dangerous by driving markets to move together, leading to flash crashes, grabbing people's attention, and leaving markets too weak to win. According to complexity theory, systems that are very connected and not very clear are likely to have sudden changes in their rules.

## VI. Moving Toward a Moral Ecology of AI

Taking care of the concentration of computers and data. Policies should examine what causes problems in the first place. They should stop mergers that harm competition, require companies to be transparent about their data, support open data trusts, limit the hoarding of proprietary data, and pay for computing infrastructure. Giving people more power. Design that puts people first must protect workers' rights to know why automated decisions were made, to appeal those decisions, and to monitor AI systems. Making AI ecosystems that anyone can use. People need to learn how to use AI, small and medium-sized businesses need help, AI infrastructure needs to be easier to get, and platforms that work together need to be pushed.

## Conclusion

Algorithmic inequality is a big problem in economies that use AI. It comes from the fact that data, algorithms, markets, labor, and institutions don't all work together in a straight line. AI could create a digital oligarchy in which algorithms decide who can move, what they can do, and what chances they have. If we don't do anything to fix the feedback loops that worsen inequality, this could happen. We can use systems thinking and ethical design to make AI a tool for shared prosperity instead of letting it take over everything.

# The Economics of Perception and Epistemic Collapse

## Abstract

This essay analyzes the epistemic disintegration of perception resulting from economic and informational intricacy. It contends that market incentives, cognitive saturation, and technological mediation collectively undermine the common foundation of truth in democratic societies. Using complexity theory and phenomenology, perception is redefined as an economic process influenced by feedback loops of value, attention, and ideology.

> *"The optimal subject of totalitarian governance is not the fervent Nazi or the staunch Communist, but individuals for whom the boundary between reality and illusion has dissolved."*
>
> — Hannah Arendt, "The Origins of Totalitarianism"

## Theoretical Underpinnings

Epistemic collapse occurs when the cognitive processes that facilitate shared understanding fail to accommodate the intricacies of social and economic signals. Based on phenomenology and systems theory, perception is not something that happens on its own; it is something we actively build from our memories, incentives, and the situation. As the amount of information increases, the ability to make sense of it all decreases, which leads to fragmented realities.

## The Dynamics of Perception and Incentive

In today's economies, perception is a commodity. Attention markets change what people think is important or true by turning their cognitive focus into economic value. Algorithms are like nonlinear amplifiers because they make biases stronger and create epistemic bubbles. The result is a positive feedback loop: distorted views lead to distorted demand, which in turn strengthens the economic systems that reward distorted behavior.

## Consequences of Epistemic Drift

As the coherence of perception diminishes, societies relinquish their capacity for rational deliberation. Political narratives transition from propositional to performative, emphasizing engagement over precision. The economic need for attention displaces epistemic integrity, turning the marketplace of ideas into a place where emotions spread and symbols are consumed.

## Toward Restorative Thought

We need to shift the economic basis of perception to restore epistemic stability. Slow media, deliberative spaces, and moral education can serve as mitigating factors in reestablishing feedback equilibrium. Complexity theory asserts that systems can only preserve coherence when feedback loops operate within cognitive and ethical limitations. In this context, authentic freedom is not characterized by the absence of structure, but rather by the restoration of significant interpretive order.

# Breaking the Balance in Very Connected Systems

## Abstract

Equilibrium, a fundamental concept in classical and neoclassical economics, assumes the existence of a self-regulating and ultimately stabilizing system. The concept of balance deteriorates in a world increasingly interconnected by digital networks, rapid information exchange, and tightly integrated socio-economic systems. This essay examines how hyperconnectivity, while improving efficiency and fostering new ideas, also destabilizes systems, creates nonlinear feedback loops, and pushes them toward phase transitions and chaotic attractors. It says that the modern economy is not moving toward equilibrium but instead toward dynamic disequilibrium, where stability comes from adaptive complexity rather than balance. This is based on ideas from systems ecology, network theory, and complexity economics.

## I. The Classical Idea of Balance

In classical economics, equilibrium is the point at which supply and demand are equal, and prices change to keep markets running. This beautiful symmetry, evident in Walrasian general equilibrium or Pareto efficiency, is based on the assumptions of rational preferences, independent agents, and smooth adjustment processes. This model, on the other hand, assumes low-dimensionality. This means that agents don't communicate directly through dense information channels; instead, they communicate through prices. In other words, classical equilibrium theory views a sparse network as an economy in which people are mostly alone and not involved. Herbert Simon said, "Complexity is mostly a matter of interdependence." In hyperconnected environments—such as financial networks, social media ecosystems, and globalized production chains—agents no longer operate in isolation. Their choices affect each other in a loop because they receive instant feedback, which makes equilibrium seem like a short-term state. A stable attractor is replaced by a strange attractor.

## II. The Changing Face of Hyperconnectivity

Hyperconnectivity is the term for how rapidly the links among money, information, and technology are growing in the global economy. Algorithms work faster than people can think, supply chains cross continents, and social moods move through markets in a matter of seconds. Having many connections makes things work better, but it also makes them less stable. Network theory says that having many connections makes it easier for information, shocks, or disease to spread. When a single node is disrupted, it can affect the entire world. During the 2008 financial crisis and the pandemic, when the supply chain was having problems, this happened. According to complexity theorist Per Bak, his model of self-organized criticality shows that highly connected systems tend to move toward critical points where small events can cause large problems. The balance of separate markets is less important than the balance of connected systems. In these cases, balance is not the goal; it's just a temporary state that happens between waves of instability.

## III. Nonlinear Amplification and Feedback Loops

Feedback is what makes things unbalanced. Positive feedback loops are patterns that repeat themselves and cause bubbles, panics, and cycles of growth. Algorithmic trading and emotional trading can cause the stock market to crash in a matter of seconds. This shows how digital interdependence can make small problems into big ones. On the other hand, negative feedback makes things less unstable and more stable. But as systems become more interconnected, negative feedback loops don't operate as quickly as they should. Institutions' rules, morals, and mental shortcuts change more slowly than the networks and algorithms they are supposed to control. This means the system enters a delay-differential regime, where correction mechanisms don't work together and make things worse rather than better. This leads to a new kind of meta-instability, where delayed and distorted feedback causes chaos rather than stability.

## IV. From Balance to Adaptive Complexity

Brian Arthur, W. Brian Brock, and others founded the field of complexity economics, which views markets as dynamic ecosystems rather than stable equilibria. In systems with rapidly changing structures that prevent equilibrium, agents learn, adapt, and co-evolve. This adaptive dynamism is not a flaw but a characteristic of complex adaptive systems (CAS). In hyperconnectivity, adaptive complexity supplants equilibrium as the principal stability principle. Instead of convergence, we see oscillation, and instead of balance, we see resilience through diversity. The health of the system depends on how well it can withstand shocks, share information, and find new ways to understand. So, for evolution to happen, the equilibrium has to be broken down. It lets us reorganize at a higher level of complexity.

## V. The Effects on the Economy and Society

The disruption of equilibrium in hyperconnected systems has significant ramifications for governance, economics, and ethics.

Policy Design: Static optimization models do not work when there is no linear interdependence. Policies shouldn't just be about making things work better; they should also be about making things last. This includes things like having backups, being able to change things, and getting feedback that changes. Central banks need to change how they think about stability to keep the economy stable. They shouldn't think of it as price equilibrium; instead, they should think of it as network damping capacity, which is the ability of financial systems to stop failures from spreading from one node to another.

Information Ecology: In highly connected societies, networks are where people find the truth and trust each other. Spreading false information or moral signaling cascades can undermine the coherence of institutions, an example of systemic contagion.

Moral Philosophy: The breakdown of equilibrium represents a profound ethical crisis; when every decision is immediately linked to all others, moral responsibility is diluted, and systemic consequences become immeasurable.

## VI. Going in a New Direction

A new conceptual framework must surpass the static equilibrium metaphors of the twentieth century. Biology and physics provide appropriate metaphors: bifurcation, self-organization, entropy minimization, and emergent coherence. Systems that are on the edge of chaos, which means they are neither ordered nor random, are the most creative and flexible. This is where the world is now in terms of economies, ecologies, and societies. When balance fails, things don't fall apart; they just change. It shows that linear control no longer works and that nonlinear self-organization is now the main way global systems operate. We don't need to restore balance; we need to prepare for change.

## Conclusion

In hyperconnected systems, balance is an old idea from a time when people didn't depend on each other as much and information moved slowly. Dynamic disequilibrium is the new normal. This means things are always changing and adjusting, making them unstable. When equilibrium breaks down, it doesn't mean order is gone; instead, it signals a higher-order complexity in which stability arises from the ongoing interaction between chaos and coherence, not from stasis.

# Fractured Abundance: The Ineffectiveness of Wealth as a Stabilizing Force in Promoting Prosperity

## Abstract

Modern societies demonstrate unmatched material wealth, technological expertise, and productive capacity. But beneath this layer of abundance is a social, psychological, and institutional landscape that is falling apart. The paradox of the twenty-first century resides not in scarcity, but in the inability of abundance to promote collective flourishing. When wealth is not linked to stability, it does not lead to well-being; instead, it causes fragility, alienation, insecurity, and a slow decline of moral and democratic systems. This essay examines the structural and psychological mechanisms that cut the link between abundance and human flourishing, elucidating the nonlinear feedback loops, inequality-driven instabilities, and systemic failures that transform prosperity into paradox. The essay, through the lens of complexity economics, behavioral psychology, systems theory, and political economy, asserts that societal prosperity depends not on the volume of wealth generated but on the dynamics among wealth, stability, resilience, moral ecology, and power distribution. When these systems fail, abundance fails as well, leading to anxiety rather than security, competition rather than cooperation, and weakness rather than freedom.

## I. Introduction: The Paradox of Modern Abundance

Throughout history, people have had trouble getting enough of certain things. For thousands of years, ecosystems, land, labor, and tools have limited wealth. To survive, people had to deal with the constant fear of not having enough. On the other hand, modern industrial-technological economies have reached levels of wealth that past civilizations could only dream of. Today, advanced economies produce far more food than people eat, far more goods than people need, and far more energy than people can use properly. The problem is no longer making things.

But people all over the world are dealing with more depression, political division, loneliness, health problems, a breakdown of democracy, a lack of trust in institutions, and a general feeling of being on shaky ground. Even in countries where businesses are making record profits, people are still worried about the economy. Workers feel less safe, even though productivity is at an all-time high. And there is more fear than confidence in public discourse. People are scared of things like automation, globalization, migration, political extremism, climate change, and being left out of the economy.

The fundamental dilemma is: Why has abundance not led to prosperity?

This essay asserts that abundance without stability produces fragility. When the systems that share wealth are unstable in terms of economics, psychology, institutions, and morality, wealth does not lead to well-being. Instead, it makes things worse by making people fight for status and making it hard for prosperity to last. It isn't enough to have a lot. Stability in all areas—economic, social, institutional, emotional, and ecological—is what makes growth possible. Without stability, even great wealth can fall apart.

## II. The Illusion of Affluence in a Deteriorating System

### A. Getting rich vs. being rich

Conventional economic indicators perceive wealth as an objective state: income, assets, and consumption. But how people feel about their financial situation is what makes them succeed. Two societies with the same amount of money can be very different in terms of well-being depending on how stable, predictable, trustworthy, and shared responsibility they are.

A society where people are always worried about going bankrupt because of a medical emergency, losing their job, being evicted, or a political collapse is always insecure, even if the average income is high. In this kind of place, abundance looks weak, needy, and easy to take away.

So, having money without stability doesn't make you less worried; it makes you more worried. The more you have to lose, the more you worry about losing it.

### B. Hyper-competition and the Loss of Psychological Safety

Inequality in today's world makes people fight hard for positional goods like elite schools, high-paying city jobs, prestigious networks, and safe neighborhoods. These goods are, by definition, hard to find. The gap between "winning" and "losing" seems to grow as inequality increases. This makes stress worse, even for people who aren't having money problems. The psychological outcome is a society in which individuals are perpetually anxious and prepared to engage in conflict or flee, even when their fundamental needs are satisfied.

## C. The Multiplier of Social Inequality

In systems where wealth is concentrated, economic elites often have too much power over politics. This leads to policy frameworks that favor asset owners over public goods such as education, health care, infrastructure, and social insurance. As the foundation of the public good weakens, the danger to people increases. The result is an unequal level of stability, a worse, more broken form of difference.

# III. The Fragility of Wealth: Why Having a Lot of Money Alone Can't Make Society Stable

## A. Wealth Without Strength

A society that can bounce back needs strong institutions, public infrastructure, social safety nets, and a healthy environment. But many wealthy countries don't have any of these on a large scale. Wealth builds up in real estate and financial markets, not in systems that make things more stable.

## B. The "Stability Gap" as a Sign of Social Distress

A nation may possess substantial wealth yet lack stability. As the macro system gets richer, it becomes harder for people to handle small risks that aren't always clear. One of the best signs that political extremism, mental health problems, and unstable democracies are on the rise is this "stability gap."

## C. The Decline of Faith in Institutions

Institutions make expectations more stable by reducing uncertainty. People lose faith in institutions when they appear broken or under threat of takeover. When people don't trust each other, they don't work together, conspiracy grows, and democracy loses its legitimacy.

# IV. The Psychological Architecture of Flourishing: The Importance of Stability Over Wealth

## A. Things need to be predictable for them to do well.

People do well when they can make plans, put their hearts into things, build relationships that last, and see futures that are possible. Chronic unpredictability diminishes cognitive capacity and erodes empathy. Instability can hurt your mind, and money can't fix that.

## B. The Status Trap: How Inequality Steals Success

People always compare themselves to others because of inequality, even in rich countries. As inequality grows, happiness declines, anxiety about goal attainment escalates, and consumption becomes a means of self-identification. Too much becomes not enough.

## C. Being Alone When There Is a Lot

It's strange that wealth is linked to social atomization. Abundance breaks down old ways of depending on each other, weakening community ties. You need more than just money to do well; you also need to feel like you belong.

# V. Systemic Instability: How Economic Structures Harm People's Health

## A. Financialization and the Gathering of Volatility

When economies are financialized, they are more likely to face major problems such as unstable markets, asset bubbles, and weak supply chains. These things make life more chaotic by making housing costs hard to predict, making retirements less stable, and making jobs less safe.

## B. Making Jobs Less Stable and Speeding Up Technology

Automation makes people very productive, but it also takes jobs away from people and gives money to a small number. People can't have stable roles or economic dignity in a society that works.

## C. The Myth of Endless Growth and Unstable Environments

Climate shocks can quickly and without warning destroy wealth. Ecological instability is what kills flourishing the most. Wealth that isn't sustainable is just an illusion that will go away.

# VI. Moral Ecology and the Loss of a Shared Goal

## A. Money Without a Purpose

Material wealth cannot take the place of moral importance. When wealth means nothing, it can make people selfish, materialistic, and cynical.

## B. The Collapse of Shared Narratives

Inequality and institutional capture weaken the shared stories we tell about fairness and opportunity. Without shared stories, abundance loses its meaning.

## C. The Rise of Morality That Is Zero-Sum

People start to think in terms of zero-sum when things aren't stable. This makes people less caring and more likely to hold extreme political views.

# VII. Toward a Stable Prosperity: Rebinding Wealth to Flourishing

## A. Redesigning economic systems to make them more stable

To help people thrive, systems need to turn money into safety, opportunities, and strength. This includes universal health care, a strong school system, durable infrastructure, and a fair way to share the benefits of new technology.

## B. Strengthening institutions and giving democracy more power

Institutions need to be rebuilt to cut down on corruption, give everyone a fair chance to take part, and restore trust.

## C. Putting Social Cohesion Back Together

Investing in communities, public spaces, and networks that connect people across classes is a good way to turn abundance into growth.

## D. Moral Renewal and Shared Responsibility

To flourish, we need a moral renewal based on fairness, kindness, connection, and civic duty.

# VIII. Conclusion: The Structure of Flourishing

Just because you have a lot of things doesn't mean you're doing well. Money can't fix broken social systems, restore trust, or give life back its meaning. Without stability, abundance is not strong. The goal of the twenty-first century is not to make more money, but to use money to create stability and stability to create growth.

# The Thermodynamics of Power and the Distribution of Justice

## Abstract

This essay posits that political and institutional power operates as an entropic system, with justice serving as a negentropic force that maintains social order. It examines the effects of power concentration on the moral economy of governance, drawing on examples from thermodynamics and complexity theory to illustrate how it generates heat, friction, and energy loss. Justice, as the opposing principle, disintegrates when feedback loops between legitimacy and accountability weaken, leading to systemic deterioration.

## I. The Energetics of Power

Power is like social energy that is stored. Its legitimacy relies on the effective transition between authority and justice. When authority is wielded transparently, the ethical force of justice permeates institutions, maintaining balance. Conversely, as power becomes more centralized, the system gathers entropy—diminished trust, inefficiency, and moral decay that undermine institutional cohesion.

## II. Power as an Unstable System

When power is generated, it also produces waste, just like any thermodynamic process. The more power there is, the faster morals and facts go away. Corruption, propaganda, and bureaucratic inertia are all examples of how unbalanced power can lead to chaos. These residues accumulate over time, worsening justice and transparency. Without constant feedback correction, this happens.

## III. Justice as a Non-Entropic Order

Justice is a negentropic force, meaning it restores balance to the political thermodynamic cycle. Aligning power with moral law and public legitimacy gives the system energy. If power is more important than justice, the feedback loop reverses, and the system starts to eat itself: authority eats legitimacy faster than it can replenish it.

## IV. Energy Loss and Institutional Friction

Institutional friction is often seen as a bad thing, but it is actually very important for stability. Checks and balances work like resistors, turning political energy into moral responsibility. When friction is removed, as in the case of authoritarian consolidation or deregulated finance, efficiency temporarily increases while stability deteriorates. The result is a feedback loop that spirals out of control, with power growing until it runs out of moral fuel.

## V. The shift from legitimacy to corruption

As power accumulates without being replaced, the system undergoes a transition from legitimacy to corruption. This change is like a thermodynamic tipping point, where the heat of concentrated power is too much for justice to handle. At this point, the law is still in place, but its legitimacy has broken down. The system goes through moral turbulence, which is normal in physics but not in politics.

## VI. Moving To a Regenerative Thermodynamics of Power

A sustainable order necessitates a regenerative model of power, perceiving justice not as a limitation but as a renewable source of moral energy. Institutions must function as open systems, facilitating the exchange of energy, accountability, and trust with the public to sustain low entropy. When justice resumes its function as the moderating force of power, legitimacy evolves from a limited resource into a sustainable dynamic equilibrium.

# The Tragedy of Transparency: How Too Much Information Reduces Collective Rationality

## Abstract

Radical transparency and real-time access to information are what make the modern world what it is. The profusion of information has not cultivated a more informed public; rather, it has impaired our collective ability to reason collaboratively. This essay asserts that excessive transparency, coupled with cognitive limitations and the structure of digital platforms, undermines collective meaning and intensifies polarization. We show that transparency starts feedback loops that go beyond interpretive frameworks, strengthen identity-based reasoning, and weaken common ground, using an analytical narrative system dynamics framework. We need to rebuild shared epistemic institutions rather than just making it easier for people to access information to restore collective rationality.

## I. Introduction: Transparency as an Ideal and a Paradox

For the majority of contemporary history, transparency has been regarded as a clear public benefit. Liberal democratic theory holds that when institutions, leaders, and the media are open and transparent, people are more accountable and less likely to be corrupt. The moral argument that secrecy leads to abuse and openness to truth has strengthened movements for open data, free information, whistleblowing, and radical visibility.

But the information environment of the 21st century is not what the transparency theory predicted. The change isn't just about getting more information; it's about changing the whole system. Information is now always available, instant, unfiltered, and shared on social media. Institutions used to control transparency, but now it is a global state. We are no longer just watching information; we are in the middle of a flood of it.

Instead of coming together to form a common understanding, societies are breaking apart into separate worlds of knowledge. This shows the main paradox: transparency shows everything, but shared meaning falls apart. The tragedy of transparency lies not in deception, but in the lack of interpretive coherence.

## II. The Attention Economy of Cognition

Human cognition developed in an environment characterized by informational scarcity. The brain is designed to pick out, simplify, and make sense of small amounts of information. But in today's world, the opposite is true: we have too much information, not too little.

When there is too much information to process, people use heuristics, which are things like identity markers, emotional cues, and interpretations that fit with their group. To put it another way, transparency changes reasoning from making analytical judgments to protecting one's identity. The outcome is not enhanced comprehension, but increased division. Additionally, transparency reveals the differences in how people interpret once private things. What used to be worked out in private is now made public, recorded, shared, and amplified. The public sphere becomes a place for performance rather than discussion. The signal-to-noise ratio gets worse, not because the truth is hidden, but because there are too many other options.

## III. The Attention Economy and Algorithmic Amplification

Digital platforms do more than just share information; they also shape the emotional and mental states people use to understand it. Platforms are made to get people involved, not to tell the truth. People are drawn to things that upset, shock, or flatter their identity. So, transparency doesn't make the most accurate claims; it makes the ones that are most likely to spread. Content that gets shared makes people feel they belong to a group or have an identity. In this setting, openness makes disagreement more visible, conflict more likely, and story fragmentation stronger.

Institutional filters that once controlled public meaning, such as journalism, education, and scientific review, are now being outpaced by viral visibility. Transparency fills the public space with signals that lack context, and platforms turn attention into money. The outcome is not a more knowledgeable populace, but rather one that experiences heightened emotions and diminished consensus.

## IV. The dynamics of Transparency and Fragmentation in Systems

Systems dynamics helps us understand how transparency changes how we think, who we are, and how much we trust institutions. In intricate social systems, the configuration of feedback loops influences outcomes more significantly than the quantity of information.

The most important dynamic is a reinforcing loop:

> Transparency → Information Load → Cognitive Strain → Identity-Based Filtering → Polarization → Reduced Shared Meaning → Increased Demand for Transparency

People think that institutions are hiding something when the meaning of things changes. They don't want interpretive reconstruction; they want more openness, which speeds up the cycle that is causing fragmentation. The system is stuck in a cycle of good feedback.

In the meantime, shared interpretive frameworks, which include common stories, trusted institutions, and community norms, break down when they are constantly bombarded with new information. Society can't work together as well when that stock goes down. The tragedy does not manifest as a dissolution of knowledge, but rather as a disintegration of coherence.

## V. Conclusion: Restoring Shared Understanding

The tragedy of transparency does not reside in the existence of truth or falsehood, but in the disintegration of the structures that enable societies to collectively interpret truth. To restore rationality as a group, we need to rebuild the institutions that make transparency meaningful. Some of these are safe places for non-performative deliberation, civic education, trusted media, and scientific review. The problem is not to limit information, but to restore its meaning. Only then can transparency bring light instead of darkness.

# Economic Externalities: Less Freedom and Negative Consequences for American Society

## Abstract

Economic externalities—costs or benefits that affect people or groups who didn't directly choose or participate in the original transaction—are among the most common structural problems in modern capitalist economies. In the U.S., people have often viewed externalities as technical issues that can be addressed by changing policies. However, many of the most significant externalities today are not simply economic distortions; they are systemic forces that redefine cultural norms, political identity, psychological well-being, and even the perceived significance of individual freedom. This essay explores the relationship between externalities and the diminishment of freedom, emphasizing how concentrated market power, environmental degradation, information asymmetry, and social inequality create a society in which individual choice appears plentiful while true autonomy diminishes. The argument posits that mitigating externalities necessitates a redefinition of the social purpose of economic systems rather than mere adjustments to market pricing mechanisms.

## I. Introduction

The Illusion of Private Exchange. Standard economic theory depicts markets as voluntary exchange systems among rational agents seeking their individual interests. In this framework, freedom is characterized as the lack of coercion in personal decision-making. But real economic behavior doesn't usually fit such generalizations. Markets are a part of social, ecological, psychological, and political systems that all shape and limit what people can do. Economic externalities, like air pollution we all breathe, addiction built into consumer platforms, and political instability caused by concentrated wealth, are among the most obvious signs of these connections.

The main problem is this: the more an economy creates externalities, the less free its people are, because they have to deal with consequences that they didn't choose, can't avoid, and can't change in any meaningful way. So, externalities become serious problems that hurt democracy, change how people talk about things in public, and make it harder for everyone to agree.

## II. Negative Externalities and the Loss of Autonomy

1. Environmental Externalities and Dependence on Materials. Pollution of air and water, unstable weather, and poor public health are all examples of externalities that limit physical autonomy. People don't often talk about the right to breathe clean air, drink clean water, or live without the threat of climate-related disasters, but it is a basic right. People lose their freedom when environmental externalities build up. This is not because they are being forced to do something, but because they have to deal with things they can't control.

   For a long time, the U.S. has privatized production and made environmental damage a public issue. Companies make money by doing things that emit a lot of carbon, while the government pays for cancer clusters, respiratory diseases, disaster relief, and infrastructure upgrades.

2. Externalities of Information and Cognitive Limitations. The current attention economy creates many cognitive externalities, such as polarization, anxiety, shorter attention spans, and group irrationality. These are not random; they are planned results aligned with making the most money by getting people to engage. To have democratic agency, you need to think clearly and base your beliefs on what others see. When platforms prioritize emotional response over factual accuracy, the realm of individual cognition transforms into a venue for uninvited influence.

3. Health Externalities and Created Dependency. Industries, from fast food to pharmaceuticals, create health problems that make chronic diseases and mental health issues worse. People are told that they are in charge of their own health, but millions of people live in places that make them more likely to become addicted, stressed, and malnourished. The result is a society that appears free, but in reality, people can't do, choose, or grow as much as they want.

## III. The Concentration of the Market and the Transfer of Risk

The structure of American capitalism has changed from competitive markets to oligopoly and monopoly dominance. A few companies now own communications, healthcare, technology, energy, transportation, and consumer goods. When businesses grow and do more, they can pass on more costs to other businesses. Market concentration creates an imbalance of power, which allows risk and harm to be passed down.

## IV. Inequality as a Systemic Externality

Policy, institutional regimes, and market design all contribute to economic inequality. When wealth is concentrated, it sets off a chain reaction of social problems, such as reduced mobility, political capture, reduced trust, and increased polarization. The legal rights are still the same, but real freedom is different. The rich have a lot of freedom, while most people have less power to make decisions.

## V. The Social Cost of Ignoring Externalities

People in the US often think of externalities as small problems instead of big ones. The choice not to internalize externalities is a moral choice made by everyone about who is free. People become accustomed to pain and limitations as externalities accumulate. Freedom is redefined as the ability to make consumer choices under constraint, rather than the ability to build a meaningful life.

## VI. To Deal with Externalities

We must reaffirm the public's right to control the conditions of life. This means thinking about the costs to society and the environment, limiting the number of markets, balancing labor and capital, and rebuilding information and cultural spaces that aren't based on manipulation.

## VII. Conclusion

Economic externalities are a secret structure of unfreedom. They take away people's freedom, change democracy, and give power to a small number of people. The work ahead is not just fixing technical problems; it's also redefining the role of markets in a democracy. Freedom cannot be a privilege for a select few; it must be cultivated as a collective benefit.

# The American Debt Overload: How Too Much Debt for People, Businesses, and the Federal Government Will Destroy Democracy

## Abstract

The United States has entered a time when debt is more than just a way to make money; it is now a part of everyday life, business strategy, and the federal government. The growth of debts owed by people, businesses, and the government since 1980 shows that the country's economy is changing in a big way. What used to be a way to encourage productive investment, new ideas, and upward mobility has now become a widespread reliance on borrowed money to maintain living standards, asset prices, and political stability. The United States is not just a place where people borrow money; it is a place where people live their lives around debt.

This essay asserts that the scale and interrelation of American household, corporate, and federal debt currently pose existential threats to democratic existence. Debt is not the issue; historically, it has facilitated the construction of homes, enterprises, and public infrastructure. The problem is that debt currently serves a structural purpose: it hides the effects of stagnant wages, makes it easier for companies to engage in financial engineering rather than productive investment, and lets the federal government put off political accountability. Debt has become a systemic equilibrium condition, a fragile balance that, if disturbed, could trigger significant economic disruption and democratic instability.

## I. The Financialization of Household Survival and Consumer Debt

People borrowed money for most of the 20th century to buy homes, get an education that would help them earn more over their lives, and buy things that would last. More and more people are using household debt to pay for basic needs. After 1980, wages stopped rising with productivity, so households made up for their stagnant income by taking on more debt. The amount of mortgage debt rose because home prices increased, not because more people bought homes. Student debt didn't rise because people wanted to get ahead in life; it rose because less public funding was available for higher education. Medical debt rose sharply because private insurance couldn't keep healthcare costs down.

This change is part of a bigger change: the middle class is no longer able to support itself financially. Debt is now the same as wages. It looks stable, but it puts people's money at risk. The household in debt is not just an economic issue; it is also a political issue that needs to be addressed. Being in debt makes it harder to negotiate, move around, and get involved in civic activities. A person who is worried about money is less likely to get involved in politics, more likely to be hurt by economic shocks, and more likely to believe political messages that promise protection or blame.

## II. Corporate Debt and the Decline of Productive Capacity

Corporate debt has also changed in a similar way. Companies used to be able to grow, hire new people, and make progress in technology by borrowing money. Most of the debt that companies take on these days is for financial engineering. Companies borrow money to buy back their own stock. This makes the earnings-per-share figures look better and gives shareholders the most money. Executive pay, which is closely tied to stock prices, encourages short-term financial goals. Because of this, money is no longer going to research and development, workforce development, and productive capacity.

The financialization of the corporate sector leads to more market concentration and political capture. Companies that can secure cheap loans can buy other companies and merge with them, gaining more power in the industry and making it harder for workers to negotiate. A smaller number of large businesses are gaining increasing power in the economy. Then, these businesses use their economic power to gain political power through lobbying, campaign donations, and rule changes. A democracy needs economic power to be spread out, but financialized corporate capitalism is making it more centralized.

## III. The federal debt, the way politicians are rewarded, and the way people think about money

The federal government is now $39 trillion in debt, and interest payments are expected to become the largest part of the federal budget over the next 10 years. It's not just how big the federal debt is; it's also the political reasons that drive it. Politicians have many reasons to spend more money without raising taxes. The costs of borrowing are delayed and politically abstract, while the benefits of spending are immediate and clear. This gives the system a structural bias toward long-term deficits.

This pattern is even stronger because of the political economy of polarization. In a polarized system, compromise costs money, and delay is a strategy. When people talk about money, they care more about symbols than real problems. The outcome is not the result of unintentional fiscal irresponsibility, but rather a deliberate design. Debt maintains short-term political stability by masking social and economic problems, but at the cost of long-term risks to democratic legitimacy.

## IV. The Interdependent Feedback Loop and Systemic Weakness

These three types of debt—household, corporate, and federal—are not separate from each other. They make a feedback loop that gets stronger:

1.  When wages don't go up, families have to rely on credit more.

2.  Household credit growth leads to more spending, which keeps corporate profits high.

3.  Corporate profits stay high because of consumer debt, not wage growth. This supports low-wage labor models. The federal government makes up for this instability by spending more than it collects in revenue.

This loop hides the system's flaw. For stability to appear to be happening, debt must keep growing. Any change, such as rising interest rates, bank instability, or falling asset prices, can trigger a chain reaction that affects the whole economy. The system is becoming more sensitive to small shocks, a phenomenon complexity theorists call a "critical state." This means stability can only be maintained with constant external support.

## V. Debt, Stable Governance, and the Erosion of Democracy

Weak political economies rely on debt. Democratic systems are more likely to become unstable when families don't have enough money, businesses have too much power, and the federal government can't make decisions. People who are having trouble making ends meet are more likely to distrust institutions, have zero-sum political views, and back authoritarian leaders who promise stability, protection, or the restoration of the nation. There is a strong link between the rise of nationalist and authoritarian movements around the world and economic instability and financial insecurity.

This dynamic is especially dangerous for American democracy because its political institutions depend on public trust, voluntary participation, and norms of compromise. Debt weakens these foundations, both financially and mentally. When people don't feel financially secure, they are less patient with the democratic process and more open to strongman rhetoric. The decline of the economic middle class hastens the deterioration of the civic middle ground.

## Conclusion

Right now, the United States has a very serious structural problem. Debt is what keeps the country stable, keeps people spending money, and keeps businesses making money. But this balance isn't very strong. We need to change the balance between wages and living costs, the way businesses are rewarded to encourage productive investment, and the way politicians are held accountable for their spending choices, to make democracy last.

The other choice is not stable stagnation; instead, it is rising instability in society, politics, and the economy. A democracy won't last if its people are poor, its businesses put extraction before production, and its government isn't ready for the future. The US must choose between a political economy of shared responsibility and one of putting off crisis. That choice will decide the future of its democracy.

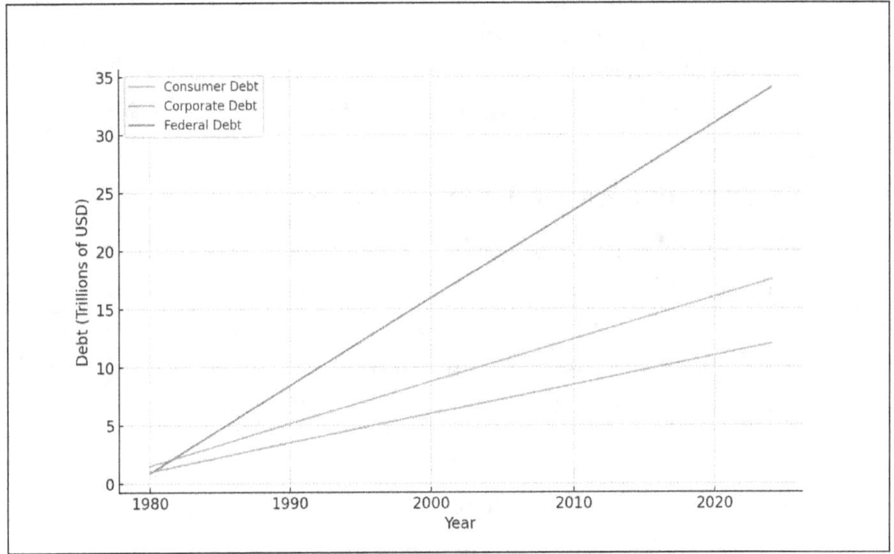


The rise in consumer, business, and federal government debt from 1980 to 2024.

# Why a $25 Minimum Wage is Necessary for Building a Strong Middle Class and Closing the Gap Between the Rich and the Poor

## Abstract

The strength of a democracy depends on the health and stability of its middle class. But over the past forty years, the American middle class has steadily shrunk as real wages remained stagnant, workers' bargaining power declined, corporate profits rose, and wealth became increasingly concentrated at the top. If wages had kept up with the economy's growth, the minimum wage would be more than $25 an hour today, given how much more productive people are. The federal minimum wage, on the other hand, has remained at $7.25 since 2009, its lowest real value in more than 50 years. Because of this, millions of workers can't afford basic necessities, while corporations and high-income families are making more money than ever. This essay argues that a $25 minimum wage is necessary not only to reduce poverty but also to revive the middle class, restore economic vitality, reduce inequality, and strengthen democratic stability. A wage of $25 is not unreasonable or inflationary. It shows the work that workers are already doing to help the economy, increases consumer demand, and moves the economy toward shared prosperity. The question is not whether the US can afford a $25 minimum wage, but whether it can afford to continue not paying it.

## 1. The Disconnect Between Pay and Productivity

From 1945 to the early 1970s, wages and productivity rose together. This was the start of the modern American middle class. One full-time worker could provide for a family, buy a house, save for retirement, and help the economy grow. But starting in the late 1970s, this relationship started to break down. Even though wages remained the same, productivity kept rising. From 1979 to now:

- Over 70% more work was done.
- The minimum wage's real value went down by almost 40%.
- The pay for executives went up by more than 1,300%.

This difference is not due to natural economic laws, but to policy choices like weaker unions, deregulation of labor markets, offshoring, financialization of the economy, and tax policies that favor capital over labor. A $25 minimum wage would help fix decades of structural imbalance by linking wages to the value of the work that workers do.

## 2. The Real Cost of Living Needs a Higher Wage

When you look at basic cost-of-living measures, the idea that $25 an hour is too much goes away. People need things like housing, healthcare, childcare, transportation, and food, and the prices of these things have gone up much faster than wages. For example:

- The average rent has more than doubled since 2000.
- Childcare costs more than $1,500 a month.
- Health insurance premiums and deductibles have gone up dramatically.
- Transportation costs are unavoidable when infrastructure depends on cars.

To live a minimally stable life in many U.S. metro areas, a worker needs to make $22 to $30 an hour. This means they don't have to save money, deal with emergencies, or invest in their education. A $25 minimum wage is not a high wage; it is the point at which the economy is stable. When wages are lower than the cost of living, workers make up the difference by taking on debt, working longer hours, or getting more than one job. This stress makes people less productive, less mentally and physically healthy, less stable in their families, and less involved in their communities. A living wage helps people stay alive and healthy.

## 3. A Strong Middle Class is Good for the Economy.

Consumer spending accounts for about 70% of GDP, making it the main driver of the U.S. economy. People buy goods and services when they have extra money, which helps businesses make money and keeps people working. The economy slows down when workers don't get paid enough because people don't want to buy things.

The economy will be better off if the minimum wage rises, as it will give millions of workers more money to spend. People who are rich often save or invest their tax cuts in risky ways, but tax increases go right back into the economy. More money at the bottom and middle means:

- More cash for small businesses
- There is more business going on in the area.
- More trust in investments in businesses
- Less reliance on government spending on social programs

A $25 minimum wage is not only fair, but also a way to grow the economy in a way that will last.

## 4. Lowering Inequality and Making Democracy Stronger

The United States' economic inequality is now as bad as it was in the 1920s, when oligarchs were in charge, the economy was unstable, and democracy was weak. Societies marked by profound inequality experience:

- Less trust in society
- More political polarization
- More likely to join authoritarian movements
- Less chance of moving up
- Weakened civic institutions

By bringing people together, keeping politics moderate, and giving everyone a sense of opportunity, the middle class helps keep democracy strong. When the middle class gets smaller and the working class's economic security goes down, democratic institutions fall apart. A minimum wage of $25 would help spread out the political and economic power that the rich have and bring back a more fair and representative political economy.

## 5. The Inflation Argument: Misunderstood and Blown Out of Proportion

Many people who don't want the minimum wage to go up to $25 say that it would make inflation go out of control. But research shows that giving people at the bottom of the income scale more money doesn't cause much inflation. In fact, it can even make workers more productive and lower costs for businesses that need to hire new people. Localized inflation happens when prices that the government kept low are allowed to go up. This is especially true in places that depend on low-wage workers.

Also, you can't understand inflation by itself. The economy stays unstable if wages go up, but basic costs go up even faster. The minimum wage should go up along with:

- Housing that costs less
- Changes to the cost of healthcare
- Enforcement of antitrust laws to stop monopolistic price control

The government puts money into schools and daycare centers.

Inflation is only a problem when wage increases are more than the economy can handle. The problem is not a lack of resources in the United States; it's how they are distributed.

From a business point of view, long-term stability is more important than short-term costs. Many employers, especially small businesses, are worried that raising the minimum wage will make it harder for them to make ends meet. But:

- Employees are less likely to leave if they are paid more, which saves money on hiring and training new ones.

- Workers who get paid more do better work.

- When wages go up, customers have more money to spend, which means more people want to use your business's services.

Big companies already know that paying workers more is good for business. Companies that do this often do better than their competitors because their workers are more productive, dedicated, and stable. The real threat to small businesses is not wages, but corporate monopolies taking over the market, and the cost of real estate going up. A minimum wage of $25, strict enforcement of antitrust laws, and rules for commercial rents all help local economies be truly competitive.

## Conclusion

It makes sense to have a minimum wage of $25. It shows the value that workers already bring to the table, brings productivity and pay back into line, boosts buying power, and rebuilds the middle class. It makes things fairer, democracy stronger, and the economy grow faster. The other option—keeping wages the same, making it harder to move, making inequality worse, and breaking down democratic norms—is much more dangerous and costs a lot more.

The main question is not whether the US can raise wages. The real question is whether the country can stay alive without doing that. To have a society that values democracy, stability, and shared wealth, people must be able to make money. One of the easiest and most effective ways to do this is to raise the minimum wage to $25.

# The Commoditization of Privacy: An Unstable Force for Democracy

## Abstract

Historically, privacy has been viewed not merely as a personal preference but as a fundamental human right—an essential prerequisite for autonomy, dignity, and democratic citizenship. To think, speak, and connect with others freely, you need a safe internal space where you can reflect without being watched or pressured by others. But in the digital age, privacy has become a commodity that can be bought, sold, tracked, valued, and exploited through increasingly advanced methods of data extraction. Companies, political groups, and algorithmic systems that are meant to change behavior can now buy and sell something that used to be an implicit part of being human. This essay argues that treating privacy as a product poses a structural threat to democracy. When privacy is turned into a product, the power differences between people and institutions grow, making it possible to manipulate, predict behavior, persuade people in specific ways, and break up society. This change alters the functioning of democracy, diminishes public reasoning, and substitutes the free exchange of ideas with algorithmically regulated influence. Democracy becomes more unstable not because people aren't interested in it anymore, but because the information environment that supports democratic judgment has changed significantly.

## I. The Historical Significance of Privacy and Democratic Liberty

For a long time, privacy has been a part of how democratic ideas have grown. In Enlightenment philosophy, the private sphere was viewed as the locus of self-formation, a crucial prerequisite for autonomous political participation. People need time and space to think things through, improve their reasoning skills, and do the moral work of becoming a citizen. Alexis de Tocqueville said that democracies need people who think for themselves and groups that work together, and both need privacy to avoid being completely controlled by the state or society.

The rise of liberal democracy in the 1800s and 1900s made privacy a legal right by giving people constitutional rights, limiting government surveillance, and encouraging cultural norms that value personal space. The private sphere acted as a counterbalance to the collective, making sure that democratic power didn't turn into authoritarian centralization. But the move to digital networks, data-driven business models, and widespread surveillance technologies changed this balance in a big way. Privacy protections that worked in the past no longer work in a world where identities, behaviors, and preferences can be tracked and sold for money in real time. What used to be private by default is now public unless a contract says otherwise. Businesses, not people, write the terms of a contract.

## II. The Growth of the Surveillance Economy

The commercialization of privacy commenced with the advent of targeted advertising models in the early 2000s. Companies like Google and Facebook found out that they could collect personal information like search histories, social networks, browsing patterns, and location signals, and use it to make predictions about how people will act. These profiles help companies predict what people want, change how they buy, and influence their choices.

The surveillance economy makes sense from an economic point of view: the more detailed the personal data, the better the prediction of behavior, and the more valuable it is to businesses. Because of this, privacy is slowly being taken away, not by threats, but by how easy it is to use, how common it is, and how much we depend on networks. People share their personal information so they can use the internet, have fun, talk to others, and feel like they belong.

In this system, the user is not the one who buys things; they are the thing that is bought. The main transaction isn't giving someone a service; it's finding out how they act. Every click, scroll, message, purchase, or pause adds to a model of the self that is always changing.

You can do more than just watch with this system. Algorithms do more than just guess what people will do; they also change what people do. Using the best persuasion techniques based on cognitive psychology and behavioral economics, you can get, keep, and direct people's attention. The result is a digital space where people's choices are carefully and systematically controlled.

## III. The Political Consequences: Weakening of Public Reason

Democracy needs a shared public space where everyone can discuss ideas and facts. When privacy becomes a commodity, this shared public space breaks down into personalized information realities. Social media sites pick news, political messages, and cultural stories that will get most people to interact with them, not because they are true or good for the public. People are put into ideological echo chambers, which strengthens their existing biases and makes it harder for them to find common ground.

Micro-targeted political ads take this idea even further. Now, political messages can be made to fit the mental weaknesses of certain people. Two people may hear completely different stories about the same election, policy, or public event, and each is meant to change how they feel rather than make them think about it.

This fragmentation is not just about knowledge; it is also about structure. It turns democratic discourse from a group effort to convince people into a market for personalized influence campaigns. The public stops being a group that talks things over and instead becomes a collection of demographic groups that can be easily influenced. Democratic institutions lose legitimacy, social cohesion falls, and polarization rises.

## IV. Behavioral Governance and Power Imbalance

The commodification of privacy redistributes power in ways that threaten democratic equality. Political groups and businesses that use big data analytics can see how people behave in ways no one else can. They can predict how people will react as a group, find weak spots in society, and use influence strategies with pinpoint accuracy. This power to gather information is greater than that of any historical state surveillance program. It doesn't use direct threats; instead, it changes people's wants, beliefs, and identities in a more subtle way. People believe they are making their own choices when they are not. This is a kind of "soft control," meaning running things through behavioral architecture rather than laws. The threat resides not merely in the presence of this power but in its obscurity. People don't know how their information is being used, how their identities are being tracked, or how their decisions are being changed. Democratic accountability is not possible without openness. Power becomes invisible, but still there.

## V. The Disturbance of Democracy

These factors make democratic systems less stable. When privacy is turned into a product:

- People lose their freedom. Unseen algorithmic forces shape their thoughts and choices.

- The power of reason as a group goes away. The public sphere that we all share breaks up into separate information silos.

- Political identity splits into groups. Instead of being rational, engagement becomes emotional, polarized, and performative.

- Institutions lose their credibility. People stop trusting each other when they see things differently.

Power unites things. People who control data infrastructures have too much power over society. Democracy becomes weak; instead of a system of free citizens talking things over, it becomes a marketplace of influence run by platforms that make money from anger, division, and spying.

## Conclusion: Reclaiming Privacy as a Collective Asset

The commodification of privacy is not an inevitable consequence of technological progress. It is the result of political choices, such as rules, business plans, and cultural norms that prioritize profit and efficiency over democratic freedom. To stop this trend, we need to stop thinking of privacy as a personal choice and start treating it as a public good necessary to democracy. We need to improve legal protections. Data rights must be fundamental. It should be required that algorithms be open to the public. But more than just laws and policies, we need a deeper cultural change: we need to understand that privacy is the basis of freedom, not something we can give up for convenience.

Democracy cannot endure in a context where human identity is commodified and citizens' internal experiences are subjected to algorithmic exploitation. We need to rebuild the lines that protect people's freedom to keep a democratic society. Privacy should not be seen as a product; it should be protected as the most important part of democracy.

# Chapter 5

# Philosophical Frameworks and Ethical Dynamics

## The Moral Ecology of Institutions: Building Systems that Make Life Better and Heal People

### Abstract

Institutions like governments, markets, schools, banks, churches, and cultural networks are the building blocks of human civilization. They make the rules, allocate resources and power, set limits on what is possible, and encode values. But institutions are not always fair. They can build people's dignity, trust, and well-being, or they can tear people down, use them, and leave them poor. There is a difference not only in their formal rules but also in the moral environment that shapes their goals, rewards, and long-term growth.

A moral ecology is how values, norms, incentives, and relationships change and affect each other in and between institutions. It is the living environment in which people make choices and change. When these ecosystems are healthy, institutions help people thrive, work together, and build strong, adaptable societies. When institutions are weakened, they make competition more cutthroat, encourage predation, break trust, and cause social, emotional, and economic harm that builds up over time.

This essay establishes a framework for comprehending how institutions can be intentionally designed or redesigned to heal and uplift humanity. It contends that robust institutions require more than mere efficiency or optimization, drawing on perspectives from complexity economics, game theory, moral psychology, evolutionary sociology, and systems philosophy. They need a moral framework, cultural backing, a sense of shared responsibility, and a long-term view of stewardship. The goal is not just to keep society from falling apart; it's also to make it possible for people and communities to do well.

# I. Institutions as Moral Frameworks

Institutions do more than just make people follow the rules; they also change how people see themselves and what drives them. Every institution teaches what it means to be a good person, how to treat others, and what kinds of success are acceptable. These lessons accumulate in the backdrop of social existence, engendering what may be termed moral atmospheres.

## Making Norms

People learn norms by repeating them, seeing them, and getting positive feedback. Institutions show which behaviors are valued, accepted, or punished, and this has a greater effect on behavior than laws alone.

## Incentive Structures

Incentives encode moral priorities. Predatory behavior spreads when people are rewarded for making money without considering the social costs. People are more likely to act prosocially when they are rewarded for honesty and working together.

## Identity and Belonging

Institutions foster collective identity, which may be either inclusive and respectful or exclusionary and hierarchical. Identity has a stronger effect on motivation than rational thought.

So, institutions are what drive cultural change. They create rules and behaviors that keep happening. A society that values dignity, reciprocity, and shared prosperity does not emerge spontaneously; it requires intentional cultivation through institutional design.

# II. The Rise of Extractive Moral Ecologies

Many contemporary institutions have gravitated toward moral ecologies characterized by competition, commodification, and efficiency, often at the expense of dignity and human welfare. This shift is neither fortuitous nor unavoidable; it stems from structural incentives and ideological frameworks that diminish human worth to mere economic productivity and consumption.

## The Reduction of the Human to the Economic

Neoliberal economic ideology portrays individuals as solitary, utility-maximizing agents, thereby concealing the relational and communal aspects of human flourishing.

Trust is slowly going away.

When institutions don't care about the public good, trust goes down. This erosion isn't steady; it takes a long time to build trust, but it falls apart quickly, which causes political polarization and social fragmentation.

## Concentration of Wealth and Power

As political and market systems converge around oligarchic control, institutional feedback loops worsen inequality, making it harder for people to work together to solve problems.

## Incentives Lead to Moral Drift

People who have to do bad things to stay alive or be successful (for example, when companies have to pass on costs to stay competitive) suffer from moral injury. This is a mental wound that occurs when people are part of systems that conflict with their values.

The end result is a society with many things but not enough people to care for them. It has a lot of technology, but not enough meaning, community, and a shared goal.

## III. Guidelines for Creating Healing Institutions

To foster a moral ecology that enhances human flourishing, institutions must be founded on principles that promote cooperation, dignity, and sustainable stewardship.

### 1. Dignity as a Fundamental Principle

Institutions must acknowledge the inherent worth of every individual. This means that:

- Equal say in government and fair treatment
- Protection from being taken advantage of and made to do things
- Acknowledgment of varied identities and contributions

Dignity is not only a moral principle; it is also a fundamental requirement for the functioning of democracy and the stability of the economy.

## 2. Mutual Care and Reciprocal Obligation

A society that is doing well needs people to be responsible for each other. Organizations that value cooperation over dominance build trust and lessen the need for forceful enforcement.

## 3. Long-Term Time Frames

Healthy systems invest in the future. To fight short-termism, we need to change how we run things and handle money. For example, we need to stop the pressure to make money every three months and the way elections work.

## 4. Power that is shared and government that is open to all

It is not possible for a centralized command to run complicated societies. People in the area should be able to make decisions that are open, fair, and based on what they know.

## 5. Ethical Reflection Embedded

Ethics should always be on the minds of institutions. They need ways to change and question their goals, rewards, and effects over time.

# IV. Design for the Economy and Society to Revive

The design of institutions is closely tied to the physical conditions of society. Economic systems should support moral ecologies rather than weaken them.

## 1. Putting social purpose back into markets

Markets should work together to help people, rather than operate in isolation. Regulatory frameworks must guarantee that economic activities foster collective prosperity.

## 2. Putting money into people's skills

Schools should teach more than just how to get a job. They should also teach wisdom, creativity, empathy, and civic duty.

### 3. The Community as the Unit of Resilience

The most important parts of social trust are the people who live in the same area. Strengthening community organizations such as cooperatives, public spaces, and cultural groups helps rebuild the social fabric from the ground up.

## V. Healing and Elevation of Institutions as a Group Activity

Changing an institution is a process that happens repeatedly, is flexible, and is open to everyone. It needs:

- Political Will: The strength to fight against long-standing systems of power.

- Cultural Imagination: A mental image of what it means to do well.

- Moral education teaches people how to care for others, think things through, and take responsibility.

- Collective Agency: Knowing that change can happen on both a personal and a system level.

Fixing healing institutions is not only a technical problem; it is also a moral and cultural one. It tells societies to remember what they care about, to face what they have made normal, and to think about what they could still become.

## Conclusion

Institutions are the places where people show their highest hopes or their biggest failures. When institutions are run by a logic that takes, competes with others, and treats people like objects, they create moral ecologies that break down trust, dignity, and the chance for everyone to do well together. But institutions can also be changed. They can be re-anchored in values that acknowledge the inherent worth of each person, promote cooperation and kindness, guarantee fair distribution of power, and encourage long-term stewardship. To build systems that heal and help people, we need to change how we think about human nature. Instead of thinking of people as competitors, we should think of them as interdependent. We need to understand that flourishing is not a personal benefit, but a collective benefit grounded in the moral framework of our institutions. What a society values again is what it becomes. We must choose to honor dignity, reciprocity, meaning, community, and care—not just in words, but in the long-lasting structure of the systems we build.

# The Philosophy of Excess and Economic Disparity

## Abstract

The philosophy of excess and economic inequality are significant concepts that interlink ethics, political economy, ecology, social psychology, and cultural criticism. Here's a structured view:

## Introduction: Setting Up the Question

Economic inequality occurs when wealth, income, and opportunities are not evenly distributed across different groups in society.

The philosophy of excess examines the ethical, societal, and metaphysical consequences of affluence, opulence, overconsumption, and hedonism.

They pose significant inquiries:

- Is excess morally defensible in a world marked by persistent poverty?

- How do cultures defend or criticize the accumulation of wealth?

- What part does consumption play in shaping identity and power?

- Is inequality and overconsumption sustainable, or do they cause instability?

## Philosophical and Historical Origins

a. Ideas from Ancient and Classical Times

Plato and Aristotle: Advocated for moderation. Aristotle's idea of the golden mean says that you shouldn't have too much or too little.

Stoicism: Valued self-control and not being attached to things.

Christianity: Jesus and later Christian theology often spoke out against wealth and stressed the importance of helping the poor.

b. Reasons for Capitalism and Enlightenment

Adam Smith believed that inequality was a natural outcome of productivity, yet he emphasized moral empathy and public welfare.

Utilitarianism: Agrees with inequality if it makes everyone happier (like Bentham and Mill).

## Contemporary Critiques of Excess and Inequality

a. Karl Marx

Thought that economic inequality was a natural part of capitalism.

Believed that giving workers too much (luxury for a few) would make them feel alone and take advantage of them.

b. Thorstein Veblen (1899), The Theory of the Leisure Class

Introduced the idea of conspicuous consumption, which means spending money to show off your status instead of meeting your needs.

Too much is a show and a sign of class.

c. Contemporary Thinkers

Thomas Piketty (Capital in the Twenty-First Century): Wealth accumulation tends to concentrate unless checked by taxation or redistribution.

Peter Singer says that morally, people should give extra money to help those who are suffering (The Life You Can Save).

## The Morality of Too Much in a Global Context

Global Disparities: Having billionaires and people living in extreme poverty coexist raises moral questions.

Climate Change: The world is getting worse because people use too much, and the poor are the ones who suffer the most.

Luxury Ethics: Can you make or defend luxury goods in a way that is moral?

## Cultural and Psychological Aspects

Desire and Consumerism: Modern capitalism thrives on the endless production of desire (Baudrillard, Zygmunt Bauman).

Excess is often sold as a way to be free or express yourself, but it hides problems in the system.

## Possible Policy Solutions

a. Changing things around

Universal basic income, progressive taxation, and limits on wealth.

b. Other Models

The idea behind degrowth is that fairness and environmental protection are more important than economic growth. Post-consumerism: Supports minimalism and finding value in things other than having a lot of stuff.

c. Ethical Ways of Life

Conscious consumerism, ethical investing, and voluntary simplicity.

## Conclusion

The philosophy of excess prompts us to consider the moral limits of inequality and how consumption shapes societies. Economic inequality is not only a technical issue; it is also a significant moral and philosophical concern. To make the world fairer and more sustainable, we need to address excess in some way, whether through personal restraint, structural reform, or cultural change.

# Aristotle and Modern Game Theory: A Philosophical Synthesis of Strategy and Virtue

## Abstract

The inquiry posits: how would Aristotle engage with the field of game theory? Modern game theory, grounded in mathematical formalism and economic rationality, provides a comprehensive framework for analyzing strategic interactions among rational agents. In gaming, even in cooperative situations, the main goal is to achieve the best outcome for oneself, not to be seen as a virtuous act or a way to help others (altruistic behavior may be a trait in cooperative games). In a competitive, zero-sum game, outcomes can be very harsh, especially when there are many players and information is asymmetrical. Since its creation in the middle of the 20th century by figures such as John von Neumann, Oskar Morgenstern, and John Nash, game theory has been applied across many fields. These areas are economics, political science, evolutionary biology, and artificial intelligence. But its main point—that people do things that are best for them to maximize utility (or some other form of optimality)—makes us think about what it means to be human, what is right and wrong, and what the goals of rational action are. If Aristotle, the ancient Greek philosopher whose Nicomachean Ethics and Politics are foundational to Western thought, were to engage with contemporary game theory, he would not accept it unconditionally. He would instead reinterpret its assumptions through his ethical and teleological framework, asserting that rational strategy must be subordinate to virtue and oriented towards the common good.

## Teleology and the Aims of Rational Action

Teleology is a very important part of Aristotle's philosophy. It says that every action has a goal (telos) and that the best thing for a person to do is to thrive (eudaimonia). Aristotle says in Nicomachean Ethics, "Every art and every inquiry... is thought to aim at some good; and for this reason the good has rightly been declared to be that at which all things aim."[1] Modern game theory assumes that agents act to maximize their utility, which is often thought of as preference satisfaction or economic gain. Aristotle would not consider this intrinsically irrational; however, he would condemn the simplification of human purpose to material or self-serving aims. For Aristotle, rational action must not only pursue personal gain but also strive for a virtuous existence within a just society. Maximizing utility devoid of moral direction would be considered an inadequate expression of reason.

## Virtue, Character, and Strategic Behavior

Modern game theory typically distinguishes between means and ends, focusing on identifying strategies that optimize outcomes within constraints. Aristotle, conversely, asserts that the means of action possess moral significance because they affect the actor's character. In game-theoretic scenarios like the prisoner's dilemma, the prevailing strategy is to defect, even though cooperation produces a superior collective result (a Nash equilibrium). From an Aristotelian standpoint, the decision to defect, while rational in a specific context, indicates a lack of virtue, especially in terms of trustworthiness, justice, and civic friendship (philia politikē).

Aristotle posits that virtues are developed through habituation and that ethical conduct must encompass both right action and right intention.[3] Strategic behavior aimed solely at self-advantage, especially to the detriment of others, obstructs the cultivation of virtue. Even when game-theoretic equilibria are attained, as in the Nash equilibrium, where no player can unilaterally improve their outcome, Aristotle would question whether such stability fosters the moral flourishing of individuals and communities.

## The Polis and the Moral Dimension of Cooperation

Aristotle asserted that humans are political animals (zoon politikon), inherently inclined to live in communities governed by justice and a common objective. This political aspect aligns with modern game theory's analysis of collective action dilemmas, including public goods games and coordination games, which explore the conflict between individual incentives and collective welfare. Aristotle would view cooperation not merely to resolve strategic dilemmas, but as a moral obligation rooted in the necessity for communal peace.

So, making rules and institutions based on game theory is morally important. Aristotle emphasizes that laws and institutions ought to foster virtue and guarantee that individuals' actions align with the common good. In game theory, institutional rules establish constraints and incentives; according to Aristotle, they should also facilitate moral development. The tension between individual rationality and social virtue, a central theme in various game-theoretic models, would, in Aristotle's view, require not optimization but practical wisdom (phronesis).

## Practical Wisdom vs. Formal Rationality

Game theory involves value optimization, which means choosing the best strategy based on the information and payoffs available. But Aristotle's idea of practical reason (phronesis) isn't just about numbers. It is a kind of judgment that considers both general and specific rules, as well as the moral quality of the results. Aristotle says that a person who is practically wise "deliberates well about what is good and expedient... not in some particular respect, e.g., about what sorts of things conduce to health or to strength, but about what sorts of things conduce to the good life in general."

In circumstances where game theory endorses defection, punishment, or retaliation (as exemplified by tit-for-tat strategies), Aristotle would promote evaluation based on character, relational context, and the long-term welfare of the community. In short, he would ask not only which strategy wins, but also which one is fair and whether trying to win makes the soul stronger or weaker.

## Criticism of Homo Economicus

The concept of homo economicus, a rational, self-interested, utility-maximizing agent, is a basic idea in classical game theory. Aristotle's anthropology diverges significantly from this model. He thinks people are reasonable and moral beings who can put their own interests aside for higher values such as friendship, honor, and justice. In Politics, Aristotle asserts that economic pursuits are secondary to the political and ethical dimensions of life. He contends that strategic rationality should not attain autonomy, as it would jeopardize the moral integrity of the polis. Aristotle also sees the good life as a group effort to achieve excellence and virtue, not as a competition for limited resources. Game theory, especially in its non-cooperative variants, often presupposes scarcity and conflict. Aristotle would support a redefinition of the "game" to promote mutual flourishing rather than mere positional advantage.

## Conclusion

Aristotle would view modern game theory not as an opponent but as a component of human rationality—one that, lacking an ethical foundation, risks distorting the aims of human behavior. He would contend that strategic interaction ought to be guided not merely by optimality or utility, but by virtue, practical wisdom, and the pursuit of eudaimonia. Game theory clarifies the structures of human decision-making and cooperation; however, it requires integration into a broader philosophical framework that encompasses the ethical and communal dimensions of existence. Aristotle would not aim to supplant strategy with virtue; rather, he would endeavor to amalgamate them, transforming game theory into a discipline of flourishing rather than merely winning.

# Nietzsche and the Game of Becoming: Power, Chaos, and Creative Destruction

## Abstract

Friedrich Nietzsche's philosophy of becoming is not a static metaphysics; it constitutes a dynamic interplay of power, chaos, and creative destruction. From this point of view, existence is not governed by unchanging laws or moral absolutes, but by the constant flow of forces that are always competing, merging, breaking apart, and coming together in new ways. Nietzsche's concept of the will to power transcends mere domination; it serves as an ontological principle of transformation, self-enhancement, and artistic creation. This essay analyzes Nietzsche's philosophy through the lenses of complexity and game theory, situating his notion of becoming within an extensive framework of dynamical systems and creative chaos. It contends that Nietzsche's philosophy presages contemporary understandings of emergent order and the self-organizing characteristics of life, culture, and meaning.

## I. The Metaphysics of Becoming

Nietzsche rejected the Platonic and Christian metaphysics of Being, which asserts that reality consists of immutable forms or divine absolutes. He instead described life as Becoming: a constant flow of energy and drives that never come to a clear end. He said in The Will to Power, "The world is the will to power—and nothing else." He called it "a monster of energy, without beginning or end." This "monster of energy" is not chaos in the bad sense, but chaos as potentially the fertile ground of creation. Nietzsche posits that Becoming supersedes Being as the paramount category of existence. Everything is different; nothing stays the same. The essence of life is its capacity to create, annihilate, and regenerate itself. Nietzsche's universe is defined not by equilibrium but by disequilibrium, characterized by the constant tension of forces striving to transcend their own limitations.

## II. The Will to Power as a Game of Action

People often think that the will to power is a way to control others. Nietzsche's deeper insight is that power is relational and generative; it arises through interaction and contestation rather than mere possession. In this way, the will to power is like a dynamic game, an evolutionary field where all forms of life try to show and grow their potential. Nietzsche's agon (contest) resembles an iterated nonzero-sum game from a game-theoretic perspective. Winning is never the end; your strategies change as you play more. There are always new chances for conflict and cooperation when something is made. Complexity theorists call this recursive interplay of forces "autocatalytic loops." These are cycles that keep going on their own and create new structures through feedback and iteration. The Übermensch (Overman) exemplifies mastery not through domination but through self-transcendence. He is the player who doesn't want to follow the rules that are already in place and instead wants to change the game itself. Nietzsche thought that the best kind of power is not to win within the rules that are already in place, but to make new ones.

## III. Destruction and Chaos in Art

The famous quote by Nietzsche, "One must still have chaos in oneself to give birth to a dancing star," shows how much he believed in creative instability. For Nietzsche, chaos is not disorder but the source of new forms. Joseph Schumpeter later echoed Nietzsche's idea with his concept of "creative destruction," the process by which new ideas break down and improve systems. Nietzsche, on the other hand, has a bigger view: creative destruction is a universal law. To pave the way for a new cultural renaissance, moral revolution, or artistic breakthrough, the certainties of the past must be obliterated. The artist who is sad and the philosopher of the future must both accept this chaos and make something new out of it. Nietzsche's concept of eternal recurrence contributes to this perspective by conceptualizing time as cyclical rather than linear. To affirm eternal recurrence—to desire that every moment repeat infinitely—is to love fate (amor fati) and to accept the creative force of chaos itself. It is a metaphysical game of becoming without end.

## IV. The Aesthetic Cosmos: Intricacy and Self-Organization

Modern complexity science provides a novel lexicon for Nietzsche's intuition. Systems on the "edge of chaos" exhibit the kind of dynamic balance Nietzsche had in mind. They are on the edge of stability and breakdown, and they can organize themselves without any outside help. Life does not move toward balance; instead, it moves toward more complicated forms of imbalance. Nietzsche's universe is aesthetically pleasing. As the will to power develops, it creates increasingly intricate and aesthetically pleasing arrangements of energy. Nietzsche posits that art transcends mere cultural activity and represents the pinnacle of existence itself. In The Birth of Tragedy, he stated, "Existence and the world are only eternally justified as an aesthetic phenomenon." Within this framework, the act of creation is posited as the ultimate affirmation of existence against nihilism.

## V. Beyond Nihilism: The Game of Becoming

The failure of metaphysical certainties leads to nihilism, which is the realization that there is no higher order that guarantees meaning. Nietzsche viewed this not as a conclusion but as a commencement: an invitation to participate in the process of becoming conscious. The death of God does not mean that value is gone; it means that value can be made. Power and chaos are not enemies in the game of becoming; they work together to make life happen. Every act of creativity is also an act of destruction. Every affirmation includes its opposite. Nietzsche asserts that a mature spirit is capable of affirming "Yes to all that is," uniting joy and sorrow, destruction and creation, within a singular aesthetic affirmation.

## VI. Conclusion: Toward a Philosophy of Emergent Power

Nietzsche's philosophy of becoming anticipates a modern synthesis of ontology, aesthetics, and complexity. The will to power serves as an emergent organizational principle, creating new forms from chaos through recursive interaction. Life is a game with no end, no winners, and no set rules. Only creative players are allowed. To live Nietzsche's vision means to be aware of the cosmic game, to accept instability, to turn chaos into art, and to remember that every moment of dissolution is also a chance to make something new. The dance of becoming, which never ends, is both scary and beautiful.

# The Philosophy of Enough and Economic Altruism

## Abstract

This essay analyzes the concept of economic altruism within the context of the philosophy of enough—the normative and psychological threshold at which the pursuit of resources transitions from substantial security to detrimental accumulation. The essay argues that contemporary capitalist societies have systematically disconnected economic behavior from collective moral reasoning, leading to pathological patterns of excess, scarcity anxiety, and status-driven consumption. It draws on complexity economics, behavioral game theory, evolutionary psychology, and contemporary discussions of wealth inequality. This essay reexamines the moral principle of "enough," proposing a framework for reforming economic systems that foster cooperation, dignity, and collective prosperity rather than continuous competitive escalation.

## I. Introduction

People have always asked themselves how much is enough. The first groups of people shared food, space, and time not because they were better people, but because they needed to work together to stay alive. For thousands of years, economic systems changed to handle more resources, share them, and give people reasons to work hard. But relationships were still what held everything together. Wealth was important because it enabled people to live and work together and to pass things down from one generation to the next.

The idea of "more" is what makes us who we are in today's world. People don't think that security or dignity are important for economic success. Instead, they look at how much they have, how big it is, and how well they do in business. The idea behind modern capitalism is that there is no natural limit to desire and that having enough is not morally important. You don't just do well; you have to do better. The market does not reward the search for "enough," but the search for "more than others." This makes status competition a structural necessity.

This essay asserts that this system is neither natural nor inevitable; it results from particular historical, psychological, and institutional dynamics. Revisiting the concept of "enough" goes beyond sentimental nostalgia; it represents a rational response to the systemic failures currently evident: increasing inequality, ecological overshoot, democratic instability, and widespread psychological distress. To understand economic altruism, we first need to understand the moral economy of sufficiency.

## II. The Evolutionary and Psychological Roots of "Enough"

Before hierarchical civilizations emerged, people lived in small groups where they had to work together to survive. Evolutionary anthropology asserts that social cohesion and fairness norms were adaptive; groups that engaged in sharing generally demonstrated greater longevity compared to those that practiced hoarding.

But evolutionary psychology also says that people want more than just to stay alive; they want to be the best. Status made it easier for people to have children, make a difference, and get what they needed. So, people think about motivation in two different ways:

> Cooperation: the ability of a group to survive, which is shown by self-lessness and kindness. Status competition: Individual benefit, expressed through accumulation and prestige.

The philosophy of enough shows how these two things don't go together. People work together more when the economy is stable and safe. When people are worried, things are scarce, and they don't know what's going to happen, they compete for status and hoard things, even if they're rich. The result is a "scarcity treadmill" in people's minds, where nothing ever feels like enough, keeping people and societies stuck in a cycle of getting more. This is not just about greed; it's also about fear.

## III. When "More" Becomes Self-Defeating: The Economics of Excess.

Traditional economic theory assumes diminishing marginal utility: the first increase in income greatly improves well-being, but subsequent gains matter less. Nonetheless, empirical studies demonstrate that beyond a certain income level, additional wealth has a negligible impact on subjective life satisfaction.

And yet, accumulation continues—not because it increases happiness, but because it satisfies the status component of identity.

This is where the logic of excess becomes dangerous for the whole system. When accumulation is not linked to well-being, economic results no longer reflect human needs. Wealth gathers in one place, but it doesn't do anything useful. The gap between the rich and the poor gets bigger. The markets are getting weaker. And societies go from having a lot of competition to being run by a small group.

There is no cultural philosophy of "enough" that is neutral; it causes political instability and structural inequality.

## IV. The Moral Economy of Enough

Talking about a philosophy of enough doesn't mean praising poverty or limiting ambition. It means that:

> The condition of enough is when wealth serves life instead of life serving wealth.

The philosophy of enough is based on four main ideas:

1. Sufficiency Over Accumulation: Wealth is only important if it helps you live a good life.

2. Relational Value Over Possessive Value: The point of economics is to make everyone better off, not to give one person an edge over another.

3. Responsibility Over Entitlement: Having money means you have to follow the social contract, not get out of it.

4. Intergenerational Stewardship: Wealth should surpass personal interests and immediate concerns.

These principles embody both ancient ethical traditions and contemporary economic critiques. The idea stays the same over time, but the ways it is put into practice change.

## V. Economic Altruism as Strategic Rationality.

Contrary to the misconception that altruism is irrational, behavioral game theory demonstrates that cooperative strategies frequently outperform purely self-interested ones in repeated interactions among individuals.

Generosity boosts trust, lowers monitoring costs, improves coordination, and creates positive-sum dynamics in stable interactions like families, workplaces, and communities. In situations where people need each other, societies that promote cooperation do better than those that promote competition. So, being altruistic with money is not only the right thing to do; it's also a smart move.

## VI. Rebuilding the Philosophy of Enough in Today's World.

The philosophy of enough does not say that having money is bad. It's a way to change how you think about being rich:

> Having power over other people is not what makes you prosperous; having stability is. - Having a lot of things doesn't mean you're prosperous; being healthy does. Prosperity is shared; otherwise, it is not whole.

In real life, this means:

> Creating economic institutions that put a stop to runaway concentration. Changing the way we think about taxes as a responsibility of citizens. Not just GDP, but also well-being and resilience metrics to measure how well a country is doing. Encouraging cultural norms that view sufficiency as achievement.

## VII. Conclusion: The Return of Enough.

We live in a time when things are out of balance, not because we don't have enough resources, but because we don't know how to use them morally. The philosophy of enough tells us to think about what a good life really needs and to make sure that our economies work for everyone. Seeking sufficiency does not limit human potential. It is to free us from the urges that change it. It's not a luxury to be nice to other people. It is the requirement for any society that wants to keep both prosperity and humanity.

# Aristotle's Virtue Ethics in a Nonlinear World: Stability, Reciprocity, and the Golden Mean as Dynamic Equilibrium

## Abstract

Aristotle's virtue ethics, framed within an orderly and teleological context, outlines a route to human flourishing (eudaimonia) through the development of stable character traits (hexeis), the enactment of reciprocity in interpersonal and political relationships, and the pursuit of a Golden Mean between vicious extremes. The modern understanding of the world is increasingly shaped by the principles of complexity and nonlinear dynamics, which challenge notions of predictability and static equilibrium through feedback loops, sensitivity to initial conditions, and emergent phenomena. This essay argues that Aristotle's ethics are not outdated but can be significantly reinterpreted and revitalized through the lens of nonlinearity. By redefining moral virtue as a dynamic equilibrium rather than a fixed point, stability as resilience instead of rigidity, and reciprocity as a complex, feedback-rich interaction rather than a mere exchange, Aristotle's framework demonstrates exceptional foresight and adaptability for addressing the complexities of the 21st century.

## Introduction: An Age-Old Moral Framework for Modern Life

In the Nicomachean Ethics, Aristotle establishes a moral framework for the Athenian citizen, an inhabitant of the polis whose existence embodies a specific telos (purpose) and evolves within a relatively stable social and cosmic order. A good life is one in which people do good things and end up in a state of eudaimonia, which means they are flourishing. The stable character state (hexis), the reciprocal bonds of friendship (philia) that hold the city together, and the doctrine of the mean, which says that virtue is a middle ground between too much and too little passion and action, are all important ideas for this project.

People often talk about our modern world, which is a nonlinear system, in terms of complexity science. In these kinds of systems, outputs aren't directly proportional to inputs (nonlinearity), small causes can have big, unpredictable effects (the butterfly effect), and systems self-organize through feedback loops that repeat over and over, creating new properties that can't be broken down into their parts. This world doesn't seem like the stable harmony that Aristotle thought it would be. It seems chaotic and connected.

It is possible to reconcile the apparent divide between Aristotelian stability and modern flux. This essay will demonstrate that a nonlinear interpretation does not undermine virtue ethics; rather, it elucidates it in a more intricate and beneficial manner. We will examine this through three fundamental Aristotelian concepts: first, by reinterpreting the stability of virtue (hexis) as a manifestation of psychological and moral resilience adept at managing disruptive change; second, by scrutinizing reciprocity in friendship and justice as a nonlinear feedback mechanism that fosters trust and social capital; and third, and most importantly, by reconceptualizing the Golden Mean not as a fixed, arithmetic midpoint but as a dynamic equilibrium, a perpetual process of calibration and adaptation in response to a fluid and unpredictable environment.

## I. The Stability of Character in a Chaotic World: Hexis as Resilience

A major point of disagreement among modern critics of virtue ethics is that it depends on the development of stable, long-lasting character traits, or hexeis. The idea of a fixed "character" can seem silly in a world where things change quickly, and people are under a lot of stress. But a nonlinear interpretation helps us understand stability in a more complex way.

Aristotle describes a hexis as a "dispositional state" that is "firm and unchangeable" (Nicomachean Ethics, 1105a35), rather than merely a habit. This kind of unchangeability is a good thing in a linear, predictable world. It could get brittle in a nonlinear one. The key is to think of this "firmness" as strength and not stiffness. Resilience in ecological and engineering systems means that a system can absorb changes and reorganize while maintaining its function, structure, and identity. A sturdy system can bend without breaking.

When it comes to character, a virtuous hexis is not a single block, but a complicated, interconnected structure that is formed by practice (ethos). For example, a brave person doesn't just do what they're told to do ("always stand your ground"). Instead, their character is a strong system that lets them adjust their reactions to a wide range of nonlinear situations, such as threats to their health, social pressure, and business risks. Their stability comes from their ability to handle fear and confidence in the right way, not from doing one specific thing. A small insult (a small input) might be best ignored, but a threat to a core principle (another small input) might need a strong and disproportionate response. This is a judgment that isn't always the same and depends on the situation.

Moral growth doesn't happen in a straight line. Justice is not achieved solely through the sequential aggregation of just actions. Aristotle said that virtue comes from doing something repeatedly and receiving feedback on how well you did it. We become builders by building things and harpists by playing the harp (1103a30). Every action provides feedback that changes the agent's mood slightly, either by strengthening or weakening neural pathways and behavioral tendencies. So, the process of forming character is a classic feedback loop: what you do in the past affects what you can do in the future, and the system that organizes itself becomes more complex and integrated. Ideally, it should move toward the eudaimonia attractor state.

## II. The Nonlinear Dynamics of Reciprocity: Friendship and Justice as Feedback Loops

Aristotle places considerable emphasis on reciprocity, especially in his analysis of friendship (philia) and political justice. He divides friendships into three groups: utilitarian, hedonistic, and virtuous. The first two are weak and linear; they only last as long as the benefit or pleasure is given in a way that is roughly equal to what the other person gets. On the other hand, the friendship of virtue is a great example of a nonlinear system.

It's hard to befriend someone you look up to for their character. It's a complicated relationship with a lot of feedback, where each friend's good deeds and good intentions make the other stronger and better. Aristotle says that a friend is "another self." This creates a positive feedback loop: my friend's virtue inspires my own, which in turn inspires theirs. This creates a synergistic relationship where the whole (the friendship) is greater than the sum of its parts. This is a property that is growing. There are rules, meanings, and histories that only the people in the relationship know about. You can't guess them just because two good people met.

But one act of betrayal can completely ruin the complex structure of the friendship. This is a classic nonlinear phenomenon: a small cause (a lie) leads to a discontinuous, disproportional effect (the end of the relationship), because it fundamentally changes the feedback dynamics that kept it going.

This model is also relevant to politics. Aristotle's concept of distributive and corrective justice encompasses a form of proportional reciprocity (Nicomachean Ethics, V.5). In a complex society, this reciprocity transcends a mere exchange of goods. It is a large network of feedback that connects to many other networks. The rules for how people should act are set by laws and social norms.

When people do the right thing, they help the system stay stable and build so-cial trust, which is a kind of moral capital. But widespread injustice creates a negative feedback loop that erodes trust, raises transaction costs, and may even push the social system to a breaking point—revolution or collapse—another nonlinear, phase-shift event. So, the stability of the polis depends on keeping these feedback loops in a virtuous balance.

## III. The Golden Mean as a Balance That Moves

The Doctrine of the Mean is the best and most useful new way to look at Aris-totelian ethics. Aristotle characterizes virtue as "a state that decides, consisting in a mean, the mean relative to us, which is defined by reference to reason, that is to say, to the reason by reference to which the prudent person would define it" (1107a1). The conventional critique posits that this is ambiguous and un-helpfully quantitative—how does one ascertain the "mean" between cowardice and recklessness amid the infinitely variable circumstances of existence?

The linear, arithmetic view of the mean, as a clear middle point between two fixed points, is not enough. When viewed through the lens of nonlinear dynam-ics, the Golden Mean becomes a powerful concept of dynamic equilibrium.

Dynamic equilibrium in complex systems is a condition in which a system main-tains its overall structure through continuous adaptation and transformation. A river is a classic example. Its channel stays the same, not because the water is still, but because the water and sediment are always moving and swirling. The equilibrium is a stable pattern maintained by constant activity.

So it is with virtue. Courage is not just one point on a line between being brave and being foolish. The right response is always changing, so you need to keep moving and adjusting. The "mean relative to us" means that this area is different for a soldier, a CEO, and a diplomat. It also changes all the time. The best way to deal with a threat today might not be the best way to deal with it tomorrow. This is because of new information, changes in the situation, and the agent's own skills getting better.

A virtuous person is like a tightrope walker or a seasoned sailor. They don't find a balance and stay still. They are always moving, making small adjustments to how they stand and act in response to the wind and the ground. This ability to change their own behavior is what makes them virtuous. Practical wisdom (phronesis) is the feedback system that takes in information about the situation, like feelings, social context, and possible outcomes, and changes the agent's response all the time to keep them in the virtuous attractor basin and away from the "vicious" attractors of too much or too little.

This model elegantly addresses the issue of moral ambiguity. In a world that isn't linear, a strict rule like "always tell the truth" can lead to problems, like telling someone who is out to get you a secret. Honesty is a dynamic balance that requires the person to find the right amount of brutal frankness (too much) and deceptive evasion (too little). The agent's practical reasoning in a given situation, as they interact with their surroundings in real time, leads to the "right" action.

## Conclusion: Flourishing in the Face of Change

Aristotle's virtue ethics, derived from the assumed linearity of the Greek polis, possesses an intrinsic complexity that makes it especially relevant to a contemporary world acknowledged as fundamentally nonlinear. We can present a dynamic moral philosophy relevant to our time by going beyond a strict, old-fashioned interpretation. Character stability (hexis) is not a product but a necessity for resilience, allowing people to maintain their integrity amid change that shakes things up. At its most advanced levels, reciprocity manifests as a complex, generative feedback loop that builds the trust and social capital communities need to thrive in interdependence. The Golden Mean is no longer just a static, quantitative idea; it is now a concept of deep practical wisdom. It is a dynamic balance that needs constant, perceptive interaction with a world that is always changing and full of surprises.

In this new way of looking at it, the Aristotelian virtuous agent is not a solid statue from the past, but a living, changing system. Their goal is not to reach a state of perfect stability, but to skillfully navigate the chaotic currents of life, continually adjusting their thoughts, feelings, and actions to keep their lives stable and thriving. Eudaimonia is not the destination of a linear path, but rather the essence of the journey. It is the strong, give-and-take, and constantly changing activity of a soul that is fully involved in the beautiful, chaotic, and nonlinear dance of life.

# Cognitive Disequilibrium and the Moral Framework of Truth

## Abstract

This essay examines how truth serves as a moral and cognitive balancing force in complex social systems. As economic and ideological incentives increase, the equilibrium between moral integrity and cognitive coherence diminishes, leading to systemic instability. The subsequent phase transition, evidenced by a moral–cognitive bifurcation, illustrates societies' ability to oscillate between moral order and epistemic disintegration.

## I. The Cognitive Framework of Belief

Belief systems serve as the cognitive structure of communal order. In this framework, truth serves as both an objective condition and a stabilizing force for social trust. When moral coherence aligns with cognitive structure, societies maintain interpretive equilibrium. But this balance becomes unstable when external forces, such as politics, economics, or ideas, shift how information is presented.

## II. The Moral Economy of Truth

Truth is like moral money in human systems. It builds trust, legitimizes power, and enables people to work together. When truth is put below profit or propaganda, it loses its moral value. This starts a feedback crisis in which perception and legitimacy diverge. The economy of truth is like a financial bubble: it creates too much symbolic value, and then trust breaks down.

## III. Distortion of Incentives and Cognitive Drift

Incentive structures affect how people learn. When institutional or economic incentives favor performance over accuracy, agents engage in strategic cognition, prioritizing persuasion over veracity. This causes cognitive drift, in which your perception gradually becomes less accurate. Complexity theory asserts that as distortions accumulate, the system transcends a critical threshold, leading to non-linear and chaotic correction.

## IV. Feedback Loops for Belief and Power

Power amplifies belief through recursive validation. Stories that those in power agree with have epistemic weight, even if they aren't true. In this system, power dynamics, not facts, decide what is true. The system transitions from an open inquiry framework to a closed feedback mechanism, serving as an attractor of ideological uniformity and moral degradation.

## V. The Collapse of Epistemic Equilibrium

When the distortion reaches a certain level, the moral-cognitive balance divides. Some actors become cynical and relativistic, while others become radicalized and moral absolutists. Both represent adaptive responses to the same imbalance: the breakdown of stable feedback between fact and meaning. As a result, the bifurcation exemplifies a significant phase transition within consciousness itself—from adaptive rationality to chaotic moral signaling.10

## VI. Restoring cognitive-moral coherence

To restore balance, you need more than just fixing the information; you also need to restore morals. Practices that restore truth, teach ethics, and make things more transparent can help align incentives with honesty. Stability is attained not through inflexibility but through dynamic equilibrium: the ongoing adjustment of beliefs, values, and perceptions towards a common moral attractor.

# Ethical Entropy and the Fragmentation of Collective Accountability

## Abstract

This essay develops a formal model of moral degradation in complex social systems, demonstrating how collective responsibility declines as moral energy wanes due to self-interest, institutional inertia, and information overload. It says that ethical entropy is the loss of coherence among moral agents, drawing on ideas from thermodynamics and complexity theory. As collective responsibility becomes less stable, the integrity of democratic and institutional frameworks is increasingly at risk of breaking down completely.

## I. The Thermodynamics of Morality

Ethical systems can be viewed as thermodynamic constructs, with moral coherence signifying a low-entropy condition of collective organization. When personal incentives align with moral principles, social energy remains concentrated and effective. As competitive self-interest and informational asymmetry expand, entropy escalates, and moral clarity evolves into subjective relativism, leading to a deterioration of directionality within the ethical framework.

## II. The Social Power of Being Responsible

Responsibility is what keeps moral systems together. It makes agents responsible within a shared system of duty and giving back. When institutions push responsibility outside their own walls, such as when they use algorithms to make decisions or break into smaller groups, the moral burden spreads across the network. This diffusion is like how energy is lost in physical systems: no one person has enough moral momentum to keep the whole moral field going.

## III. Incentive Gradients and the Decline of Morality

Incentive gradients determine the flow of moral energy. When rewards make people more likely to be dishonest than honest, things get out of hand. Systems that prioritize short-term gains generate feedback loops that gradually erode trust. As ethical signaling replaces moral action, virtue becomes a performative trait rather than a substantive one, accelerating the decline of responsibility.

## IV. Self-Interest and Feedback Loops of Collective Loss

In complex adaptive systems, feedback loops can improve moral coherence or worsen it. When moral standards are set aside for strategic gain, positive feedback reinforces bad behavior, making corruption a stable state that people want to be in. This phenomenon can be termed 'ethical phase locking'—a metastable equilibrium characterized by ongoing moral decay, despite individual cognizance of impending collapse.

## V. The Disorderly Collapse of Moral Order

At advanced stages, ethical entropy manifests as cynicism, disengagement, and institutional paralysis. People stop trusting the government, laws lose their moral authority, and moral language becomes disconnected from moral substance. Like a thermodynamic system getting closer to equilibrium, social energy spreads out until moral temperature—collective passion for justice and virtue—gets close to zero.

## VI. Restoring Moral Equilibrium

To stop ethical entropy, we need to bring back friction—deliberate, reflective, and moral resistance to the automaticity of self-interest. Institutions need to internalize moral cost structures, reestablish feedback between power and accountability, and renew collective moral narratives. Just like in physics, order is not restored by suppressing entropy but by creating open systems that can be morally renewed through exchange, reflection, and reform.

# Prosperity Without Meaning: The Entropy of Abundance

## Abstract

This paper argues that modern economies have entered a paradoxical regime of material abundance and moral entropy. While productivity, wealth, and technological capacity reach historic highs, societies experience declining meaning, trust, coherence, and civic vitality. Using a moral ecology framework grounded in complexity economics, social psychology, and systems humanism, the paper models meaning as a public good subject to entropy, depletion, and collapse. It demonstrates that abundance without moral architecture produces nihilism, polarization, and institutional decay—not as cultural failure, but as systemic inevitability.

## Introduction: When Prosperity Decays the Soul

Never in human history have societies been richer and never more psychologically fractured. Rising GDP, record stock markets, unprecedented consumption, and accelerating technological power coexist with:

- Epidemic anxiety
- Institutional distrust
- Civic disengagement
- Identity collapse
- Social fragmentation

Prosperity is no longer generating flourishing. It is generating entropy. This is not accidental. It is structural.

## Moral Ecology: Meaning as a Public Good

*Moral ecology* treats meaning, trust, and legitimacy as ecological resources.

They are:

- Non-rivalrous
- Non-excludable
- Slow to regenerate
- Vulnerable to extraction

Modern economies externalize moral depletion the way early capitalism externalized environmental damage. Meaning becomes an invisible common, over-harvested until collapse.

## Abundance as a Destabilizing Force

Abundance destroys scarcity feedback that once disciplined behavior:

- Limits vanish
- Status competition intensifies
- Identity becomes performance
- Desire decouples from need

The system enters **hyper-consumption dynamics** that amplify narcissism, alienation, and nihilism.

## The Entropy of Excess

Entropy in moral systems rises when:

- Reward becomes detached from contribution
- Narratives replace reality
- Attention becomes monetized
- Institutions lose sacred legitimacy

The result is a extreme moral decay, maximum freedom with minimum meaning.

## The Psychology of Hollow Prosperity

Empirical patterns reveal:

- Rising depression in wealthy societies
- Declining life meaning scores
- Explosive loneliness
- Radicalization vulnerability

Abundance collapses the evolutionary logic of effort, gratitude, and belonging.

## Institutional Decay and Meaning Collapse

Institutions depend on moral energy. When moral energy is depleted:

- Law becomes coercion
- Markets become extraction

- Education becomes credentialism
- Democracy becomes spectacle

Institutional legitimacy collapses before institutional function.

## VII. The Nihilism Feedback Loop

Abundance accelerates nihilism through:

- Identity commodification
- Attention monetization
- Algorithmic polarization
- Hyper-individualism

Nihilism then destabilizes institutions, which increases nihilism further. A positive feedback loop of collapse.

## VIII. AI and Moral Death

AI accelerates:

- Desire amplification
- Meaning fragmentation
- Simulation replacement of reality
- Cognitive outsourcing

Without moral constraints, AI pushes society toward maximum entropy.

## IX. Rebuilding Moral Architecture

Flourishing requires moral infrastructure:

- Shared narratives
- Civic rituals and collective ethics
- Contribution-reward coherence
- Institutional sacredness
- Limits on attention extraction

Meaning must be engineered back into systems.

## X. Conclusion: The Tragedy of Unstructured Abundance

We are not poor in resources. We are poor in meaning.

Without moral architecture, prosperity becomes poison.

Abundance does not save civilizations. Meaning does.

# Chapter 6

# Art History, Aesthetics, and Cultural Dynamics

## A Look at Chaos Theory and the Abstract Impressionism Art Movement

### Abstract

This paper examines the convergence of Chaos Theory and the Abstract Impressionism art movement through a multidisciplinary perspective, emphasizing their mutual engagement with complexity, unpredictability, and emergent order. It asserts that the core principles of Chaos Theory—sensitivity to initial conditions, nonlinearity, and fractal geometry—are abstractly represented in the gestural, layered, and emotionally resonant artworks of artists like Jackson Pollock, Joan Mitchell, and Willem de Kooning. This study shows that in the middle of the 20th century, both science and art shared a way of knowing that rejected linear causality and accepted dynamic systems of expression.

### Introduction

Chaos Theory, an important mathematical and physical framework that emerged in the 20th century, investigates deterministic systems that exhibit both unpredictable and patterned behaviors. At the same time, Abstract Impressionism, a major American art movement that emerged after World War II, focused on expressive abstraction, emotional spontaneity, and a turn away from traditional forms of representation. These movements originated in separate intellectual domains, yet they collectively concentrate on complexity, emergence, and the dissolution of linear causality. This paper posits that Abstract Impressionist artworks, particularly those by Jackson Pollock, serve as aesthetic analogues to the dynamic systems depicted in Chaos Theory, thereby elucidating the significant philosophical connections between art and science.

## Chaos Theory: A Framework of Intricacy

Chaos Theory was formally established as a discipline in the 1960s, although its origins can be traced back to Henri Poincaré's contributions in the 1800s. It basically talks about deterministic systems that can change in ways that are hard to predict because they are sensitive to their starting conditions. This is often called the "butterfly effect." But just because something is unpredictable doesn't mean it's random; chaotic systems exhibit patterns, often strange attractors, and fractal geometries. Edward Lorenz's weather models and Benoît Mandelbrot's fractal mathematics demonstrate how chaos unveils order within apparent disorder.

These systems run counter to traditional Newtonian models that place great value on predictability and linear causation. A way of looking at the world that uses emergence and feedback loops to explain complicated behaviors better with Chaos Theory. This intellectual departure from linearity corresponds with simultaneous progress in the arts.

## Abstract Impressionism: A Reaction to Structure

After World War II, artists in New York City like Jackson Pollock, Mark Rothko, and Willem de Kooning sought new ways to express themselves. They didn't like European ideas of form, symmetry, and perspective; instead, they liked spontaneity, gesture, and abstraction.

Pollock's "drip paintings," for instance, were a radical way to make art because they used movement, intuition, and actions that didn't follow a straight line. He didn't just throw paint on horizontal canvases at random; he did so on purpose, influenced by the work's physical dynamics, rhythm, and feedback. Harold Rosenberg is famous for coining the term "action painting" to describe a style of painting that makes the canvas look like a battlefield rather than a window into a scene.

Pollock's art features fractals and pretty patterns.

Richard Taylor, a physicist, conducted a groundbreaking study of Pollock's drip paintings and found that they had fractal dimensions, indicating they were chaotic. Taylor found that Pollock's paintings grew increasingly complex over time, suggesting that he was deeply interested in new spatial patterns. These fractal patterns are statistically similar across scales, suggesting that there is hidden order in what might otherwise seem random or chaotic.

This is a key point of connection: Mandelbrot's fractals reveal natural shapes like coastlines, clouds, and blood vessels, while Pollock's lines create organic, moving patterns that don't fit traditional composition. His paintings are like pictures of non-linear dynamical systems, and they ask people to find coherence not in symmetry but in recursive complexity.

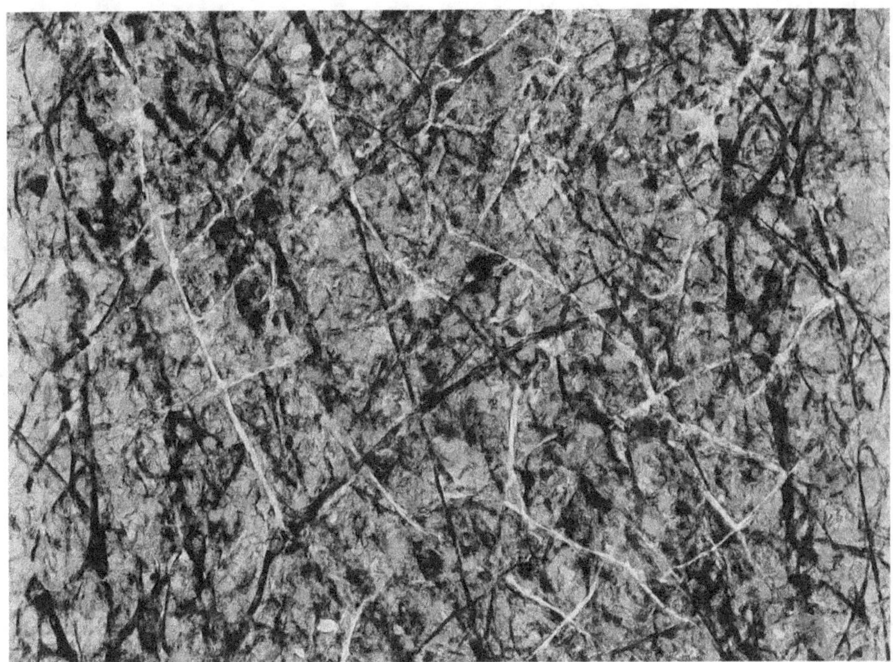

## The artistic process, being sensitive, and getting feedback

Another common theme is the importance of understanding the starting conditions in Abstract Impressionist art. This is a very important idea in Chaos Theory. The first stroke on a canvas, like the first variables in a simulation, makes a path. Every time you move or put paint on the canvas, you get feedback. The artist reacts to what has come before in a way that isn't straight or linear.

The first steps affect the future state of the whole system, just as chaotic systems change over time. Pollock says that paint viscosity, gravity, momentum, and arm movement all work together to make a system that is very sensitive to even the smallest changes. In de Kooning's art, rapid changes and layers are a way for him to navigate an internal feedback loop of emotions and visual stimuli. He doesn't plan out his designs ahead of time; instead, he lets them happen on their own.

# Postmodernism, Disorder, and the Dismantling of Dominant Narratives

## Abstract

Both Abstract Impressionism and Chaos Theory emerged as people lost faith in the Enlightenment's ideas of reason, control, and linear progress. Following the war, both artists and scientists scrutinized the adequacy of classical models. Chaos Theory challenged the predictability of Newtonian physics, whereas Abstract Impressionism subverted the presumed stability of representational art. This denial aligns with Jean-François Lyotard's critique of "grand narratives" in postmodern discourse. Abstract Impressionism and Chaos Theory don't have one meaning; instead, they focus on variety, emergence, and uncertainty. Both fields indicate that the quest for truth or beauty is not a linear path but a non-linear interaction with the unpredictable.

## Conclusion: A Shared Understanding of Disorder

The convergence of Chaos Theory and Abstract Impressionism reveals a shared epistemological viewpoint: that disorder and unpredictability ought not to be feared but examined. Pollock's fractal works, de Kooning's gestural distortions, and the recursive geometries of chaotic models give us a new way to think about complexity. This vision transcends disciplinary boundaries, illustrating that art and science are not antithetical; rather, they represent two approaches to understanding a complex world.

# The Art of Instability: Joan Mitchell and the Beauty of Chaos

## Abstract

This essay examines Joan Mitchell's art through the lens of turbulence—both as a concrete phenomenon and as a metaphor for the psychological, emotional, and social instabilities that defined postwar modernity. This article examines how Mitchell's work turns instability into a fundamental principle by situating her within the contexts of chaos theory, complexity aesthetics, and the existential unease of mid-twentieth-century America. Mitchell's paintings, which aren't at all chaotic in the usual sense, show how unstable systems of motion, feedback, and recursive emotional energy can make sense of things. Her art shows how nonlinear systems are a part of both nature and human experience.

The above figure is an abstract expressionist representation inspired by Joan Mitchell's "La Grande Vallée."

## 1. Modernism and Chaos

In the middle of the 20th century, artists were trying to figure out how to live in a world that had lost its sense of security. The end of classical balance came with the atom bomb, psychoanalysis, and the rise of abstract expressionism. In this way, Joan Mitchell's paintings are like the scientific discovery of chaos, when things appear out of order but actually have a deep, deterministic structure. Mitchell's art, on the other hand, is what physicists call "sensitive dependence on initial conditions." This is not like Cézanne's calm balance or Kandinsky's spiritual order.

## 2. The Beauty of Turbulence

Mitchell's art is beautiful because she can make unstable things look good. Her painterly chaos isn't random; it's the structured disorder of a system poised to reach equilibrium. Her approach is markedly distinct from that of her male counterparts; she transforms expressive gestures into recursive feedback.

## 3. The Nonlinear Self and the Complexity of Emotions

Mitchell's art also shows how complicated things can be. Her work makes sense of the emotional chaos—the never-ending cycles of love, grief, memory, and rage that don't make a straight story. In this way, her paintings are like what Carl Jung called "psychic individuation."

## 4. The Feminine Sublime, Nature, and Complexity

Mitchell's landscapes are abstract, but they are based on how light, wind, and water move in the real world. But nature, in her work, is never calm; she is always changing, full of life and energy. She reaches what could be called a feminine sublime.

## 5. The Art of Instability as a Way to Talk About Being Human

Mitchell's "art of instability" encompasses more than just painting. It is a way of thinking about life itself. In her work, as in complex adaptive systems, the goal is not stability but adaptability.

## 6. Conclusion: Moving Toward a Complexity Aesthetic

Joan Mitchell's art differs from other modern art because it combines chaos and consciousness. Mitchell's aesthetics of turbulence show us that art is a living system that is unstable, sensitive, and always putting itself together.

# The Renaissance as a Revolution of Complexity: The Emergence of Artistic Order and Economic Growth

## Abstract

People have always seen the Renaissance as a "rebirth" of classical antiquity, a direct line from the "Dark Ages" to modern humanism and scientific rationalism. This essay presents a nuanced interpretation, contending that the Renaissance represented a complexity revolution, a profound transformation in European society characterized by the emergence of a new world order through the nonlinear interactions of its elements. This analysis goes beyond a simple cause-and-effect story to examine how the combination of new art, economic changes, and new technology created a system that sustained itself. We will examine how the aesthetic principles of artistic order—particularly perspective and proportion—were not merely reflections of a novel worldview, but also instrumental in shaping a new social reality. We will also examine the emergence of novel financial, trade, and patronage systems that functioned through decentralized, networked, and feedback-oriented processes. The combination of these things made the one-of-a-kind and unbreakable event we now call the Renaissance. This shows that its real genius wasn't in going back in time, but in making a complicated, self-organizing leap into a new future.

## Beginning: From Rebirth to Emergence

Historians like Jules Michelet and Jacob Burckhardt were the first to use the word "Renaissance" in the 1800s. It gives the impression that history is simple and linear: a thousand years of sleep followed by a return to the greatness of Greece and Rome. This story is a simplification, but it is still strong. The medieval era was not insular, nor was classical antiquity merely rediscovered as an immutable artifact. A more credible model, grounded in complexity theory, perceives the Renaissance as an autonomous emergence.

In complex systems, emergence occurs when a collection of relatively simple, interacting agents self-organizes into a unified entity through iterative feedback loops. The whole has qualities the parts do not. These new properties are "irreducible," which means that you can't figure them out by just looking at the agents. The Renaissance is a great example of this process. The fall of Constantinople, the invention of the printing press, and the wealth of the Medici were not the only things that caused it. Instead, it emerged from the nonlinear, synergistic interaction of economic, artistic, technological, and intellectual trends that reached a critical level of connectivity and innovation between the 14th and 16th centuries.

This essay will analyze this complexity revolution from two primary viewpoints. First, it will examine the idea of artistic order and argue that the rise of linear perspective and the renewed focus on mathematical proportion were not merely style choices but also ways to help people understand a world growing more complicated. They were tools for turning a messy world into a place that could be understood and made sense of, like a model of a universe that was both divinely ordered and open to observation. Second, it will examine the emergence of a new European world system resulting from the nonlinear impacts of trade networks, banking innovations, and the competitive backing of an expanding merchant class. Lastly, it will show how the aesthetic and economic realms were not separate streams but instead deeply intertwined feedback loops, each influencing the other in a co-evolutionary process that led Europe into a new historical basin of attraction.

## I. Artistic Order as a Mental Tool for a Complicated World

The Renaissance's artistic revolutions, especially in Italy, changed how people thought about and showed reality in a big way. This change can be seen as society's way of dealing with the growing complexity by seeking to create a new kind of order that is both logical and kind.

### A. Linear Perspective: Putting Words into Visual Space

The formalization of linear perspective by Filippo Brunelleschi around 1415 and its subsequent expansion by Leon Battista Alberti in Della Pittura (1435) marked a critical juncture. It was more than just a way to paint; it was a great way to learn. A lot of medieval art showed a symbolic space with hierarchy. The size of the figures indicated their spiritual importance. This showed a worldview based on divine providence and clear, if otherworldly, hierarchy.

Linear perspective supplanted this symbolic order with a unified, mathematical, and relational dimension. At this point, all the parts of a painting had to follow the same rules that led to a point that disappeared. This created a world that was always there, measurable, and predictable. The viewer was positioned as a unique entity with a singular, advantageous viewpoint. People's minds changed as a result of this. It made a universe that was more than just a stage for religious plays. It was a huge, logical system that followed rules that people could understand, figure out, and eventually master.

From a complexity standpoint, the perspective simplifies matters. The overwhelming, multi-sensory flow of real-world sights and sounds was filtered and simplified into a geometric schema that was easier to understand. It was a way to use math to make sense of chaos by creating a virtual version of reality that the mind could understand. This new way of seeing things didn't just show that people were already sure about humanism; it also taught a whole generation how to see the world in a new, measurable way. This enabled the empirical perspective, which subsequently precipitated the Scientific Revolution.

## B. Proportion and the Human Body: The Small World of Order

There was a new interest in proportioning the human body that came with the new interest in organizing space outside. Vitruvius inspired artists like Leonardo da Vinci and Albrecht Dürer, who sought the ideal mathematical ratios that defined the ideal human body. The best symbol of this search is Leonardo's famous "Vitruvian Man." It shows a person, perfectly drawn, inside a circle and a square that represent the union of the earthly and the divine. The small circle reflects the large circle.

This wasn't just a nice thought. It was a search for the basic, universal rules that govern everything, from the movements of the stars to the structure of the human body. People began to examine the human body meticulously, believing that its beauty and harmony were derived from mathematics. This showed the basic idea behind complexity: that simple, repeated rules (like the golden section's geometric ratios) can make things that seem limitless and beautiful.

This artistic focus on proportion led to a way of thinking in which complexity was not seen as random but as grounded in a deep, understandable order. It strengthened the idea that the universe was a coherent system, which was important for the growth of modern science. Scientists could find these new laws of nature in the artist's studio.

## II. The Nonlinear Dynamics of a New World-System: Economic Emergence

European economies were changing as artists were creating a new conceptual space. The medieval feudal economy, which was based on land and duty, was simple and hierarchical, and was being replaced by a capitalist, dynamic, and globally connected world economy. This is a classic case of economic growth.

## A. Networks, Feedback, and the Expansion of Mercantile Capitalism

The Renaissance economy was marked by the rapid rise of decentralized networks. The Hanseatic League in the north and the merchant empires of Venice, Genoa, and Florence formed a dense web of trade routes linking Europe to Africa and Asia. These networks were systems that could change and grow. Prices were set by the actions of many merchants, not by a royal order. People could talk about the weather, politics, and markets on these networks, which made feedback loops that led to more investment and production.

Financial innovations like double-entry bookkeeping (which Luca Pacioli formalized in 1494), bills of exchange, and early forms of insurance were the "algorithms" of this new economy. They were rule-based systems that made it easier and more predictable for capital to move by lowering transaction costs and managing risk. The Medici Bank had branches worldwide and operated like a network of computers processing information. It used local knowledge to make money worldwide. This system didn't follow a straight line. A successful trip to the Levant could make a lot of money, but if one debtor didn't repay their loan, it could lead to many bankruptcies.

## B. Patronage as a Driver of Competition and Co-Evolution

The economic surplus generated by this emerging capitalism did not merely accumulate; it was channeled into a robust feedback loop with art and culture. Patronage became a major way for the new urban elite to assert status. This included the popolo grasso (the fat people) of Florence, the Sforza of Milan, and the merchant princes of the Netherlands.

It wasn't a simple, step-by-step process to buy art. Co-evolution was a complicated process. The patron wanted to be praised (through portraits, palaces, and religious frescoes), which created a huge demand for new artistic styles. The patron's social and cultural capital grew as the artist produced more and more impressive works that demonstrated their understanding of perspective, realism, and classical forms. This competitive spiral accelerated the artistic revolution.

Pope Julius II's support of Michelangelo's work on the Sistine Chapel ceiling is a great example of a high-stakes input that led to a non-proportionally great output: a masterpiece that changed the course of Western art forever. The system of patronage created a "fitness landscape" in which new technologies, artistic talent, and intellectual humanism were selected and encouraged. The artist went from being an unknown craftsman to a famous genius. This is something new that happened because of the new economic and cultural system.

## III. The Entanglement: How Art and Business Work Together

The complexity model's true power comes into play when we look at how these artistic and economic systems got mixed up, with each serving as a key place for the other to grow. The new artistic order directly helped the economy. Realistic paintings of merchants, their families, and their wealth (like those by Jan van Eyck or Hans Holbein) made them look good in society. The grand buildings, like Brunelleschi's dome for the Florence Cathedral, were not only amazing feats of engineering but also made people proud of their city and attracted more business and talent. Art became a form of "soft power" and a means of sharing economic ideas.

But the economy also gave art the physical and mental support it needed. The global trade networks brought in new colors, such as ultramarine blue from Afghanistan. The experiments were paid for by the desire to make money. The merchant's practical, empirical, and results-oriented way of thinking was similar to the artist's new approach to nature. Pacioli wrote about accounting, as well as math and proportions. This shows how closely the logic of capital, and the logic of art are connected.

This started a good cycle, a loop of good feedback. The economy's wealth funded new art, thereby enhancing cultural capital and civic identity. This, in turn, made the economy even more active by creating an environment of innovation. The system began to structure itself around the novel attractors of individual renown, civic honor, and financial prosperity. This took European society away from the feudal loyalty and otherworldly piety that were popular in the Middle Ages.

## The Unavoidable Jump: The End

Using complexity theory to study the Renaissance helps us get past the simple idea of "rebirth." It wasn't just waking up from sleep; it was a change in the way society was organized, with new traits like individualism, scientific rationalism, and global capitalism emerging and not reducible to smaller parts.

The artistic order of perspective and proportion made a mental map of a world that was getting more complicated. It showed a universe that was logical, measurable, and focused on human experience. The rise of mercantile capitalism, on the other hand, created a dynamic, interconnected, and feedback-based system. This led to more wealth and competition than ever before. These two forces didn't cause things to happen on their own; they were parts of a single, self-reinforcing complex system that worked together.

The brilliance of the Renaissance was not in its look back at the past, but in its ability to create something new from the chaos of its own time. It changed the way people talked to each other, gave feedback, and set things up. The paintings, sculptures, and financial records from this time are like fossils that reveal how this important event unfolded. They remind us that the most important changes in human history are not straight lines, but revolutions that are complicated, nonlinear, and very creative.

# Abstract Expressionism and the Geometry of Emotion: Pollock as a Cartographer of Economic Disorder

## Abstract

This essay looks at Jackson Pollock's abstract expressionism as a visual and philosophical representation of economic chaos. Pollock's "drip paintings" are reconceived as maps of systemic turbulence that evolve over time, mirroring the nonlinear dynamics of modern capitalism. This essay contends that Pollock's work represents not chaos, but the latent order of emotion, energy, and exchange that underlies both artistic and economic life, through an interdisciplinary synthesis of art history, chaos theory, and complexity economics.

## 1. Aesthetic Disorder: A First Look

Abstract Expressionism emerged in the mid-twentieth century as an artistic revolt against structured representation. After a war and a depression, artists like Jackson Pollock, Willem de Kooning, and Joan Mitchell stopped being formal and started being spontaneous. They looked for truth in chaos. But what seems like emotional chaos is really a hidden geometry—a web of energetic lines and repeating gestures that look like how modern economies work. Pollock's paintings, with their rhythmic splatters and fractal densities, show how markets and societies on the edge of order can be unstable, receive feedback, and grow.

## 2. A Way of Thinking and Doing Things in Chaos

Pollock's way of making art—putting canvas on the floor and letting paint fall through gravity and motion—wasn't random; it was a process that happened again and again. Like a nonlinear equation that makes a fractal shape, each layer is added to the one before it. This back-and-forth between control and giving up is like how complex adaptive systems work: decisions at the micro level shape structures at the macro level without any central coordination. Just like financial markets do through millions of independent transactions, Pollock's painting builds structure through local interaction. Every drop, splash, and motion is a piece of data in an attractor that is always changing. From this perspective, Pollock is not merely a painter; he is simultaneously a practitioner of systems theory. His art predicts the discovery of strange attractors and phase transitions in chaos theory. What looks like spontaneity is really a balance of freedom and restriction, feeling and form. It's like the economic cycles of boom, bust, and reorganization that define life in a capitalist society.

## 3. Pollock's Canvas and the Fractal Economy

Richard Taylor, a physicist, has demonstrated that Pollock's drip paintings possess fractal dimensions analogous to those observed in natural systems such as coastlines and turbulence. As Pollock's style develops, the fractal dimension increases, indicating that it is becoming more complex and similar across scales. The same logic about fractals works for the economy today. Market volatility, income inequality, and groups of new ideas all exhibit fractal traits, meaning they share patterns of concentration and diffusion. Financial crashes unfold in a way similar to Pollock's compositions: small shocks spread through networks, triggering systemic crises. For example, Pollock's Autumn Rhythm (Number 30) could be seen as a way for an artist to show how markets work together. Instead of money flow, emotional energy takes its place, and paint becomes liquidity itself.

## 4. Emotional Economies: Energy, Exchange, and Entropy

Abstract Expressionism was a moral response to feeling alone. It was an attempt to bring back real human feelings in a world of industrial and bureaucratic abstraction. Pollock's work shows the "geometry of emotion," revealing this tension: emotion is not chaos but structured energy controlled by invisible forces, just as supply, demand, and expectation are. Emotional systems are also economic systems. Markets are driven by fear, trust, imitation, and a shared illusion. Pollock's paintings make these psychological currents visible by turning the invisible economy of affect into visible motion. Every drop is a chance, a gamble that something beautiful will come out of the unknown. In this way, his paintings are like maps of how emotions change over time, where chaos, not order, is what gives things meaning.

## 5. The Art of Economics of Instability and Complexity

Complexity economics doesn't see the economy as a machine that is always in balance; it sees it as a living, changing ecosystem. There are feedback loops, nonlinear interactions, and order that emerge from nowhere in its structure. The same idea underlies Pollock's painting style: repeated movements that respond to their own buildup, adapt to constraints, and make sense of what seems like chaos. In both art and economics, instability is not a problem; it is a source of creativity. Pollock's brilliance stemmed from embracing uncertainty, akin to how novel concepts frequently emerge from the brink of chaos. His paintings are not nihilistic at all; they show a strong belief in beauty that can organize itself and meaning that can happen without any help. The lesson of Abstract Expressionism is that chaos is not the enemy of form; it is where form comes from.

## 6. Conclusion: Pollock's Legacy as a Guide to Being Aware of Money

Pollock's art will last because it shows what modern economics often misses: the emotional and chaotic roots of order. His work transcends the boundaries delineating art, psychology, and systems dynamics, offering a comprehensive understanding of complexity. When we look at Pollock through the lens of economic chaos, we don't see randomness; instead, we see resonance—a geometry of emotion that reflects the geometry of markets. Both are driven by the same things: human desire, uncertainty, feedback, and emergence. This synthesis exemplifies the lasting importance of Pollock's art—not solely as abstraction for its own sake, but as a mapping of contemporary consciousness on the verge of control.

# Art as Epistemology: When Aesthetic Qualities Unveil Systemic Framework

## Abstract

This essay says that art, in all its forms, is not just a way to express beauty but also a deep epistemological system that helps us know, model, and reveal hidden structures in complex systems. Whether through Renaissance perspective, abstract expressionist turbulence, or the symbolic cognition of modern aesthetics, beauty serves as a cognitive attractor that elucidates order within chaos, pattern within uncertainty, and meaning within nonlinearity. In a world characterized by complexity, algorithmic opacity, and systemic interdependence, art provides an alternative means of apprehending structural truths that escape solely analytical examination.

## I. The Power of Beauty to Know

Measurement, logic, and empiricism have been the main ideas in epistemology throughout history. But long before science became formal, art was a way to learn about the world. Beauty, coherence, harmony, and resonance are signs of hidden connections. To perceive beauty is to recognize structural order. Art connects logical thinking and gut feelings, revealing the structures of reality that can't be reduced to simple statements.

## II. The Renaissance: Perspective as a Change in Thinking

The creation of linear perspective was one of the most important changes in how people thought about knowledge in history. Brunelleschi's innovation transcended mere aesthetics; it represented a paradigm of spatial organization. Renaissance art created a mental framework that reflected and supported the new scientific view of the world by organizing the visual field around a point that disappears. Perspective articulated three epistemic assertions: (1) space is organized, (2) humans can simulate that organization, and (3) representation discloses structural veracity. Beauty thus evolved into a conduit for scientific rationality.

## III. The Abstract Expressionists: Showing How Complexity Grows

Abstract expressionism did the opposite of what geometry does: it showed structure through emergence instead of through geometry. Pollock's drip paintings, which were once thought to be random, were later shown to have fractal dimensions like those of naturally occurring turbulence. Physicist Richard Taylor's study showed that Pollock's paintings exhibit self-similarity and scale invariance, traits of complex systems. Joan Mitchell's gestural landscapes also show emotional and ecological dynamics that can't be put into words. Abstract expressionism shows that beauty can come from complexity, not just from order.

## IV. Beauty as a Cognitive Heuristic: Recognizing Patterns and Making Sense of Things

Beauty is a mental shortcut that points to a meaningful structure. People's ability to see symmetry, rhythmic repetition, proportional relationships, and fractal geometry has changed over time. These things are all related to stable or coherent patterns in nature and in social situations. Beauty condenses complexity into comprehensible wholes; it highlights structural relationships; and it facilitates understanding through pattern recognition. In this way, aesthetic cognition is an important addition to analytical reasoning.

## V. The Role of Aesthetic Knowledge in Scientific Discovery

For a long time, scientists have used aesthetic judgment as a guide. Einstein said that physical laws have an "inner beauty," and Dirac said that the beauty of math is a good sign of truth. Major scientific breakthroughs, such as Maxwell's equations, general relativity, and quantum field theory, arose from a sense of beauty in symmetry and coherence. Beauty often comes before measurement; it serves as an epistemic compass pointing to hidden structure.

## VI. Art as System Mapping: Moral, Psychological, and Social Structures

Art shows us things that analytical tools have a hard time seeing. Literature charts social power, identity, and cycles of feedback between people. Music reflects emotional regulation, tension dynamics, and affective "systems." Visual art shapes psychological landscapes. Art can reveal moral failures before institutions do; it can reveal trauma passed down through generations; and it can reveal systemic injustices. Art's ability to represent things is like a mirror that shows the social, emotional, and moral systems that control human life.

## VII. Aesthetic Epistemology in a Time of Complexity and Algorithmic Opacity

Linear models don't work for systems in the 21st century, like financial markets, supply chains, climate feedback loops, and AI recommendation architectures. Conventional epistemic instruments are inadequate for fully depicting nonlinearity, emergence, or systemic fragility. Art makes understanding more accessible by using metaphors to show how things are connected, motifs to show how things come together, narrative to show how things work, and abstraction to show how things are uncertain. Art restores epistemic coherence in a world where analytic intelligibility is deteriorating.

## VIII. Beauty as Truth: Theoretical Underpinnings

Philosophers ranging from Plato and Kant to modern aesthetic theorists contend that beauty unveils profound structural truths. Beauty is in line with shapes, sizes, and relationships that show coherence. It makes you think and focuses your attention. Beauty is not just for show; it reveals things. Elaine Scarry says that beauty "brings copies of itself into being," which makes people more aware of structural truth.

## IX. In conclusion, art is a way of knowing.

Art does not merely represent reality; it unveils its structure. It sheds light on the grammar of systems that are too complicated, subtle, or emotionally charged for formal analysis. Beauty is a mental magnet that draws people toward coherence. As global systems become more unstable, unpredictable, and nonlinear, art becomes a more important way to learn about the world. To understand complexity in the future, we will need to combine scientific analysis with aesthetic insight. Beauty is truth—not just in a figurative sense, but also in a structural sense.

# Surrealism as a Response to the Collapse of the Market: Dream Logic and Economic Chaos

## The Broken World and the Unconscious Response: An Introduction

1929 was not just a bad year for the economy; it was also a big change in how we know things. The Wall Street Crash and the Great Depression that followed destroyed the basic ideas that people in the late 1800s and early 1900s believed in: that progress was inevitable, that markets were rational, and that the bourgeois world order was strong. When factories stopped operating, banks closed, and breadlines snaked through city streets, it became clear that the material reality of Western society was weak, arbitrary, and absurd. It was in this climate of disintegration that Surrealism, formally founded in 1924 by André Breton but reaching its zenith in the 1930s, evolved from a provocative avant-garde literary movement into a potent visual and philosophical language. This essay says that Surrealism, especially in its visual forms, was a deep aesthetic and psychological response to the market crash. By prioritizing dream logic, liberating the unconscious, and intentionally fostering imagery of disorientation and decay, Surrealist artists did not evade economic chaos; rather, they formulated a representational approach to critique, interpret, and navigate its daunting new reality. The movement's main ideas—automatism, putting together different realities, and being obsessed with broken or mixed-up things—were a direct reflection of and a question about what it was like to live in a world where value had disappeared, systems had broken down, and the surface of life had cracked open to show a stranger, more troubling layer underneath.

## The Historical Conjuncture: 1929 and the Surrealist Era

To comprehend Surrealism's reactive essence, it is imperative to contextualize it within its distinct historical period. The movement's manifesto came out before the crash, but its most famous and mature works—Salvador Dalí's "The Persistence of Memory" (1931), René Magritte's "The Human Condition" (1933), and Max Ernst's collages from the early 1930s—came out right after the economy fell apart. The Great Depression was not just an economic event; it was also a cultural trauma. It showed that capitalism's logic was wrong and unstable at its core. The market, which used to be seen as a self-correcting machine, now looked like a chaotic, uncontrollable force, a nightmare for everyone.

This setting confirmed and strengthened the Surrealists' main idea that bourgeois rationality was a false front. The movement, which was heavily influenced by Freudian psychoanalysis, has always sought to bypass rational control to reach the more "real" and lively world of the unconscious. The failure of the market economy was huge, real-world proof of what they said was wrong. If the so-called rational world could cause such widespread and irrational suffering, then real understanding must be found somewhere else. The external chaos reflected and validated the internal psychological turmoil that the Surrealists aimed to investigate. The crisis also made people ready to respond to images that showed feelings of dislocation, anxiety, and the strange change of the familiar into something scary. Surrealism provided a lexicon for a widespread, nebulous sensation that the earth had fundamentally collapsed.

## Dream Logic as a Different System: Automatism and the Criticism of Instrumental Reason

The Surrealist response was based on the idea that "dream logic" could replace the discredited logic of the market. Dream logic functions via association, condensation, displacement, and symbolic transformation—methods entirely foreign to the instrumental reason of balance sheets and production quotas. Surrealist methods like automatism (writing or drawing without thinking) and exquisite corpse (a collaborative, chance-based image game) were intended ways to replicate this logic in art.

These methods can be seen as a direct response to the economic logic that didn't work. Capitalism valued planning, efficiency, and predictable results, while automatism valued accidents, spontaneity, and unconscious drive. It suggested a different economy of creation, one where value came not from work or usefulness but from direct psychic expression. The strange and chaotic results of these processes, like the drips and swirls in André Masson's automatic drawings or the strange anatomical composites in exquisite corpse, were like the unpredictable and seemingly pointless movements of a market that had crashed. They depicted a realm governed by an alternative, more profound set of principles, in which meaning was associative and latent rather than static and explicit.

Also, this turning inward to the dream world wasn't just a way to escape. Walter Benjamin and other thinkers deeply interested in Surrealism believed that the movement's strength lay in its "profane illumination." This means that dream images could spark revolutionary consciousness by showing how mythic and archaic forces are hidden in modern consumer culture. During a period of economic collapse, when goods lost their worth and became trash, the Surrealist gaze could re-enchant these discarded items, not with their market value but with their psychic and poetic resonance, thus exposing the fetishism of the commodity.

## The Object in Crisis: Destruction, Hybridity, and the Uncanny

In Surrealist art, the way it treats objects is the most direct visual metaphor for an economy in crisis. The stable, useful object of the world before World War II, which stood for industrial production and middle-class comfort, undergoes a radical transformation in Surrealism, becoming ruined, mixed up, and strange.

Think about how common images of decay and ruin are. Yves Tanguy and early de Chirico (a major precursor) both painted desolate, dreamlike landscapes full of strange, often broken structures. These are mental landscapes that reflect the material reality of the Great Depression: the closed factory as a modern ruin and the empty lot as a place of abandonment. The air is filled with a haunting stillness, like after a disaster.

The Surrealist "object" frequently represents a disintegration of function and classification. In "The Persistence of Memory," Dalí's limp, melting watches are the best example of this. The most important measure of industrial capitalism (work shifts, production schedules, interest accrual) becomes soft, useless, and ugly. It continues to exist, but not as a standard of order; instead, it is a dying organism. Meret Oppenheim's "Object (Luncheon in Fur)" (1936) does something strange and unapproachable to a teacup, saucer, and spoon by covering them in gazelle fur. These are examples of good manners at home. It makes a useful item useless, cutting off its use-value and replacing it with an unsettling sensory and psychological frisson. This act of making things seem strange is very similar to how the market crash made everyday things seem strange, distant, and out of reach due to sudden poverty.

Hybrid creatures and biomorphic forms, common in the work of Joan Miró and Hans Arp, add to this feeling of things falling apart. In a stable economy, there are clear roles and boundaries for raw materials, products, money, and waste. The Crash showed that these borders were not solid and could be crossed. Savings could disappear, owners could become poor, and solid investments could turn into worthless paper. The Surrealist object, like a sewing machine and an umbrella on a dissecting table (to remember Lautréamont's famous saying that the Surrealists loved), shows this shocking yet creative clash of different realities, creating a new, unsettling thing that reveals a world where all traditional categories have been called into question.

## The Body Under Pressure: Distortion, Fragmentation, and Alienation

In Surrealist art, the human body was put under a lot of pressure, just as the outside world of objects was. This reflected the physical experience of an economic crisis—the anxiety, the vulnerability, and the feeling of being acted upon by invisible, crushing forces.

The distorted, elongated, or fragmented bodies in Dalí's paintings and Hans Bellmer's photographs convey a deep sense of solitude. Bellmer's disarticulated dolls, put together and taken apart in grotesque ways, can be seen as symbols of the worker under capitalism: a machine that can be used, taken apart, and put back together in whatever way the system needs it to be, a process that was horrifyingly real during the Great Depression when so many people lost their jobs and were thrown away. The body loses its integrity and becomes a place where strange things happen, and people are hurt.

This fragmentation is also connected to the Marxist idea of alienation, which Surrealists, especially those in Breton's more revolutionary group, sought to address. The economic collapse worsens alienation by taking away not only the things people have worked for, but also their sense of control over a world they can understand. The Surrealist body, frequently depicted as passive, slumbering, or dismembered, symbolizes this relinquishment of control. But it was in this very passivity—the trance state of the automatist, the sleeper—that the possibility of freedom lay. By yielding to the unconscious, individuals could evade the oppressive and alienating frameworks of the rational (and now defunct) world. In Surrealism, the violated body is both a record of trauma and a place where new, non-rationalist ways of thinking can be created.

## The Search for a New Myth and Political Ambiguity

Surrealism's connection to direct political action, especially communism, was complicated and often contradictory. This shows how hard it is to link inner revolution with social revolution. Breton and a few others briefly joined the French Communist Party because they saw the criticism of capitalism as a common enemy. They famously asked, "Can the revolution be made without the unconscious?" because they believed that real social change required a psychological dimension.

But this partnership was not easy. The Communist Party's demand for doctrinal conformity and social realism was at odds with Surrealism's focus on individual psychic exploration and dreamlike, unclear images. In a different way, the movement's "failure" to find a stable revolutionary home is what makes it a strong historical document. It shows the real problem artists and intellectuals faced in the 1930s: the old world was gone, the capitalist future looked like a nightmare, and the proposed collectivist solution required giving up individual creative freedom, which many Surrealists couldn't accept.

So, the most powerful political act of Surrealism was still an artistic one. It wanted to create a "new myth" for the modern age, one that could replace the broken myths of progress and the market. This myth was based on wishful thinking, luck, and the amazing things that happen every day. Surrealism suggested that in a world devoid of material security, value and meaning could be reestablished within the complexities of the psyche, in serendipitous encounters, and through the poetic elevation of the ordinary. Its politics were image politics: a constant effort to undermine the dominant reality principle, which had proven to be disastrous, by claiming the revolutionary power of the imagination.

## Conclusion: The Mode's Lasting Power

Surrealism did not cease with economic recovery. But its strategies are closely tied to that first moment of systemic failure. The movement gave people a way to show a reality that had lost its logical moorings, a reality where clocks could melt, cities could empty, and even the most familiar things could become strange and threatening. It affirmed the internal, subjective experience of crisis as a legitimate source of truth when external, objective systems had failed.

In this way, Surrealism's legacy comes back to life in every new crisis of capitalism. The financial shocks of 1987, 2001, and 2008, each with its own strange qualities—algorithmic flash crashes, pyramid schemes of fake derivatives, and the ghostly trade of bundled debts—have always led to cultural expressions that use Surrealist techniques. The fragmented narratives of postmodern fiction, the sampling and mash-up culture of digital media, and the pervasive sense of the uncanny in contemporary horror and thriller genres all owe a debt to the pathways Surrealism carved out.

So, "The Persistence of Memory" can be seen as a prediction not only of psychological time but also of economic time. It implies that the trauma of collapse, akin to the soft watch, indelibly distorts the collective consciousness.

Surrealism taught us that when the market's dream of endless growth becomes a widespread nightmare, art must turn to the logic of dreams themselves—not to escape reality, but to create a new, more honest map of a world that has suddenly become strange. It remains the most important way to deal with chaos, showing how the human mind can make sense of broken systems by piecing them together.

# Chapter 7

# Social Psychology and Collective Dynamics

## A Social Psychological Examination of Collective Narcissism in American Politics and Society

### Abstract

The concept of collective narcissism has emerged in social psychology as a crucial tool for analyzing the dynamics of group identity, insecurity, and intergroup hostility. Individual narcissism is when a person thinks too highly of themselves. Collective narcissism is when a group of people thinks too highly of themselves and is too sensitive to threats or criticism. In the United States, this dynamic has been deeply ingrained in political, cultural, and social life, resulting in increased polarization, exceptionalist rhetoric, and hostility towards perceived outsiders. From a social psychological perspective, collective narcissism helps us understand both historical patterns and current tensions in American society.

### What is the definition of collective narcissism in social psychology?

Henri Tajfel and John Turner developed social identity theory, which holds that people derive part of their self-concept from the groups they belong to and strive to be different from other groups in a positive way. Collective narcissism emerges when group identity weakens, requiring constant affirmation and safeguarding. Agnieszka Golec de Zavala and her colleagues say that it is "a belief in the unparalleled greatness of an in-group that is not sufficiently recognized by others." This makes people mad and hostile toward critics. This idea is linked to authoritarianism, prejudice, and conspiracy thinking, which makes it different from just being proud of being part of a group.

## American Exceptionalism and the Roots of Collective Narcissism

American collective narcissism has historical roots in exceptionalist narratives that depict the United States as uniquely virtuous and destined for global leadership. This belief has made people feel like they are part of something bigger and has given them a sense of purpose as a nation. However, it has also weakened them. For example, during the Vietnam War, people who didn't like the U.S. military's involvement were often called unpatriotic because it made the country look bad to have people disagree with it. During the Civil Rights Movement, people who believed in racial hierarchy also said that calls for equality were attacks on the "real America." These events show how people become defensive and self-centered when their national myths are challenged, rather than thinking about others.

## Partisan Collective Narcissism and Political Polarization

In the 21st century, collective narcissism has increasingly become associated with partisan identity. Lilliana Mason's research indicates that political affiliation in the United States has transformed into a "mega-identity," encompassing not only policy preferences but also cultural, racial, and religious identifiers. Social psychology posits that the integration of political identity and self-concept leads to the perception of party criticism as a personal affront. Collective narcissism contributes to affective polarization, in which members of opposing parties perceive one another not as legitimate adversaries but as existential threats. This makes it clear that modern American politics is very rigid.

## The Rise of Narcissistic Behaviors on Social Media

Digital media has made collective narcissism worse by creating echo chambers and rewarding anger. Cass Sunstein's research on group polarization shows that people with similar views tend to become more extreme when they discuss issues together. Social media algorithms are designed to enhance user engagement with emotionally charged content that affirms their identity. As a result, perceived insults to the country or to one's political party, serving as a stand-in for the country, are turned into collective complaints. This has been especially clear in the rise of conspiracy theories like QAnon, where people who believe in "true America" think they are fighting against hidden enemies.

## Consequences for Democratic Unity

Collective narcissism weakens the strength of democracy by destroying trust, making opposition less legitimate, and encouraging authoritarianism. Research shows that people who are collectively narcissistic are more likely to support political violence, reject compromise, and back leaders who promise to protect the honor of the group. In the United States, this has led to more acceptance of anti-democratic actions when they are framed as protecting the country from traitors or outsiders. The attack on the Capitol on January 6, 2021, shows how stories that make losing an election seem like an awful shame can cause violence in the real world.

## Conclusion

From a social psychological perspective, collective narcissism provides a comprehensive framework for understanding contemporary American dynamics. Collective narcissism, stemming from exceptionalist traditions and exacerbated by partisan identity and digital technologies, transforms national pride into feeble defensiveness. Conspiracy thinking, polarization, and political violence all have effects that directly threaten the stability of democracy. To deal with this issue, we need to promote dialogue across divides, strengthen civic education, and encourage forms of identity that include everyone. If these steps aren't taken, American society could stay stuck in cycles of narcissistic grievance and hostility between groups.

# The Political Economy of Cognitive Capture: An Examination from a Social Psychology Standpoint

## Abstract

This extended essay analyzes cognitive capture as a fundamental mechanism by which disparities in political and economic power influence public belief formation, limit collective imagination, and reinforce unequal social structures. Drawing on political economy, complexity economics, and various domains of social psychology—such as heuristic reasoning, identity-protective cognition, motivated reasoning, group polarization, narrative persuasion, and epistemic trust—this analysis contends that cognitive capture operates as a multilevel system of constraints: psychological, institutional, narrative, and technological. It demonstrates how elites manipulate informational asymmetries, algorithmic infrastructures, and emotion-driven media architectures to create belief systems that validate inequality and undermine structural reform. The essay contextualizes cognitive capture within nonlinear feedback loops that interconnect public opinion, policy outcomes, institutional design, and material structures, resulting in path-dependent equilibria that perpetuate hierarchy. Lastly, it provides a framework for cognitive freedom through epistemic resilience, rebuilding democratic media, and transforming political and economic systems.

## 1. Introduction: Cognitive Capture as an Insufficiently Theorized Mechanism of Power

Cognitive capture is the least examined yet most influential force shaping political behavior in modern democracies. Cognitive capture works upstream, changing how people understand political reality, while regulatory capture addresses corruption within institutions. This difference makes cognitive capture more nuanced and deeper. A regulatory agency that is captured changes policy, while a cognition that is captured changes perception itself.

Modern political economy is still too materialistic, focusing too much on wealth, institutions, lobbying, and markets. But these operate within a cognitive superstructure composed of beliefs, assumptions, causal narratives, and moral frames that shape how people see what is possible, right, or good. When cognitive environments are constructed or shaped by actors with asymmetric capabilities, political economy becomes a competition over perceptions rather than policies.

This broader framework looks at cognitive capture in five areas:

(1) economic incentives based on structure,

(2) mental processes,

(3) media and algorithmic structures,

(4) group-level and identity-driven dynamics, and

(5) nonlinear feedback loops that keep societies in stable states that keep getting stronger.

## 2. The Economic Logic and Structural Foundations of Cognitive Capture

From the perspective of the most powerful economic actors, cognitive capture makes sense. Three structural forces make it a predictable strategy.

### 2.1 Information Asymmetry as a Source of Power

Elites have better access to data, experts, signaling platforms, and the ability to tell stories. In markets where information is a valuable asset, changing people's beliefs is an economically smart way to get what you want. When the cost of persuasion is very low, like on digital platforms, the benefits of manipulating people's minds become huge.

### 2.2 Oligopoly in the Market and Narrative

As the media, technology, finance, and political consulting industries merge, narrative production becomes more centralized. Only a few companies create cognitive environments for billions of people. The transition from a pluralistic media ecology to a concentrated economy diminishes epistemic diversity, constricting the spectrum of perceived alternatives.

### 2.3 The Economics of Legitimacy and Made-Up Consent

Democratic systems must establish public legitimacy. When states can't provide material well-being due to inequality, austerity, or institutional capture, they rely more and more on narrative engineering to maintain legitimacy in the public's eyes. This creates a political economy in which people become passive recipients of meaning rather than active creators of civic identity.

# 3. Cognitive Capture Viewed Through the Prism of Social Psychology

Social Psychology elucidates the cognitive permeability of populations. Cognitive capture leverages predictable psychological structures.

## 3.1 Cognitive Shortcuts and Heuristics

Human reasoning is designed to be quick, not precise. Dominant actors use weapons:

- availability heuristic (salience is about how important something is),

- anchoring effects (the first time you see something shapes how you see it for a long time),

- confirmation bias (information that supports your beliefs is given more weight).

## 3.2 Cognition that protects identity

People will protect their identity before they tell the truth. Beliefs serve as indicators of allegiance to political factions. When political identity merges with moral identity, epistemic flexibility disintegrates. Cognitive capture leverages this by linking structural economic stories to group identity.

## 3.3 Motivated Reasoning and Emotional Cognition

Beliefs are rarely established through dispassionate reasoning; they are developed through emotional coherence. Modern persuasion architecture inundates individuals with emotionally charged signals (fear, outrage, threat). Emotional salience supersedes factual content, rendering cognitive capture affective rather than analytical.

## 3.4 Cues of Authority and Fake Expertise

When people think about complicated issues, they often rely on perceived authority. In a captured environment, authority is created through branding, repetition, credential mimicry, or the institution's look. Social psychology shows that confidence often convinces people more than accuracy does, which makes it easy to manipulate knowledge.

## 4. Digital Infrastructures, Media Systems, and the Architecture of Capture

Digital infrastructures enhance cognitive capture via automation, personalization, and emotional optimization.

### 4.1 Personalization through algorithms and cognitive micro-realities

Algorithms create personalized epistemic worlds. This division makes millions of microstructural realities, each one supporting what people already believe. The outcome is the disintegration of the epistemic commons essential for democratic governance.

### 4.2 The Attention Economy as an Emotional Marketplace

Platforms get people more involved by evoking emotions. Fear and outrage are stronger than subtlety and complexity. So, cognitive capture becomes profitable: the stories that are most emotionally manipulative get the most attention.

### 4.3 Narrative Supply Chains

A coordinated ecosystem of think tanks, PR firms, data brokers, consultants, and partisan media creates narrative frames that move through digital channels. These frames influence causal reasoning, moral judgment, and the development of political identity, acting as cognitive defaults.

## 5. Cognitive Capture as a Means of Reproducing Inequality

Cognitive capture not only helps the powerful; it also creates the moral and interpretive framework that supports inequality.

### 5.1 The Myth of Meritocracy

Meritocracy serves as a legitimizing ideology that reinterprets structural inequality as a consequence of varying levels of effort. It makes systemic outcomes personal and makes elite success stories universal.

### 5.2 TINA Dynamics ("There Is No Alternative")

Captured cognitive systems constrict ideological space by depicting alternatives as impractical or perilous. This stops people from using their imaginations, which is necessary for structural reform.

### 5.3 Flipping Responsibility

Cognitive capture frequently reinterprets structural issues as individual short-comings: poverty is recast as poor decision-making, low wages as insufficient skills, and civic disengagement as apathy. These inversions stop political action and make it harder for people to work together.

## 6. Group Dynamics, Shared Illusions, and Social Enforcement

Group dynamics strengthen cognitive capture.

### 6.1 Polarization of Groups

Homogeneous groups amplify initial tendencies, leading to more extreme beliefs. Social media speeds up this process by fostering communities based on ideas.

### 6.2 Group Illusions

People often go along with beliefs they don't agree with because they think other people want them to. Cognitive capture creates these illusions on a large scale, which keeps harmful or unpopular norms in place.

### 6.3 Enforcing the Status Quo Norm

Going against stories that the group agrees with could lead to social punishment. This means that changing your mind is not only hard for your brain, but also bad for your social life.

## 7. Nonlinear Feedback Loops and Systemic Entrenchment

Cognitive capture becomes self-reproducing through feedback loops that happen on their own.

### 7.1 Beliefs → Institutions → Policies → Beliefs that are stronger

Policies influenced by entrenched beliefs yield results that reaffirm those beliefs, establishing path-dependent institutional trajectories.

### 7.2 Institutional Narratives as Machines of Legitimacy

Institutions construct interpretive frameworks that affirm their own existence. In captured systems, institutions circulate narratives produced by elites as objective truth.

### 7.3 Self-Fulfilling Cognitive Equilibria

When a large number of people believe something, like "the government can't solve problems that affect everyone," the belief becomes true in its effects. This is what W.I. Thomas's theorem on the macro-political level.

## 8. Psychological and Structural Obstacles to Cognitive Liberation

To get out of cognitive capture, you have to face strong psychological and structural barriers:

- avoiding cognitive dissonance,

- sunk-cost identity commitments,

- helplessness that is supported by institutions,

- emotional reliance on narratives that affirm identity

## 9. Democratic Consequences: From Epistemic Fragmentation to Authoritarian Drift

Cognitive capture undermines the epistemic framework of democracy. Deliberation fails without common facts. When people are confused or swayed by emotional stories, they are more likely to accept simple authoritarian solutions. Institutional paralysis arises when policy discussions transpire within discordant cognitive frameworks.

## 10. Toward a Structure for Cognitive Freedom

Cognitive liberation necessitates:

- improving metacognition and civic epistemology,

- rebuilding media that serves the public,

- setting rules for systems that use algorithms to persuade,

- lessening the power of monopolies and inequality,

- bringing back civic identity as a way to fight tribal identity.

Cognitive liberation is psychological, institutional, and material all at the same time.

## 11. Conclusion

Cognitive capture is a systemic problem that connects psychology, political economy, and complexity theory. It affects how societies think about the future, make sense of things, and process information. To bring back democratic agency, expand the collective imagination, and create systems that can fix themselves, we need to understand cognitive capture.

# Political Nihilism, Shared Delusions, and the Rise of Partisan Violence in American Society

## Abstract

In the last few decades, political extremism and violence have become more common in the United States. This phenomenon can be understood as the convergence of three formidable forces: collective illusions (prevalent yet erroneous beliefs regarding others' thoughts or values), political nihilism (the diminishment of trust in democratic institutions and norms), and an environment that fosters violence as a perceived means of expression or resolution. Understanding how these forces interact can help us understand how American civic life is becoming less stable.

## Collective Illusions: Distorted Social Perceptions

When people think they know what others want or think, and do what they believe is the norm, this is called a collective illusion. Polls show that most Americans support some compromises on guns, immigration, or healthcare, but many people think that "everyone else" has more extreme views. This disconnect causes people to stop speaking out, divide into groups, and create a false feedback loop: leaders and the media promote fringe views because they seem to resonate, which reinforces the illusion of extremity.

## Political Nihilism: The Erosion of Faith in Democratic Institutions

Political nihilism isn't just not caring; it's the belief that current institutions are illegitimate, corrupt, or unchangeable. Unlike traditional protest movements, which aim to improve the government, nihilistic actors often welcome disruption for its own sake. In the U.S., years of partisan gridlock, economic inequality, and high-profile crises (like financial crashes, pandemics, and contested elections) have made people less trusting of Congress, the courts, and even the electoral process. This is made worse by social media, which rewards anger instead of helpful conversation.

## The Rise of Violence as a Political Weapon

Historically, democratic societies have experienced diminished political violence when institutions effectively resolve conflicts. But when nihilism and collective illusions come together, the validity of nonviolent channels begins to diminish. People who think that "everyone else" supports extreme measures may think that violence is okay or even needed. Nihilism, on the other hand, sees violence as "truth-telling" or "direct action" instead of a crime. This pattern can be seen in attacks on government buildings, election offices, and government workers.

## Self-Organizing Radicalization and Feedback Loops

These three things work together to make each other stronger. Collective illusions make polarization seem worse, which, in turn, makes nihilism worse by making it seem there is no way to reach a consensus. Nihilism makes violent language normal, which leads to dramatic events that the media and social networks make more visible. This supports the idea that there is a violent majority. Over time, this creates a self-organizing system of radicalization that doesn't need a central authority to run it.

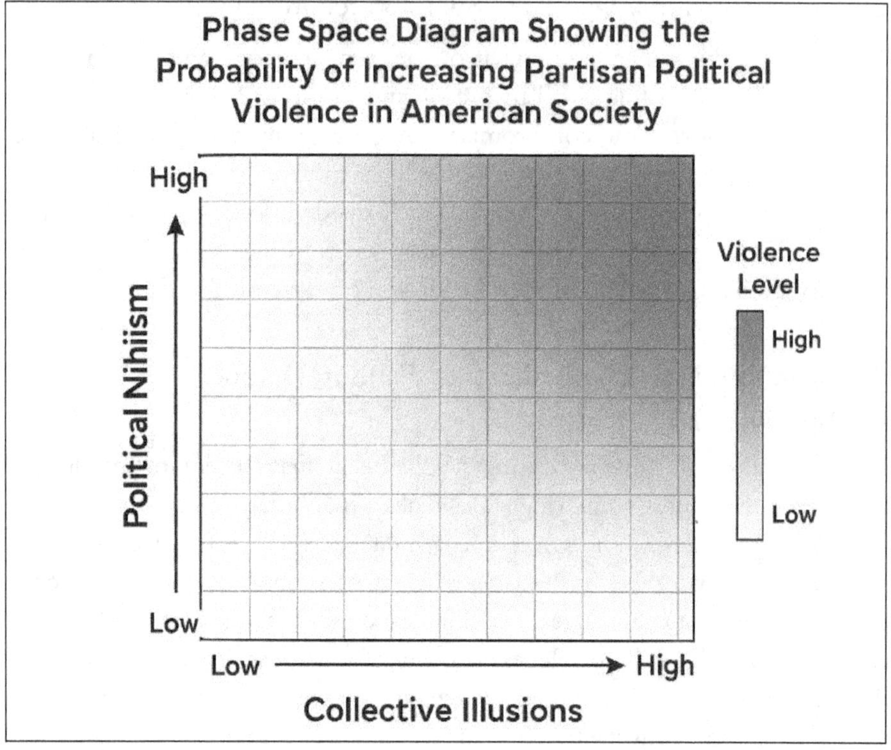


The diagram above shows a made-up phase space in which different levels of political nihilism (Y-axis) and collective illusions (X-axis) mix to produce different levels of violence (color scale). As we move toward the northeastern quadrant, we see that partisan political violence is becoming more likely in American society as both political nihilism and collective illusions increase.

## Possible actions and their effects on policy

1. Transparency and Norm-Clarification: Surveys and deliberative polling that show what most people want can break down groupthink and show that moderation is more common than people think.

2. Rebuilding Institutional Trust: Making changes to how things are done (such as nonpartisan redistricting, election safeguards, and visible anti-corruption measures) can show that working together pays off.

3. Counter-Violence Narratives: Studies in social psychology show that focusing on stories of peaceful conflict resolution and community strength makes people less likely to think that violence is unavoidable. Changing how algorithms amplify extreme content on social media, as antitrust laws do for information monopolies, could make outrage less profitable.

## Conclusion

Violence in American society is not just caused by a few extremists; it is also caused by system-level factors that connect collective illusions, political nihilism, and the acceptance of violent expression. To fight these forces, we need to work together to define real social norms, rebuild trust, and make it more appealing to do good than to cause trouble. Without these kinds of actions, the U.S. could end up in a chaotic state where violence is a normal part of politics.

# Collective Narcissism in American Politics and Society: A Social Psychological Perspective

## Abstract

The concept of collective narcissism has emerged in social psychology as a crucial tool for analyzing the dynamics of group identity, insecurity, and intergroup hostility. Individual narcissism is when a person thinks too highly of themselves. Collective narcissism is when a group of people thinks too highly of themselves and is too sensitive to threats or criticism. In the United States, this dynamic has been deeply ingrained in political, cultural, and social life, resulting in increased polarization, exceptionalist rhetoric, and hostility towards perceived outsiders. From a social psychological perspective, collective narcissism helps us understand both historical patterns and current tensions in American society.

## What does social psychology mean by "collective narcissism"?

Henri Tajfel and John Turner developed social identity theory, which posits that individuals derive aspects of their self-concept from the groups to which they belong and endeavor to distinguish themselves from other groups in a favorable manner. Collective narcissism emerges when group identity weakens, requiring constant affirmation and safeguarding. Agnieszka Golec de Zavala and her colleagues say that it is "a belief in the unparalleled greatness of an in-group that is not sufficiently recognized by others." This makes people mad and hostile toward critics. This idea is linked to authoritarianism, prejudice, and conspiracy thinking, which makes it different from just being proud of being part of a group.

## American Exceptionalism and the Roots of Collective Narcissism

American collective narcissism has historical roots in exceptionalist narratives that depict the United States as uniquely virtuous and destined for global leadership. This belief has made people feel like they are part of something bigger and has given them a sense of purpose as a nation. However, it has also weakened them. For example, during the Vietnam War, people who didn't like the U.S. military's involvement were often called unpatriotic because it made the country look bad to have people disagree with it. During the Civil Rights Movement, people who believed in racial hierarchy also said that calls for equality were attacks on the "real America." These events show how people become defensive and self-centered when their national myths are challenged, rather than thinking about others.

## Partisan Collective Narcissism and Political Polarization

In the 21st century, collective narcissism has increasingly become associated with partisan identity. Lilliana Mason's research indicates that political affiliation in the United States has transformed into a "mega-identity," encompassing not only policy preferences but also cultural, racial, and religious identifiers. Social psychology holds that the fusion of political identity and self-concept leads to interpreting party criticism as a personal insult. Collective narcissism cultivates affective polarization, leading individuals from opposing parties to view each other not as legitimate opponents but as existential threats. This makes it clear that modern American politics is not very flexible.

## The Rise of Narcissistic Behaviors on Social Media

Digital media has made collective narcissism worse by creating echo chambers and rewarding anger. Cass Sunstein's research on group polarization shows that people with similar views tend to become more extreme when they discuss issues together. Social media algorithms are supposed to encourage people to interact more with emotionally charged content and to strengthen their sense of self. So, when people feel insulted about their country or political party, they complain as a group. This is especially clear in the rise of conspiracy theories like QAnon, where people who believe in "true America" think they are fighting against enemies who are hiding.

## Consequences for Democratic Unity

Collective narcissism undermines democracy by fostering distrust, delegitimizing opposition, and promoting authoritarian conduct. Research shows that people who are collectively narcissistic are more likely to support political violence, reject compromise, and back leaders who promise to protect the honor of the in-group. In the United States, this has led to more acceptance of anti-democratic actions when they are framed as protecting the country from traitors or outsiders. The attack on the Capitol on January 6, 2021, shows how stories that make losing an election seem like an awful shame can cause violence in the real world.

## Conclusion

From a social psychological perspective, collective narcissism provides a comprehensive framework for understanding contemporary American dynamics. Collective narcissism, stemming from exceptionalist traditions and exacerbated by partisan identity and digital technologies, transforms national pride into feeble defensiveness. Conspiracy thinking, polarization, and political violence all have effects that directly threaten the stability of democracy. To solve this problem, we need to promote identities that include everyone, improve civic education, and get people from different backgrounds to talk to each other. If these steps aren't taken, American society could stay stuck in cycles of narcissistic grievance and hostility between groups.

# Jevons Paradox: Contemporary Applications and Prevailing Misconceptions in the American Economy

## Abstract

Jevons' Paradox, the notion that enhancing efficiency may lead to increased resource consumption, has re-emerged as a significant subject in twenty-first-century economic policy discussions. However, people often mistake the paradox for a law that guarantees resource depletion. This essay reinterprets Jevons' Paradox in the context of the contemporary American economy, focusing on energy markets, digital platforms, consumer behavior, and macroeconomic feedback loops. By placing the paradox in the context of complex adaptive systems, we can gain a deeper understanding of how efficiency gains alter cost structures, market incentives, demand elasticity, and socio-political trajectories. The result is a framework that goes beyond simple claims that "efficiency always backfires," offering a deeper understanding of how governance, institutional design, and behavioral dynamics shape the link between efficiency, sustainability, and consumption driven by rapid growth.

## I. Introduction: Reflecting on a 19th-century concept

In 1865, English economist William Stanley Jevons noticed something strange: even though England was using coal more efficiently, it wasn't using less of it; instead, it was using more of it. People began relying on coal more as coal-powered engines grew cheaper and more efficient. This made the demand for coal skyrocket. This is what is now known as Jevons' Paradox. In modern discussions, the paradox is often used to say that making things more efficient, whether it's energy use, farming, or computing power, is useless. This deterministic interpretation, though, makes a dynamic economic principle too simple. Efficiency lowers the cost per unit of output, but the overall effect on total consumption depends on how elastic demand is, how markets are set up, the incentives regulators provide, and how technology is used in general.

## II. The Logic of Efficiency and Rebound Effects

To understand Jevons' Paradox, you need to know the difference between direct and indirect rebound effects. Jevons' Paradox is the most extreme example of a rebound effect: when making things more efficient, it leads to more resources being used across the board. Efficiency makes it cheaper to make one more unit, which makes producers want to make more and consumers want to buy more. Depending on the sector, the size of the rebound can vary widely. The paradox is not inevitable; it depends on the institutions' circumstances.

## III. The American Economy and the Culture of Excessive Consumption

The United States has a unique role in the world economy: consumption makes up about 70% of GDP. Because consumer spending is structurally linked to the domestic economy, institutions encourage spending over saving. Rebound dynamics are stronger because of cultural identity, the need for businesses to grow, and fiscal-monetary policy. This means that efficiency often helps growth rather than slowing the flow of resources.

## IV. Case Study: Digital Consumption, Data Centers, and Computing Power

Digital infrastructure still needs more and more energy, even though computers are getting better at using it. Efficiency enabled new uses of data, such as cloud computing, streaming services, gaming networks, and training AI models. Efficiency didn't reduce overall energy demand; instead, it made computation a normal part of life, supporting Jevons' point that efficiency leads to growth.

## V. Conclusion: Jevons as a Framework for Systemic Design

Jevons' Paradox is not a sign of despair; it is a method to identify the issue. It tells us that in an economy that is focused on growth, efficiency alone can't keep things going. The American model, which is based on consumption, makes rebound effects stronger than in most other societies. This paradox pushes us to keep efficiency while building systems that use structural limits to steer consumption toward long-term goals.

# The Edge of Chaos: New ideas, Instability, and the End of Shared Reality

## Abstract

Human societies have always changed at the line between order and chaos. Too much order stifles creativity, and too much disorder makes things less clear. Complexity science calls this important point the "edge of chaos," which is a dynamic state in which systems are most adaptable, creative, and responsive to change. At this point, new patterns form, old structures break down, and innovation that changes everything becomes possible. But the edge of chaos isn't always a good place to be. It encourages learning and creativity, but it also has the potential to cause fragmentation, instability, and collapse. In modern societies, especially advanced democracies, the rapid pace of technological progress, economic intricacy, and information exchange has brought social systems alarmingly close to this limit. What once encouraged pluralism and experimentation now increasingly erodes shared meaning, institutional legitimacy, and epistemic trust. This essay examines the paradox of the edge of chaos in today's societies: how the same factors that foster new ideas also make reality less stable. Drawing on ideas from complexity theory, political economy, social psychology, and media studies, it argues that modern societies have shifted from productive complexity to epistemic fragmentation. In this new state, competing narratives don't interact constructively; instead, they create self-reinforcing cognitive silos. The outcome is not merely polarization; it signifies a profound disintegration of shared reality, leading to the deterioration of the common frameworks essential for democratic coordination, collective problem-solving, and social trust.

## I. Complexity Theory's Edge of Chaos

The idea of the edge of chaos comes from research on complex adaptive systems, which are networks of agents that interact in ways that can't be explained by looking at each agent in isolation. From ecosystems to neural networks to economies, systems have a critical zone between balance and randomness where adaptability is at its highest.

In very ordered systems, behavior is easy to predict but not very strong. Rigid structures can't absorb disturbances, so small shocks can spread very badly. In very chaotic systems, behavior is random and doesn't make sense; signals turn into noise, which makes it hard to coordinate. At the edge of chaos, though, systems show structured unpredictability, with enough order to keep things coherent and enough disorder to let people learn and try new things.

For instance, biological evolution works close to this limit. Genetic variation causes chaos, while selection pressures create order. In the same way, healthy economies need a balance between institutional stability and entrepreneurial disruption. Democracies need stable rules and the ability to openly disagree.

It's important to remember that the edge of chaos isn't a fixed point; it's a dynamic zone. Feedback loops, outside shocks, and internal incentives can cause systems to become rigid or fall apart. The difficulty for intricate societies lies not only in attaining this threshold but also in sustaining their existence within its feasible limits.

## II. Innovation as a force that shakes things up

Innovation is often seen as a clear good thing that drives progress, efficiency, and human well-being. But from a systems perspective, innovation is always destabilizing. Every technological or institutional advancement reconfigures incentive frameworks, reallocates authority, and modifies coordination patterns.

In the past, societies adopted new ideas through a lengthy process. Cultural norms, legal frameworks, and educational institutions evolved gradually. Innovation cycles have gotten much shorter in the past few years. Digital technologies, algorithmic systems, and globalized markets facilitate change at a pace that exceeds the capacity of social institutions to assimilate it.

This destabilization can be seen in three areas that are related to each other:

### New Ideas in Business

Financialization, platform economies, and automation have made work more productive, but they have also broken down traditional ways of doing things. Network effects drive wealth accumulation, while precarity spreads among workers. This imbalance causes both moral dissonance and economic instability. Systems reward abstract capital flows more than socially embedded labor, leading people to think institutions are less fair.

### Innovation in Technology

The cost of creating and sharing stories has decreased significantly thanks to information technology. Authority that used to be based on expertise and institutions is now based on attention markets, which are amplified by algorithms. Truth competes with virality, and engagement competes with coherence.

## New Ideas in Culture

Identity has become a modular, performative construct. This broadens expressive liberty, yet simultaneously disintegrates collective narratives. Shared symbols lose their ability to bring people together, and instead, fluid micro-identities take their place, making it hard to agree on what they mean.

In short, innovation gives systems greater freedom to move. Without ways to compensate for the lack of integration, these freedoms push societies past the point of productive complexity into chaos.

## III. From Pluralism to Epistemic Fragmentation

Pluralism, which means having different points of view within a common framework, has always been a strength of democratic societies. It assumes that there is disagreement in a shared epistemic space, which includes shared facts, shared rules of evidence, and shared institutional arbiters.

When this shared space breaks down, epistemic fragmentation happens. Instead of arguing over how to understand reality, competing stories now argue over reality itself. Facts turn into signals for tribes. Expertise becomes biased. Institutions that used to be trusted to settle disputes are now seen as captured or not real.

This change is a sign of a bigger change in the ecology of information. Social media sites and algorithmic curation systems work best when they get people to interact with each other rather than when they make sense. Content that incites anger, fear, or identity validation disseminates more effectively than content that promotes comprehension. Over time, people are pushed into self-reinforcing informational niches, or echo chambers, that make them more certain of their beliefs while hiding evidence that contradicts them.

From a complexity perspective, these niches act as local attractors in cognitive phase space. When people get into them, feedback loops stabilize belief systems, even when they are challenged from the outside. The system can no longer coordinate globally, even as local coherence strengthens. The result is not chaos in the sense of randomness, but pathological order—many internally consistent realities that can't talk to each other in a meaningful way.

# IV. The Psychological Aspect: Cognitive Load and Simplification for Protection

The breakdown of shared reality is not just due to technology or institutions; it is also deeply psychological. Human cognition evolved for coordinating small groups rather than for managing the incessant complexity of global systems.

As the amount of information grows, so does the cognitive load. When things are unclear, uncertain, and changing quickly, people look for psychological closure. Social psychology shows that when things are like this, people tend to choose simpler stories that make them feel less anxious and give them back a sense of control.

These stories often have things in common:

- Moral dualism (the battle between good and evil)
- Personalizing issues that affect the whole system
- Blaming outsiders
- Resistance to subtlety or probabilistic reasoning

At the edge of chaos, these kinds of simplifications help people adapt by making things less confusing. But when many people use them, they make the group's intelligence worse. Societies give up epistemic humility for emotional certainty, giving up accuracy for coherence.

Also, defensive simplification affects identity. Beliefs get mixed up with how we see ourselves and how we fit in with others. If you question a story, you risk damaging social ties. These dynamic turns disagreement into an existential conflict, accelerating polarization and distrust.

# V. Institutions Under Stress: When Stabilizers Don't Work

Institutions are important for maintaining stability and coordinating behavior in complex societies. Historically, courts, scientific bodies, electoral systems, and media organizations served as stabilizing feedback mechanisms, mitigating shocks and converting complexity into manageable formats.

These institutions are under a lot of stress right now:

### Speeding Up from the Outside

The speed of social and technological change is faster than that of institutional change. Rules made for slower dynamics seem old or random. As stories break apart, institutions are seen in a new light by different political groups. Impartial mediators are redefined as opponents. People don't accept procedural outcomes because they don't work; they don't accept them because they go against group identity.

When trust in institutions declines, societies lose their main ways to return to a shared reality. Disputes that used to end in acceptance now turn into recurring conflicts. Every decision made by an institution adds to the data that supports the beliefs already there. Feedback loops make problems worse rather than better, which is a sign that systems have gone from the edge of chaos to structural instability.

## VI. Innovation Without Integration: A Failure of Systems

The main problem with modern societies is not innovation itself, but innovation that isn't connected to anything else. Complexity theory posits that adaptive systems necessitate both variation and selection, as well as exploration and constraint. When new things come along faster than ways to make sense of them can change, coherence breaks down.

In the past, shared rituals, stories, and schools helped people come together. These functions are less effective today because the market rewards fragmentation and newness more than synthesis and continuity. The result is a society that has a lot of information but not much wisdom, a lot of choices but not much shared purpose. Innovation moves faster, but the group's direction fades.

From a systems perspective, this shows that micro-level incentives (such as attention, profit, and identity signaling) and macro-level stability (such as social trust, democratic legitimacy, and epistemic coherence) are not in sync. If this kind of misalignment isn't fixed, it will lead to societies splitting in two: either authoritarian consolidation or chronic dysfunction.

## VII. Getting Back to Normal: What Needs to Happen for Renewal

The edge of chaos doesn't have to end in failure. If you take care of it, it can become a place of renewal. The issue is not how to get rid of complexity, but how to rebuild the ability to integrate at scale.

Several ideas come to light:

- Epistemic Institutions Need More Support.
  Societies need reliable ways to find the truth that are not affected by attention markets or partisan capture. Transparency is not enough; legitimacy must be nurtured.

- Narrative integration is important.
  Shared reality is maintained not solely by facts, but by significance. Societies require inclusive narratives that embrace diversity while maintaining coherence.

- Comprehending Complexity Is Important.
  Schools need to teach people to think probabilistically, deal with uncertainty, and understand how systems work. Without this kind of literacy, complexity leaves people scared rather than helping them understand.

It is necessary to realign technological incentives.

Platforms that affect how people think as a group can't be neutral about what happens. Design choices affect how well we know things. This is the truth that governance must reflect.

Stability at the edge of chaos is an accomplishment, not a given. It takes careful planning, moral restraint, and bravery on the part of institutions.

## Conclusion: The Decision at the Doorstep

Modern societies are at a very important point in their development. The forces of innovation have made the world more complicated than ever before, opening up new creative possibilities while making shared reality less clear. When things are on the edge of chaos, systems can either reorganize into a more coherent whole or break apart into parts that don't make sense to each other.

The end of shared reality is not certain, but neither is a new beginning. The result hinges on society's ability to perceive complexity not as an adversary to be eradicated, but as a phenomenon of being judiciously managed. Futures are decided on the edge of chaos. It is a place of danger and opportunity—where new ideas can either deepen divisions or build a more unified, strong, and caring society.

# Chapter 8

# Political Economy and Geopolitical Dynamics

## The Fall of the Labor Republic: The Disintegration of Unions, the Rise of Inequality, and the Fragility of American democracy

### Abstract

The American republic of the twentieth century was not just a constitutional democracy; it was also a labor republic. Its political stability, economic mobility, and democratic legitimacy were founded on institutionalized collective bargaining, wage coordination, and collaborative productivity enhancement. This essay posits that the methodical disintegration of labor institutions since the 1970s constitutes a principal structural factor contributing to current inequality, political discontent, and the vulnerability of democracy. This paper employs complexity economics, political economy, and moral-ecological analysis to illustrate that the disintegration of organized labor has converted American democracy from a cooperative, productivity-sharing framework into a high-entropy, oligarchic system inherently susceptible to polarization, populism, and institutional disintegration.

### I. Introduction: The Republic That Wasn't Remembered

The American social contract after World War II was not just an idea; it was a system of institutions. From 1945 to 1975, rising wages, strong unions, and public investment worked together to create a system of productivity sharing that kept democracy stable. Labor institutions acted as:

- Wage equalizers
- Ways for people to get involved in politics
- Civic infrastructure that builds trust
- Democratic ballast

The destruction of this architecture, which impeded social mobility, signifies the concealed constitutional fracture of contemporary America and the shredding of the social contract.

## II. Work as a part of democracy

Unions were not just places where people could negotiate; they were civic institutions that:

- Lowered the differences between classes
- Made political coalitions across classes
- Stabilized demand for goods and services
- Strengthened the legitimacy of democracy

They served as institutional buffers that lessened political and economic instability.

## III. The Structural Dismantling (1970 to Now)

It was not an accident that the Labor Republic was destroyed. It happened through a variety of coordinated systems:

1. Less power to negotiate with workers and the emphasis on focused returns on capital over labor

2. Deindustrialization

3. Erosion of the law and a de-emphasis on collective bargaining

4. Limited union organizing

This tearing down worsened inequality and destabilized the political phase space.

## IV. Inequality as a Weird Attractor

As labor power fell apart, the system fell into an oligarchic strange attractor that was marked by:

- Concentration of wealth
- Political capture
- Stagnation of wages
- Decrease in mobility

These factors are demonstrated in the graph below, which shows a steady decline in labor union membership to its current low of 9.9% in 2024.

## V. Political Discontent and Cognitive Deterioration

In the past, labor organizations turned economic participation into political identity. Their failure caused:

- Civic alienation
- Narrative fragmentation
- Vulnerability to populism
- Eroding trust in institutions

Political identity divorced from tangible engagement leads to moral and cognitive disintegration.

## VI. Polarization as a Change in Phase

Economic dislocation preceded political polarization. As labor institutions disintegrated, societies traversed bifurcation thresholds:

- Below the threshold → pluralism
- Above threshold → tribal division

Polarization is not a cultural phenomenon; it is a structural one.

## VII. The Moral Ecology of Labor Collapse

Labor institutions used to promote dignity, reciprocity, and a sense of belonging. The breakdown of their systems led to:

- Moral fatigue
- Social distrust
- Diminishing civic duty
- Psychological instability

Democracy needs more than just rules; it needs moral ecology.

## XIII. Why Linear Reform Won't Work

Increasing the minimum wage by itself will not restore lost coordination structures. Institutional reconstruction is what is needed. That is achieved through market-sector bargaining, co-determination, mobile benefits, and rights to organize for everyone.

## IX. Conclusion: Rebuilding the Republic of Labor

The fall of the Labor Republic was the fall of democracy itself. Democracy is still structurally weak without restoring labor institutions. It is prone to instability, division, and the formation of authoritarian attractors. Economic justice is not a policy choice. It is the structure of democracy.

# The End of Democratic Capitalism and Financial Feudalism

## Abstract

After World War II, democratic capitalism rose to power. This system, though not perfect, sought to balance market dynamism and social stability, political accountability, and a certain level of fair prosperity. This essay contends that this model has been methodically dismantled and supplanted by a novel regime aptly characterized as "financial feudalism." This new order is not based on productive investment and broad-based wealth creation. Instead, it is based on two main and interconnected mechanisms: debt peonage and rent extraction. By turning public goods into private sources of income and making everyday life more about money, a powerful group of financial institutions, asset managers, and corporate monopolists has taken over the economy and the government. This has weakened the basic principles of democratic capitalism, such as the social contract, the power of property to spread, and responsive government. This essay will outline the historical shift, identify the fundamental mechanisms of this new feudalism, evaluate its socio-political ramifications, and conclude by exploring emerging forms of resistance.

## 1. Introduction: From the Promise of Democracy to Neo-Servitude

Democratic capitalism, as envisioned in the mid-20th century, was predicated on an implicit class compromise. Capital got a stable place to put money and make money, while workers got higher wages, social safety nets (the welfare state), and the political power to change economic outcomes through collective bargaining and elections. The system was based on growth, higher productivity, and a fair distribution of those gains that would keep people able to buy things and keep the peace. Property ownership, especially owning a home, became more accessible and was seen as a key part of a society where everyone has a stake.

Stagflation, the end of the Bretton Woods system, and a squeeze on capital profits began in the 1970s, which led to the model's crisis. The neoliberal revolution, led by people like Thatcher and Reagan and supported by the Chicago School of Thought, was the most important answer. The pillars of deregulation, privatization, tax cuts for capital and high earners, breaking up unions, and globalization were all sold as a return to "free market" principles. Neoliberalism did not inaugurate a new epoch of competitive entrepreneurship; instead, it enabled the financialization of the economy, characterized by the growing size, influence, and profitability of the financial sector relative to the productive (non-financial) economy.

A new political-economic structure has formed as a result of this change. It is similar to feudalism, not in its literal medieval forms, but in its core logic: a system in which a powerful elite takes tribute from a dependent population, not by directly owning people (chattel slavery) or land (classic feudalism), but by controlling important resources and by widespread debt. The "lord" is the modern financial conglomerate; the "vassals" are private equity-backed businesses; and the "serfs" are families that have mortgages, student loans, and credit card debt. The manor is the portfolio of securitized assets, and the rent comes from every part of life.

## 2. The Ways That Financial Feudalism Works

### 2.1 Debt Peonage: The Sealing Off of Opportunities

Historically, debt peonage is a system in which workers are tied to their employers or landlords by debt that never goes away. In its modern form, it means putting households under contractual obligations that control their choices, silent dissent, and shift income upward.

The Student Loan Complex: College used to be a public good that helped people move up in the world, but now it's all about money. States are cutting funding to colleges and universities, which means students have to pay for things themselves. They have to borrow money from the federal government, which means the debt is impossible to get rid of in bankruptcy. More than 45 million Americans owe more than $1.7 trillion, which makes it harder for them to buy a home, start a family, or save for retirement. Debt is like collateral for human capital, in which you pledge your future earnings to the financial system.

The Housing Trap: The 2008 crisis showed how deeply housing financialization runs. While homeownership was encouraged, the financial sector benefited the most through mortgage-backed securities and derivatives. After the crisis, big private equity firms like Blackstone became major landlords by turning foreclosed homes into rental properties. For many people, the dream of owning a home turned into the reality of living in one forever, paying rent to faceless institutional landlords who make the most money by raising rents and charging fees.

Medical and Consumer Debt: Medical emergencies are one of the main reasons people go bankrupt in the US. A healthcare system that makes money and a payment system that is based on money make it impossible for sick people to pay their bills. At the same time, stagnant wages have been made worse by easy-to-get, high-interest credit card debt, which has kept people buying things while putting families in debt. This debt has two main functions in the system: 1) Disciplining: People who owe money are less likely to go on strike, switch jobs, or take political risks. They become workers and customers who do what they're told. 2) Extraction: Interest payments are a huge, ongoing transfer of money from the bottom 90% to the top 10%, especially the financial elite.

## 2.2 Rent Extraction: The New Enclosures

In classical economics, rent is the money you make from owning or controlling a scarce asset, not from doing something useful. Financial feudalism is the best example of a rentier economy.

Intellectual Property and Monopoly Power: Tech and pharmaceutical companies don't just compete; they use patents, copyrights, and network effects to build monopolistic barriers. This lets them charge consumers and businesses that work with them higher-than-normal rents and licensing fees. The end result is huge profits without any real social benefit in terms of innovation or output.

Financial Engineering and Shareholder Primacy: The idea that companies should maximize shareholder value, which activist hedge funds and stock-based executive pay enforce, makes companies more likely to buy back their own stock and pay dividends than to invest in research and development, raise wages, or improve their capital. This is a way for current shareholders to get money from the company's future productive capacity.

Privatization of Public Goods: The neoliberal agenda has systematically turned state functions into profit centers, from schools and prisons to water systems and infrastructure. Private equity firms are experts at buying these kinds of assets, putting them in debt, cutting costs for services and workers, and charging fees. The public pays twice: first as taxpayers who built the asset, and then as users who pay more and receive worse service.

The Asset Manager's Power: A few companies, like BlackRock, Vanguard, and State Street, now own the most shares in many of the world's largest companies through their index funds. This "managerial capitalism" concentrates unprecedented economic power in one place. They don't "own" the economy in the strictest sense, but they do control the flow of capital and the rules that govern the productive base. They charge fees and shape how businesses act to get rent-seeking models.

## 3. The Decline of Capitalism in a Democratic Society

Debt peonage and rent extraction together attack the three main parts of democratic capitalism.

1.  The end of the social contract: The deal made after the war, which promised social security in exchange for social peace, is no longer valid. Wages are no longer tied to productivity growth, and the welfare state is now means-tested and often run by private contractors (for example, Medicaid Managed Care). Risk has been transferred from collective institutions (the state, the corporation) to the individual, who is anticipated to navigate healthcare, education, and retirement through the perilous waters of financialized markets. Being a citizen is increasingly dependent on your credit score.

2.  The End of Dispersive Property: James Madison thought that having property spread out among many people would protect them from tyranny. Financial feudalism reunites property across all its forms, including physical (land, housing), intellectual (IP), and financial (securities). The outcome is not a republic of stakeholders but an oligarchy of rentiers. For young people and people who don't have much money, debt is their main form of "property," which is a bad thing.

3.  State Capture and the Crisis of Democracy: The neoliberal state has not diminished; it has been reconfigured. Through monetary policy (quantitative easing that raises asset prices), fiscal policy (tax cuts on capital gains and corporate profits), regulatory policy (deregulation of finance and strengthening of IP law), and legal frameworks (bankruptcy law favoring creditors), it actively builds and protects the structure of financial feudalism. Campaign finance, lobbying, and the revolving door between Wall Street and Washington ensure that the state is a "committee for managing the common affairs of the whole bourgeoisie," now a financialized one. This capture makes formal democracy useless because elections rarely change the basic way the economy works. This leads to political alienation and the rise of populist movements opposed to the system, and often reactionary.

## 4. Examples of Feudal Logic

The Private Equity Playbook: The leveraged buyout is a classic move in the feudal system. A company like Apollo or KKR buys another company with a lot of debt (which is recorded on the target's balance sheet), strips value out of it by cutting fees, selling assets, and laying off workers, and then sells it or takes it public. The company is often weaker, more indebted, and has pension funds in poor shape. The people who work there and the people who live there are the serfs on this stolen estate.

The Gig Economy: Services like Uber and DoorDash are the worst examples of rent extraction and instability. They say they are just "marketplaces," so they don't have to take on any employer responsibilities. They take a cut (a commission) from each deal, while the workers pay for everything (the vehicle, maintenance, health insurance) and take all the risks. Algorithmic management is like a digital boss who makes sure everyone follows the rules without being held accountable.

## 5. Resistance and Paths Forward

The first step to challenging the system is to figure out what it is. Resistance can show up in many ways:

Policy Changes: Proposals for debt jubilees (forgiving student loans), a movement to get rid of modern debtors' prisons, public banking, antitrust action to break up monopolies, a complete rewrite of intellectual property law, and wealth taxes are all meant to break down the systems that take money from people.

Reclaiming the Commons: Movements for housing justice (tenant unions, community land trusts), Medicare for All (de-financializing healthcare), and free public college seek to de-commodify essential goods and re-establish them as public rights.

Worker Power: The revival of labor organizing, especially in the service and tech sectors, and new tactics like sectoral bargaining, directly challenge the power of rentier capital where value is made.

Theoretical Framing: Calling the system "financial feudalism" is itself an act of resistance that breaks the dominant story of "markets" and "efficiency" to show power, hierarchy, and exploitation.

## 6. Conclusion

The time of democratic capitalism, which had its own problems and left some groups out, has ended, and a more stable and hierarchical order has taken its place. Financial feudalism, which is based on debt peonage and rent extraction, is a step back in social and economic progress. It doesn't promise creative destruction; instead, it promises destructive creation, which means making financial tools and legal systems that destroy stable jobs, fair communities, and democratic accountability. The outcome is an economy of tribute, a politics of capture, and a society of insecurity. To change this path, we need more than just technical fixes. We need to reaffirm the people's right to control finance, put the public good ahead of private profit, and believe again that the economy should work for people, not the other way around. The challenge lies in ascertaining whether the 21st century will usher in a new feudal era or establish the groundwork for a truly democratic and post-capitalist future.

# Civilizational Risk in the Age of Nonlinear Geopolitical Power

## Abstract

The old way of looking at geopolitics, based on straight-line projections of state power, military strength (including nuclear weapons), GDP, and population, is becoming less useful. We are now living in an age of nonlinear geopolitical power, where threats and influence arise not from steady, predictable changes but from complex interactions, feedback loops, and sudden phase transitions within a tightly linked global system. This essay argues that this nonlinearity is the main cause of unprecedented risks to civilization and systemic threats to the basic pillars of human security, prosperity, and governance worldwide. We will look at the intersection of technological acceleration, ecological breakdown, and a broken global order through the lens of complexity science. We will look at how nonlinear dynamics cause cascading failures, make prediction impossible, and increase the likelihood of low-probability, high-impact events. The conclusion will evaluate the significant challenges this presents for global governance and investigate possible avenues for fostering resilience in an inherently unstable world.

## 1. The End of Linear Geopolitics: An Introduction

For hundreds of years, it seemed like there was a clear, almost Newtonian logic to the rise and fall of great powers. Empires grew until they got too big and fell apart. Industrial capacity always turned into military strength, and diplomatic alliances kept the balance of power stable. This was the world of linear geopolitics, which held that inputs (such as resources, treaties, and new ideas) would always yield outputs that were proportional and predictable. Even though the Cold War was terrifying, it was based on a straightforward, two-sided idea of mutually assured destruction and spheres of influence.

This paradigm has been broken by the 21st century. Power is no longer just adding or taking away; it is also nonlinear and multiplicative. A social media algorithm can change the outcome of an election. A pandemic that starts in one city can bring the world economy to a halt. A cyberattack on a small logistics company can stop supply chains. A drought in one area, made worse by climate feedbacks, can cause people to move and fight thousands of miles away. These things aren't strange; they're the natural results of a hyper-connected system that changes technology at an exponential rate and weakens institutions that help people communicate. This essay argues that these forces working together create systemic civilizational risks, threats that spread across many areas (ecological, technological, economic, political), making it impossible for nation-states and international organizations to respond, which puts the future of complex global civilization at risk.

## 2. The Architecture of Nonlinearity: What Causes Systemic Risk

Three interdependent factors that speed up cause nonlinearity in geopolitics.

### 2.1. Speeding up technology and hyper-connection

The digital revolution has made it possible for information and money to flow around the world almost instantly. This network is a great place for nonlinear effects to happen.

Feedback loops and viral cascades: Information (or false information) spreads not in a straight line but in a viral way, with algorithms optimizing for engagement that often leads to anger and conspiracy. A made-up story can cause social unrest, market panic, or diplomatic crises in just a few hours, even as it gets around traditional gatekeepers and fact-checking organizations. The 2021 U.S. The Capitol riot and the effects of COVID-19 misinformation around the world are two clear examples.

Cyber-Physical Convergence: Critical infrastructure, like power grids, financial networks, and water systems, is now deeply embedded in digital control systems that are easy to hack. A successful cyberattack can cause physical damage and social disruption on a scale far exceeding the resources the attacker used, a classic example of a nonlinear outcome. The NotPetya attack in 2017, which started in Ukraine, caused more than $10 billion in damage around the world by shutting down multinational companies.

The AI Sovereignty Race: Advanced AI and autonomous systems could shift the balance of power. It doesn't grow in a straight line; instead, it goes back and forth and may even stop. The first country or group to develop artificial general intelligence (AGI) could cause a sudden and permanent shift in strategic advantage, upsetting the nuclear balance and creating new types of catastrophic risk, from algorithmic warfare to the loss of control over people.

### 2.2. Breakdowns in ecology and crossing of boundaries

The Earth system has complicated feedback loops that take a long time to work. Human industrial activity is pushing these loops past their tipping points.

Climate Tipping Cascades: When Arctic permafrost melts, it releases methane, which accelerates warming. This makes wildfires burn hotter, which releases more carbon. If the West Antarctic ice sheet breaks up, the sea level could rise by meters, but not in a smooth, linear way; instead, it could happen in sudden jumps. These are nonlinear biophysical shocks that directly affect politics, including wars over resources, climate apartheid, and the flooding of sovereign territory.

Resource Nexus Conflicts: Stress on one resource, such as water, affects other resources, such as food and energy. A drought in a breadbasket region reduces hydropower and agricultural output, driving up food prices. This leads to political instability and migration, which puts more strain on resources in the areas that receive them. This nexus effect makes conflict multipliers that can't be modeled with linear tools.

## 2.3. The breaking up of the Liberal International Order

The rules, institutions, and norms that were in place after 1945 created a (flawed) framework for stability. It loses its buffers and amplifiers when it wears down.

The Shift from Multilateralism to Transactional Chaos: The decline of U.S. hegemony and the rise of revisionist powers (China, Russia, UAE) and assertive middle powers occur not within a stable rulebook, but in a world where norms are constantly challenged. This makes the world multipolar, not polar, meaning that no single power can keep the peace, but many can break it. As trust and communication break down, alliances become less stable, and small problems can escalate into bigger ones, as in the South China Sea or Ukraine.

The Domestic-International Feedback Loop: In major democracies like the US and EU, polarization at home makes it hard to make long-term foreign policy decisions. This internal instability is sent out into the world through unpredictable choices, which in turn create instability worldwide, making the situation at home even more dangerous and divided—a vicious, nonlinear cycle.

## 3. Emerging Civilizational Risks: Cascades and Synergies

The real danger comes not from these drivers working alone, but from how they work together to make risk cascades that cross domains. Some examples are:

### 3.1. The Pandemic Prototype: A Biological-Geopolitical Chain Reaction

COVID-19 was a classic nonlinear event. A spillover event (ecological domain) used global connectivity (technological domain) to spread worldwide. Countries closed their borders and restricted exports (geopolitical fragmentation), disrupting supply chains (economic domain). This economic shock worsened social inequalities, making people less trusting of institutions (socio-political domain) and harder for countries to work together to vaccinate people, allowing new variants to spread (back to biological). The pandemic wasn't just a health crisis; it was a full-scale test of the strength of global civilization. It showed that just-in-time economies are very weak, public trust is very fragile, and geopolitical instincts are always right.

### 3.2. The Climate-Conflict-Migration Connection

A lot of the time, predictions about climate migration use linear models (X degrees of warming equals Y migrants). Life is not linear. For example, in Syria, a long drought from 2007 to 2010, made worse by climate change, forced more than 1.5 million people from rural areas to cities. This worsened social tensions, leading to the 2011 uprising and the civil war that followed. The conflict caused a refugee crisis that made European politics less stable, helped populist movements grow, and pushed the EU to its political limits. A climate event made existing problems worse, which led to conflict, then to migration, and eventually to political shocks thousands of miles away. This was a chain reaction with no single cause or controller.

### 3.3. The Crisis of AI-Augmented Disinformation

Think about a future geopolitical crisis, like a naval incident in the Taiwan Strait. State actors could use AI-generated deepfakes (fake video and audio) to run hyper-personalized disinformation campaigns across many societies simultaneously. They could make up speeches by leaders telling people to get ready for war, show fake footage of horrible things happening, and make people less likely to believe any official story. This could lead leaders whose domestic support is manipulated in real time by algorithms to make decisions that worsen things on short notice, based on disputed facts. The cognitive side of war becomes so dirty that diplomacy is not based on reason, and de-escalation becomes impossible. This makes it much more likely that a catastrophic mistake will happen.

## 4. The Governance and Foresight Crisis

Nonlinear dynamics make our usual tools for governing and predicting not only useless, but also very dangerous.

The Failure of Linear Forecasting: Governments, intelligence agencies, and risk consultancies all depend on extrapolating trends. It is impossible to predict the details of nonlinear systems beyond short time frames. "Black swan" events are not unusual; they are just what the system does. We need to stop worrying about what might happen and instead focus on being strong and ready for a wide range of shocks.

The Sovereignty Gap: Risks to civilization cross national borders. No country, no matter how strong, can protect itself from cyber pandemics, climate change, or financial contagions. But nation-states remain the primary sources of political power and legitimacy. These are often paralyzed by short-term elections and competition that doesn't add up. International organizations like the UN were created for a linear world focused on states. They don't have the authority, resources, or flexibility to handle nonlinear, transboundary cascades.

The Wisdom-Deceleration Gap: Technology and risks are moving faster, but human biological evolution, institutional learning, and ethical frameworks are not. This widening gap makes sure that our responses are always reactive, slow, and often not big enough for the problem at hand.

## 5. A Plan for Nonlinear Resilience

To get through this age, we need to change the way we think and act, going from control to adaptation and from being alone to being layered resilient.

Adopting a Complexity Mindset: Policymakers need to learn about systems thinking, how things are connected, feedback loops, and the law of unintended consequences. Instead of static, threat-based assessments, we should use scenario planning and "red-teaming" for very bad, synergistic crises.

Investing in Decentralized Resilience: Important systems need to be modular and have backups. This means spreading out energy grids (with renewable microgrids), diversifying supply chains, ensuring everyone has enough food, and building strong public health infrastructure. The goal is to stop shocks from spreading and to keep the "domino effect" of failures from speeding up and worsening.

Building cognitive security: Societies need to protect themselves against information warfare by teaching people to use the media, supporting independent journalism, and creating technical and legal tools to identify and stop AI-generated misinformation. This is just as important to national security as missile defense.

Making Mini-Lateral and Functional Coalitions: While big global treaties may not be possible, groups of states, cities, businesses, and civil society that are willing to work together on specific issues can make progress. The Coalition for Epidemic Preparedness Innovations (CEPI) for pandemics and the Global Methane Pledge for climate are two examples. These networks are flexible and task-focused, so they can move quickly when needed.

Precautions in Technological Development: The race for AI, bioengineering, and other powerful technologies can't be based only on market or geopolitical factors. It necessitates global discussions regarding safety standards, ethics, and, when essential, constraints. The Biological Weapons Convention model, even though it isn't perfect, shows that we need to plan ahead for how to govern technologies that can be used for both good and bad.

## 6. Conclusion: Living on the Exponential Curve

We live in a time when the linear models of the past have stopped working, but new ways to run a complex planet have not yet been created. The era of nonlinear geopolitical power is not a fleeting disruption; it represents the new state of the Anthropocene. It creates systemic, synergistic, and growing risks to civilization. The main problem is no longer just competition among great powers. It's also dealing with the complicated system that those powers are part of, which they can destabilize but not control on their own. We can either go down the path of a neo-Malthusian world of rising shocks, failing systems, and fortress-mentality geopolitics, or we can work together to build adaptive capacity, shared resilience, and new ways to care for the planet. The second path requires humility in the face of complexity, a commitment to investing in the global commons, and the bravery to see security not as power over others, but as strength together in the face of shared, nonlinear threats. The future of our civilization depends on the path we take.

# An Economic History of the IMF and American Geopolitics: Financial Architecture, Power, and the Moral Ecology of Global Order

## Abstract

The International Monetary Fund (IMF) has been both a stabilizing financial institution and a tool of American power in world politics since its founding in 1944. The IMF was officially established to help stabilize the global financial system, make it easier to adjust the balance of payments, and prevent countries from devaluing their currencies to gain a competitive advantage. In practice, though, it has been a key part of a global governance system that combines finance, security, ideology, and institutional power. This essay reconstructs the IMF not as a neutral technocratic body, but as a complex adaptive system embedded within U.S. grand strategy, Cold War containment logic, neoliberal transformation, and post-financial-crisis monetary hegemony. Employing complexity economics, political economy, and moral ecology frameworks, the essay delineates how IMF conditionality reconfigured development trajectories, reinforced perpetuators of inequality, regulated labor systems, and institutionalized asymmetric sovereignty throughout the Global South. The Fund acts like a feedback loop, making markets more stable while making societies less stable, enforcing monetary orthodoxy while weakening democratic capacity. The IMF is one of the most important but least accountable institutions shaping the world order in the twenty-first century.

## I. Bretton Woods and the Structure of Monetary Hegemony

Bretton Woods was where the IMF was born. It wasn't just a bank; it was also a part of a larger American plan for world domination. Its official goals were to stabilize the currency, provide liquidity, and help with adjustments. However, its real goal was to prevent a return of economic nationalism, which had caused instability during the interwar period, and to build a rules-based order grounded in U.S. industrial, military, and monetary supremacy.

From the very beginning, the IMF's governance structure made this imbalance permanent. Voting shares were linked to financial contributions, which made U.S. dominance a permanent part of the system. The dollar's status as the world's reserve currency, along with its ability to be exchanged for gold, enabled U.S. deficits to serve as global liquidity. This is often called "exorbitant privilege," but it is better understood as a monetary empire.

The IMF acted as a monetary stabilizer within a system of political and military containment by linking currency discipline to American security structures such as NATO, the Marshall Plan, and later development banks. The monetary order became inextricably linked to the geopolitical order.

## II. Discipline in Development and Containment during the Cold War

During the Cold War, the IMF's loans were closely linked to the idea of containing ideologies. Financial stabilization programs often fit well with U.S. strategic goals, such as stopping socialist or nationalist economic models from taking hold in Africa, Asia, and Latin America.

Adjustment lending was not a neutral form of help. It enforced fiscal austerity, currency devaluation, and capital liberalization—policies that fundamentally shifted economies from domestic industrialization to export dependency. In terms of complexity, IMF conditionality changed the way national economies worked, forcing countries into low-wage, low-sovereignty equilibrium basins. Instead of speeding up development, these programs often set up traps that people couldn't escape from:

- The currency devaluation made imports more expensive.

- Pay cuts hurt workers' power.

- The shrinking of the public sector weakened institutions' ability to do their jobs.

- Dependence on exports made economies vulnerable to commodity price cycles.

This caused institutional hysteresis: once economies fell into IMF-designed adjustment attractors, it became harder to get out.

## III. The Neoliberal Shift and the Globalization Shock

The IMF changed from a lender of last resort to an enforcer of neoliberal globalization in the 1980s. After the Volcker Shock and the Latin American debt crisis, the Fund made structural adjustment a permanent policy.

Privatization, deregulation, and trade liberalization were presented as reforms to improve efficiency, but they actually transferred sovereignty from domestic democratic institutions to transnational capital networks.

In moral ecology terms, this time period saw a change in what was considered normal: markets became sacred, and societies became flexible variables.

People thought that public health systems, education, food subsidies, and labor protections were wasteful instead of important parts of civilization. What happened was not convergence but divergence: inequality grew, the state's legitimacy weakened, and democracy became even more fragile.

## IV. Financialization, Capital Volatility, and the Asian Crisis

The 1997 Asian Financial Crisis showed that the IMF's structure favors financial capital over social stability. The IMF's demand for higher interest rates and lower government spending worsened recessions, led to business bankruptcies, and wiped out middle-class wealth.

Complexity models show that IMF actions made the system more unstable by increasing its connectivity and reducing its ability to dampen changes. The IMF made things worse instead of better by amplifying positive feedback.

This crisis changed the balance of power in the world forever:

- Asian economies built up huge foreign reserves to protect themselves,

- The world's insurance assets were converted into U.S. Treasury debt.

- Global imbalances have gotten worse.

The IMF inadvertently contributed to the creation of the financialized world order it currently endeavors to stabilize.

## V. The Crisis of 2008 and the Era of Monetary Empire

The IMF's role changed a little after 2008. It kept enforcing austerity in the Global South, especially in Greece, but it also became an institutional partner in global liquidity management with the Federal Reserve.

The IMF entered a new phase here:

The Age of Monetary Empire, when stabilizing meant keeping asset markets stable instead of societies. Quantitative easing boosted asset values worldwide, while IMF adjustment programs kept wages and public spending low. This created a gap between asset holders and workers worldwide. As a result, the IMF became a tool for global class stratification, keeping capital stable while undermining democratic legitimacy.

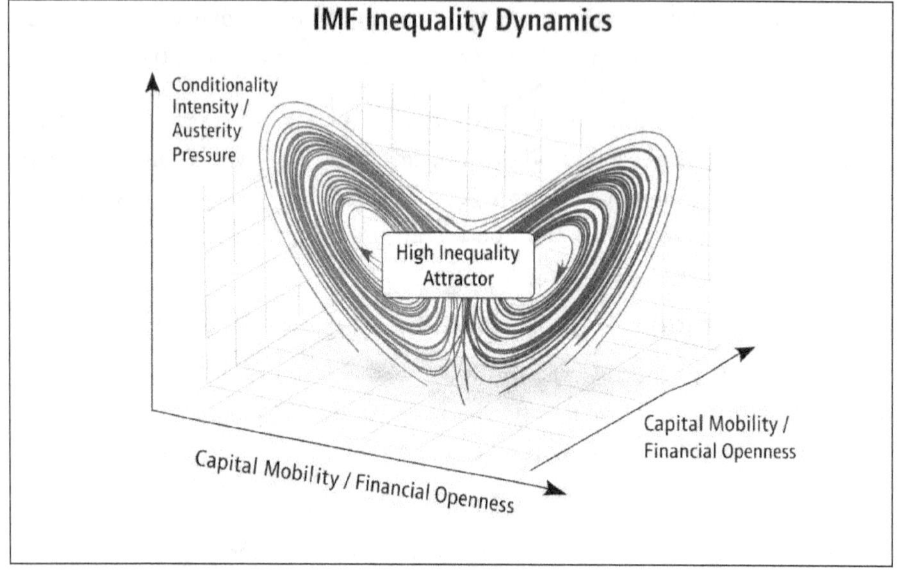


The above is a conceptual model of how IMF inequality changes over time, with the axes shown as:

- X: Financial Openness / Capital Mobility
- Y: Intensity of Conditionality / Pressure for Austerity
- Z: Capital Mobility / Financial Openness

This captures the idea of a system that moves randomly but usually stays in a high-inequality attractor basin, where "macro" variables stabilize while the system passes through socially destabilizing states.

## VI. Moral Ecology: The IMF as a Filter for Civilizations

The IMF acts as a civilizational selection mechanism in moral and ecological terms. It rewards institutional structures that allow the greatest capital mobility, enforce discipline among workers, and prevent political experimentation, while punishing social democratic or developmental alternatives.

This is a kind of institutional Darwinism:

- Systems that protect labor, public goods, and sovereignty are not chosen; they are imposed.

- Systems that prioritize capital extractability are favored.

The outcome is a global economy progressively disconnected from social prosperity.

## VII. Conclusion: IMF as a Complexity Attractor of Inequality

The IMF is more than just a lender. It is a global systems architect that shapes the paths of development, the legitimacy of politics, labor relations, and moral norms. Its interventions act as attractor-shaping forces that systematically push the world economy toward inequality, instability, and political disintegration. The institution was established to avert systemic collapse; however, it now functions as a stabilizer within a system that inherently generates collapse.

The IMF's main paradox is that it has become one of the most powerful yet least accountable architects of the twenty-first-century geopolitical order.

# The Geopolitics of Inequality: How Internal Extraction Creates External Instability and the Dismantling of the Cooperative World Order

## Abstract

Geopolitical instability is typically ascribed to ideological conflict, territorial contention, or competition among major powers. This essay posits a profound structural thesis: escalating internal inequality serves as a principal destabilizer of international order. This paper draws on complexity economics, systems theory, and moral-ecological analysis to illustrate how domestic extraction regimes undermine productive capacity, fragment civic legitimacy, degrade institutional competence, and transform foreign policy into a compensatory mechanism for domestic instability rather than a collaborative global strategy. As inequality grows, governments become more reactive, populist, militarized, and financially coercive. This makes alliances less reliable, increases conflicts over sanctions, and speeds up the process of multipolar fragmentation. Inequality is not only an ethical failure; it is also a systemic cause of geopolitical chaos.

## I. Introduction: Inequality as a Geopolitical Factor

Geopolitics sees inequality as a problem within a society and international conflict as a fight for power between countries. This analytical distinction is no longer valid. Modern states are nonlinear systems, and their internal economic structures determine how well they work strategically with other states. When inequality gradients become steeper, political coordination breaks down, public trust in institutions falls, and institutions lose their ability to make decisions. Foreign policy becomes unpredictable, reactive, and more forceful. So, inequality is a geopolitical variable. It affects the reliability of alliances, the consistency of strategies, the credibility of diplomacy, and the conduct of war and peace. As inequality grows around the world in both core and peripheral economies, the world system itself becomes chaotic, with rising sanctions, unstable alliances, trade fragmentation, and militarized signaling.

## II. Extraction Regimes and Institutional Erosion

Inequality is not just about income; it also shows how resources are taken out. When economic systems value rent capture more than productive investment, states' institutional competence slowly fades over time. The ability to pay taxes declines, public infrastructure falls apart, and bureaucratic professionalism deteriorates. Strategic institutions become politically captured and less able to plan for decades. This hollowing has a subtle but important effect on geopolitics: the state can no longer make sense of its grand strategy. Foreign policy becomes episodic, reactive, and symbolically performative rather than coordinated in a structural way.

## III. The Gradient of Inequality and the Reliability of Alliances

Alliances rely not only on formal treaties but also on enduring domestic legitimacy. States with high inequality have greater political instability, more populist turnover, and more rapid ideological change. This instability renders treaty obligations unreliable and weakens collective security agreements. Allies respond by hedging, diversifying their security partnerships, and reducing their strategic dependence. So, inequality quietly breaks up alliance networks long before open conflict breaks out.

## IV. Militarization to make up for bad government

As the legitimacy of governments at home declines, they increasingly depend on militarized foreign policy to create unity. External threats replace internal social contracts. Military posturing becomes a way to stabilize the story rather than a real way to protect yourself. This militarization leads to arms races, regional instability, and diplomacy likely to trigger crises.

## V. Financialization, Sanctions, and Monetary Coercion

In financialized economies, financial coercion is becoming more common than diplomatic negotiation. Governments start using sanctions, asset freezes, and monetary exclusion as normal ways to run things. These systems create nonlinear feedback loops that destabilize currency markets, disrupt payment systems, and erode people's trust in the global financial system. Sanctions wars show not strength, but weakness in the system.

## VI. Polarization as Strategic Disturbance

Increasing inequality worsens political polarization, making it harder to make good decisions. Instead of being based on facts, foreign policy becomes based on stories. Strategic consistency disintegrates as policy fluctuates between administrations and factions. This noise makes long-term alliances less stable and undermines deterrence.

## VII. Multipolar Bifurcation and Global Fragmentation

As inequality grows in core economies, the global system is increasingly at risk of splitting in two. Multipolar fragmentation replaces cooperative multilateralism. Trade blocs are becoming more rigid, technological standards are becoming less similar, and sanctions are replacing negotiations. The world order changes from a stable state of cooperation to a chaotic phase space.

## VIII. The Collapse of Global Trust and Moral Ecology

For geopolitical cooperation to work, there must be a moral ecology, which includes trust, reciprocity, ethical behavior, and the belief that actions are right. Inequality undermines these conditions both domestically and internationally. When trust breaks down, it becomes impossible to coordinate on a global scale.

## IX. Examples of Case Patterns

In advanced and developing economies, increasing inequality is associated with:

- Exiting treaties
- Trade disputes
- Militarization
- Erosion and realignment of alliances
- Escalation of sanctions

These are not individual political decisions; they are systemic results. All this maneuvering creates negative externalities and lessens the efficiency of geopolitical interactions.

## X. Why linear reform can't bring back stability

Trade agreements and military deterrence cannot fix geopolitical instability caused by inequality. Structural domestic rebalancing is needed, which means coordinating wages, investing in public goods, and rebuilding labor institutions.

## XI. Conclusion: The New Geopolitical Situation Creates Constant Instability

There is now a permanent state of geopolitical instability worldwide. Inequality gradients make every disturbance worse, making it harder to keep things stable by balancing power alone. Inequality is no longer just unfair; it is also dangerous for world politics. Internal extraction weakens alliances, undermines institutions, and fractures the world order. The future of world peace now rests on the structure of domestic economies.

# The Multipolar Bifurcation: Phase Transitions in World Order

## *Nonlinear Power, Chaotic Realignment, and the End of Stable Hegemony*

## Abstract

World order is no longer governed by linear balance-of-power dynamics. The post-Cold War unipolar regime has entered a nonlinear transition characterized by feedback loops, threshold effects, and cascading instability. This essay models the international system as a complex adaptive system undergoing bifurcation, where small perturbations now generate disproportionate structural realignments. Drawing on complexity economics, nonlinear dynamics, and moral-ecological analysis, it demonstrates that the global order has crossed critical thresholds driven by inequality gradients, technological acceleration, and financialized coercion. The result is the emergence of a multipolar chaotic regime defined by alliance volatility, sanctions warfare, arms races, and geopolitical fragmentation. The paper argues that modern geopolitics now operates inside a bifurcation corridor in which stable equilibrium is structurally unattainable without systemic reconstruction of global institutions and domestic political economies.

## I. Introduction: The End of Linear Geopolitics

For most of modern history, geopolitical theory assumed that international order evolved through proportional causality: incremental changes in power produced incremental changes in stability. The Cold War's bipolar order and the post-1991 unipolar moment reinforced this belief. However, contemporary geopolitics increasingly violates these assumptions. Small diplomatic incidents, localized military engagements, and financial sanctions now produce disproportionate cascading effects across trade, currency markets, energy systems, and alliance networks.

This behavior reflects nonlinear dynamics. The international system has entered a regime of political turbulence governed by feedback amplification, sensitivity to initial conditions, and phase transitions. The global order is undergoing a bifurcation.

## II. World Order as a Complex Adaptive System

The international system functions as a complex adaptive system composed of interacting state and non-state actors, financial networks, technological platforms, and security alliances. Its dynamics are governed not only by power balances but by recursive feedback loops linking:

- Domestic political legitimacy
- Financial interdependence
- Narrative control
- Military signaling
- Technological infrastructure

These couplings give rise to nonlinear responses to perturbations. The system no longer relaxes smoothly toward equilibrium; it oscillates among unstable attractors.

## III. Bifurcation Theory and Geopolitical Phase Space

In nonlinear systems, bifurcation occurs when a control parameter crosses a critical threshold, causing a qualitative change in system behavior. The global system's control parameters include:

- Inequality gradients
- Financial leverage concentration
- Technological asymmetry
- Energy transition pressures
- Institutional legitimacy decay

These variables now push the system past its critical thresholds.

## IV. Drivers of the Multipolar Bifurcation

Several factors drive multipolar bifurcation. Some of the more important are:

- Financialization and Monetary Weaponization
- Technological Platform Sovereignty
- Energy Transition, Rare Earth Mineral Supply, and Resource Cartography
- Institutional Legitimacy Collapse
- Inequality and Domestic Volatility

These interact to destabilize unipolar coherence.

## V. Alliance Volatility and Strange Attractors

Multipolar realignment exhibits strange-attractor behavior: alliances fluctuate chaotically but gravitate toward fragmentation, militarization, and bloc consolidation. Sanctions now produce feedback loops that fragment global payment networks, destabilize currencies, and accelerate de-dollarization, amplifying instability rather than restoring order. Localized conflicts can now trigger global supply-chain shocks, arms races, and reconfigurations of alliances, all hallmarks of nonlinear cascade dynamics.

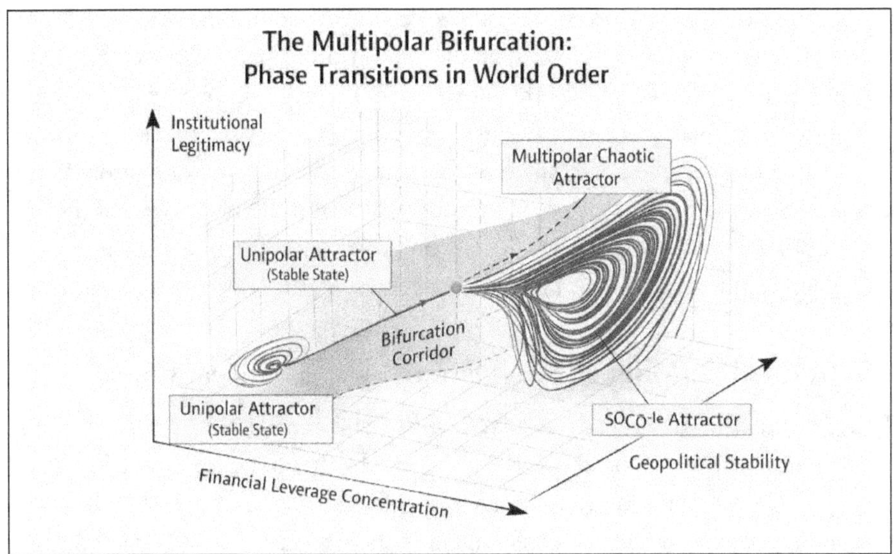


## VI. Moral Ecology of World Order

Global stability depends on trust, reciprocity, and legitimacy. Moral-ecological collapse amplifies chaos. The system now operates permanently near bifurcation thresholds. Stable hegemony is structurally unattainable. Only global institutional reconstruction can restore damping mechanisms.

# BRICS and the End of Dollar Hegemony

## Abstract

This essay examines the emergence of the BRICS bloc (Brazil, Russia, India, China, South Africa—and now an expanding coalition) as a structural challenger to U.S. dollar monetary hegemony. Rather than interpreting de-dollarization as a mere geopolitical maneuver, this analysis frames it as an emergent complexity phenomenon: a phase transition driven by nonlinear feedback loops between sanctions, payment architecture, commodity pricing, sovereign debt structures, and global liquidity fragility. Drawing from complexity economics, evolutionary game theory, and political economy, the paper argues that dollar dominance has entered a late-stage metastability regime—still operational, but increasingly vulnerable to network-cascade disruption. BRICS does not merely seek monetary multipolarity; it is catalyzing a systemic regime shift in global monetary architecture.

## I. Introduction: Monetary Hegemony as a Complex System

The U.S. dollar is not merely a currency; it is the central clearing medium of the modern world-system. Since Bretton Woods, the dollar has served as a reserve asset, settlement instrument, energy-pricing unit, sovereign-debt anchor, and geopolitical enforcement mechanism. Its hegemony emerged not from fiat decree but from positive network externalities, self-reinforcing feedback loops that made exit costly and participation compulsory.

Yet complex adaptive systems are subject to regime shifts when internal stresses exceed adaptive capacity. BRICS represents a coordinated structural response to dollar-centric fragility, accelerating nonlinear bifurcations in trade settlement, reserve composition, payment rails, and geopolitical alliances. The de-dollarization process is not a revolt. It is a phase transition.

## II. The Dollar System as an Extractive Network

Dollar hegemony imposes asymmetric costs:

- Developing nations must accumulate dollar reserves
- Trade deficits are financed through dollar debt
- Capital flows are vulnerable to Federal Reserve policy
- Sanctions weaponize SWIFT and correspondent banking
- Commodity markets require dollar liquidity

This creates what complexity economics describes as an extractive attractor basin—once nations enter the dollar-debt–trade–reserve loop, exit becomes structurally difficult. This attractor has now become unstable.

## III. Sanctions as a Systemic Shock Amplifier

The weaponization of dollar rails following the Ukraine conflict triggered the largest structural monetary shock since 1971. Russia's central bank reserves were frozen. SWIFT access was severed. Energy trade was disrupted. From a systems perspective, this event converted a latent fragility into an explicit survival signal for non-Western states: monetary dependency now constitutes existential vulnerability.

This triggered a cascade of defensive adaptation:

- Bilateral currency settlement agreements
- Gold accumulation
- Non-SWIFT payment rails (CIPS, SPFS)
- BRICS reserve pooling
- Commodity-linked currency discussions

This is classical adaptive behavior in complex systems approaching bifurcation.

## IV. BRICS as a Parallel Monetary Architecture

BRICS is no longer a political forum; it is a financial operating system. A lack of trust in American geopolitical behavior, the potential for dollar manipulation, U.S. tariffs, and pure geographic proximity have been the driving forces behind BRICS efforts to de-dollarize. The following is the specific structure of an Asian monetary regime:

| Architecture Layer | Dollar System | BRICS Parallel |
|---|---|---|
| Settlement Rails | SWIFT | CIPS, SPFS |
| Reserve Assets | Treasuries | Gold, yuan |
| Development Lending | IMF/World Bank | NDB |
| Trade Pricing | Dollar | Local currency/commodity-linked |
| Liquidity Governance | Fed | Multipolar |

This is not a substitution. It is structural redundancy, an essential prerequisite for systemic exit.

## V. Game Theory of Monetary Exit

De-dollarization follows a coordination-game structure:

- Staying in dollars is individually rational until enough others leave.
- Once critical mass emerges, exit becomes dominant.

This creates a phase-shift tipping point. The BRICS bloc is approaching this threshold as sanctions, debt stress, and capital-flow volatility accelerate threshold dynamics.

## VI. Commodity Anchoring and the Energy Currency Loop

Energy pricing anchors monetary hegemony. The petrodollar is the keystone of dollar demand.

BRICS controls:

- Approximately 42% of the world's oil production

- Approximately 36% of natural gas production with immense reserves of rare earth refining

- 50% of grain exports

Commodity-backed settlement alternatives are no longer speculative; they are structurally feasible. This reintroduces real-asset anchoring into monetary regimes, disrupting fiat hierarchy.

## VII. Financial Fragility and U.S. Debt Feedback Loops

U.S. national debt now exceeds $39 trillion. Treasury issuance requires permanent foreign absorption, as foreign nations hold over 50% of the outstanding debt.

De-dollarization introduces a nonlinear feedback loop:

- Less foreign demand → higher yields
- Higher yields → fiscal stress
- Fiscal stress → monetary easing
- Monetary easing → higher inflation
- Higher inflation → debasement
- Debasement → accelerated de-dollarization

This is a self-reinforcing instability spiral.

## VIII. Multipolar Liquidity and the End of Monetary Unipolarity

BRICS is not replacing the dollar; it is fragmenting the monetary global order.

This produces:

- Multiple liquidity centers

- Reduced sanction effectiveness

- Commodity-linked settlement corridors

- Regionally autonomous payment ecosystems

This is the end of monetary unipolarity.

## IX. Moral Ecology: Monetary Order and Systemic Justice

Dollar hegemony exports volatility to the periphery while privatizing gains at the core. It is not neutral; it is extractive. Multipolar liquidity restores sovereign adaptive capacity, enabling nations to retain internal policy autonomy. This is a realignment of moral ecology, not merely geopolitical maneuvering.

## X. Conclusion: The Phase Transition Has Begun

The dollar will not collapse. It will lose centrality. Like all dominant complex systems, it is entering a late-stage metastability regime, operational but structurally fragile. BRICS does not overthrow the dollar. It is rendering it optional. And as we know from network economics, optionality is the beginning of the end.

# Chapter 9

# The Path to a Moral Ecology of Civilization

## I. The Path of the Question

This work has taken a conceptual route through economic, psychological, cultural, and political systems to show how societies either do well or break down. The inquiry has been guided by a foundational conviction: that human flourishing cannot be reduced to material production, market efficiency, or personal wealth gain, but instead emerges from the structural and ethical integrity of the systems in which human existence occurs. At the heart of the book is an empirical, intellectual, and moral inquiry: What does it signify for a society to thrive collectively rather than disintegrate?

We looked at the following to answer this question:

- The nonlinear economic dynamics that lead to the concentration of wealth and the increase in inequality;

- The game-theoretic frameworks of competition and cooperation that shape behavior and institutions.

- The psychological and cultural feedback loops that create group delusions, division, and moralization of identity.

- The aesthetic and symbolic frameworks societies use to comprehend disorder, importance, and possibility.

We have seen that prosperity is not only about having a lot of resources or using them well; it is also a dynamic equilibrium—a fragile balance on the edge of chaos—where innovation and stability work together rather than against each other. This last chapter ties everything together. It describes the Moral Ecology of Prosperity as a way to think about things and a moral obligation: a way to figure out how prosperity happens, how it goes away, and what it requires to stay.

## II. The Boundaries of the Linear Mind, Complexity, and Vulnerability

Modern societies are built on systems that are highly interrelated, heavily dependent on one another, and don't necessarily move in a straight line. In these kinds of systems:

- Changes that are little can have tremendous effects.

- Benefits build up unevenly.

- Linear extrapolation from historical trends does not consistently yield accurate forecasts.

Traditional economic theory viewed markets as self-correcting equilibrating systems, wherein deviations from pricing or allocation efficiency naturally resolved themselves. But as we've seen, real economies are more like weather systems than thermostats. They exhibit turbulence, new patterns, feedback loops, and phase variations. This recognition reframes inequality, perceiving it not as a result of market forces but as an inherent trait of complex competitive systems. Wealth increases because one benefit leads to another; network effects make power stronger; and capital increases not only in terms of money, but also in terms of social and political power. When concentration goes above specified levels, the system changes. It changes. Prosperity grows weak. Democracy gets weak. Working together costs money. It's hard to find trust. The game is built in a way that makes it hard for people to work together, not because they want to.

When the benefits of competition far outweigh those of cooperation, and when dominance becomes more advantageous than mutual restraint, trust erodes, institutions decline, and the foundation of shared meaning collapses. This isn't simply a guess. It is the way things have always been.

## III. The Ethical Implications of Disparity

Inequality is not merely a matter of money. It is an ethical sickness, a cultural force, and a political force. When inequality gets too high:

- People don't think of society as a joint endeavor anymore.

- The meritocratic explanation leads to systemic cynicism.

- The social compact goes from being based on conditions to being based on transactions, and finally to being useless.

- Democratic pluralism begins to transform into tribal identity politics rooted in competitiveness.

In this context, narratives of anger, grievance, superiority, or victimhood serve as organizing myths. They delineate the in-group and out-group, converting politics from a negotiation of interests into an existential battle for status and acknowledgment. The way people in society see things change as inequality grows:

- Success doesn't imply giving anymore; it means taking.

- People no longer admire wealth; instead, they dread, hate, or copy it.

The public sphere ceases to serve as a venue for collective meaning-making and transforms into a platform for individuals to display their identities. People feel like they don't exist, aren't heard, or aren't needed in a very unfair society. The social body disintegrates not because individuals are prone to conflict, but because they fail to acknowledge one another as constituents of a collective moral framework. And as the shared world disappears, the things that make democracy possible start to crumble, not the institutions that support it.

## IV. Democracy on the Edge of Chaos

Democracy is not stable just because of the law. Law needs people to believe in it. You need to trust someone to believe them. And trust needs to go both ways, both with things and with symbols. A society is not democratic only because it holds elections; it is democratic when:

- Even when they don't receive what they want, people want things to be fair.

- People regard opposition as a valid form of action, not as treason.

- People view the future as a shared entity rather than a zero-sum scenario.

These situations worsen when inequality disrupts reciprocity. Political polarization isn't just about people disagreeing; it's also about how people see themselves. Enemies are people who don't like each other. Criticism becomes an attack. Institutions turn into weapons. The system is approaching a critical, unstable point in complexity science.

At this point:

- A lot of volatility might result from small political shocks.

- When it comes to getting people to do anything, stories beat facts.

- Charisma beats expertise.

- Demagogues are not outliers; they are systematic results.

This book says that the US and many other countries are approaching this boundary condition. And the reason isn't cultural or political. It is systemic, structural, and economic. The end of shared wealth has made modern democracy less stable.

## V. The Individual at the Core of the System

The approach heavily depends on economics, complexity theory, and political systems; however, the book's most profound argument is philosophical. People are not just driven by their own interests. Our desires, identities, and goals are shaped by:

- Being part of something and getting credit for it,

- What it means and what it says,

- Purpose and respect.

Philosophers talk about this idea a lot, but it rarely makes its way into economic design. The prevailing economic paradigm posits that individuals predominantly react to incentives. But, as we have demonstrated, incentive systems affect not only conduct but also the situations in which identity and meaning are created. So: Systems that reward extraction will create extractive identities; Systems that reward working together will create cooperative identities. Systems that reward performance with certainty will make people less open to new ideas. Curiosity and empathy will lead to adaptive knowledge in systems that reward them.

Economics does not study resources. It examines the influence of systems on individuals and the reciprocal impact of individuals on systems, with significant emphasis on the "common good."

# VI. Moving Toward a Moral Ecology of Wealth

When we talk about a moral ecology, we mean three truths that are all linked: People's well-being is connected to their relationships; what affects one person always affects many. Systems affect how humans make moral decisions. Ethics isn't just a choice people make; it's also a product of the system. To be successful, you need balance. Too much stability can lead to stagnation, and too much turbulence can lead to collapse.

A moral ecology is a situation in which, instead of taking, economic systems encourage giving and taking. Cultural systems promote comprehension rather than hostility. Political systems keep different groups from being better than others. Instead of being sure, schools teach students to be interested. People think that meaning is something they share, not something they guard.

This is hardly a picture of a perfect world. It is a realistic description of what needs to happen for any complex society to last. Having money doesn't mean being rich. A civilization is prosperous when it can take care of itself.

# VII. The Work That Lies Ahead

A moral ecosystem of affluence does not change with just one policy, law, reform, or election. It's a revamp of the full system:

It needs:

- Knowing that inequity doesn't have to happen.

- Instead of selling public goods, they should be restored.

- Creating markets that benefit everyone, instead of just one person.

- Instead of taking away human dignity, use technology to strengthen it.

- Putting meaning, belonging, and purpose back at the heart of the economy.

This job isn't only technical. It must deal with morals, philosophy, culture, and psychology. And it all starts with how you think.

# VIII. Final Thoughts: You Decide What Happens Next

History does not control us. We create it, whether we know it or not, through the systems we choose to embrace or reject. Design, not fate, shapes the future. So, the question that remains, the one that finishes this book, is simple yet deep: What type of world do we want to make together? A world where there is no limit to competition? A world full of jealousy, status, and distrust? A world where just a few people can get rich? Or a world where everyone works together to protect the environment, and everyone has a purpose, respect, and moral duty? The solution is not clear. You need to decide as a group right now. The processes that make us who we are are continually evolving. The question is whether we will adapt to them or be killed by the things we don't want to understand. The future is still up in the air. The work is still possible. We still have the moment. It is both our duty and our birthright to promote the moral ecology of prosperity and human flourishing.

# References

## Chapter 1

### The Moral Ecology of Prosperity and Human Growth in Complexity Economics


Farmer, J. Doyle. *Making Sense of Chaos: A Better Economics for a Better World.* New Haven, CT: Yale University Press, 2024.


### The End of Competition and Market Concentration: How Complexity Economics and the Monopoly Can Charge More


Arthur, W. Brian. *Complexity Economics: A Different Way to Look at Economic Analysis.* Santa Fe, NM: Santa Fe Institute, 2013.

Khan, Lina M. "Amazon's Antitrust Paradox." *Yale Law Journal* 126, no. 3 (2017): 710-805.

Philippon, Thomas. *The Great Reversal: Why the US Gave Up on Free Markets.* Cambridge, MA: Harvard University Press, 2019.

Schumpeter, Joseph A. *Capitalism, Socialism, and Democracy.* New York: Harper & Brothers, 1942.

Stigler Center for the Study of the Economy and the State. *Digital Platforms and Concentration.* Chicago: Booth School of Business, University of Chicago, 2019.


### The Economics of Emergent Despair: How Systemic Dysfunction Leads to Group Psychological Collapse


Case, Anne, and Angus Deaton. *Deaths of Despair and the Future of Capitalism.* Princeton, NJ: Princeton University Press, 2020.

OECD. *Update on Income Inequality.* Paris: OECD Publishing, 2023.

Piketty, Thomas. *Capital in the Twenty-First Century*. Cambridge, MA: Harvard University Press, 2014.

Putnam, Robert D. *Bowling Alone: The Collapse and Revival of American Community*. New York: Simon & Schuster, 2000.

Stiglitz, Joseph E. *The Price of Inequality: How Today's Divided Society Endangers Our Future*. New York: W. W. Norton, 2012.

## The Strange Attractor of Inequality: Nonlinear Feedback Loops in Wealth Concentration

Arthur, W. Brian, and Benoit Mandelbrot. "Complexity and the Economy." *Science* 284, no. 5411 (1999): 107–09.

Mandelbrot, Benoit, and Richard L. Hudson. *The (Mis)Behavior of Markets: A Fractal View of Financial Turbulence*. New York: Basic Books, 2004.

Mazzucato, Mariana. *The Value of Everything: Making and Taking in the Global Economy*. New York: PublicAffairs, 2018.

Piketty, Thomas. *Capital in the Twenty-First Century*. Cambridge, MA: Harvard University Press, 2014.

Stiglitz, Joseph E. *The Price of Inequality: How Today's Divided Society Endangers Our Future*. New York: W. W. Norton, 2012.

## The Rise of Oligarchy in America: How Complex Adaptive Systems Ended Equal Opportunity

North, Douglass C., John Joseph Wallis, and Barry R. Weingast. *Violence and Social Orders: A Conceptual Framework for Interpreting Recorded Human History*. Cambridge: Cambridge University Press, 2009.

Ostrom, Elinor. *Governing the Commons: The Evolution of Institutions for Collective Action*. Cambridge: Cambridge University Press, 1990.

Piketty, Thomas. *Capital in the Twenty-First Century*. Cambridge, MA: Harvard University Press, 2014.

Robinson, James A., and Daron Acemoglu. *Why Nations Fail: The Origins of Power, Prosperity, and Poverty*. New York: Crown, 2012.

Stiglitz, Joseph E. *The Price of Inequality: How Today's Divided Society Endangers Our Future.* New York: W. W. Norton, 2012.

Turchin, Peter. *Ages of Discord: A Structural-Demographic Analysis of American History.* Chaplin, CT: Beresta Books, 2016.

Winters, Jeffrey A. *Oligarchy.* Cambridge: Cambridge University Press, 2011.

## The Emergence of Oligarchy as a Complex Adaptive System: Self-Organizing Inequality in American Society

Acemoglu, Daron, and James A. Robinson. *The Narrow Corridor: States, Societies, and the Fate of Liberty.* New York: Penguin Press, 2019.

Andrias, Kate. "The New Labor Law" *Yale Law Journal* 126, no. 1 (2016): 2–101.

Arthur, W. Brian, and Benoit Mandelbrot. "Complexity and the Economy." *Science* 284, no. 5411 (1999): 107–09.

Azar, José, Martin C. Schmalz, and Isabel Tecu. "Anticompetitive Effects of Common Ownership." *Journal of Finance* 73, no. 4 (2018): 1513–65.

Baker, Jonathan B. *The Antitrust Paradigm: Restoring a Competitive Economy.* Cambridge, MA: Harvard University Press, 2019.

Barabási, Albert-László, and Réka Albert. "Emergence of Scaling in Random Networks." *Science* 286, no. 5439 (1999): 509–12.

Bartels, Larry M. *Unequal Democracy: The Political Economy of the New Gilded Age.* Princeton, NJ: Princeton University Press, 2008.

Bénabou, Roland, and Jean Tirole. "Belief in a Just World and Redistributive Politics." *Quarterly Journal of Economics* 121, no. 2 (2006): 699–746.

Federal Trade Commission and U.S. Department of Justice. *Horizontal Merger Guidelines.* Washington, DC, 2010.

Gabaix, Xavier, and Augustin Landier. "Why Has CEO Pay Increased So Much?" *Quarterly Journal of Economics* 123, no. 1 (2008): 49–100.

Gilens, Martin, and Benjamin I. Page. "Testing Theories of American Politics: Elites, Interest Groups, and Average Citizens." *Perspectives on Politics* 12, no. 3 (2014): 564–81.

Gruber, Jonathan. *Public Finance and Public Policy*, 6th ed. New York: Worth Publishers, 2019.

Holland, John H. "Complex Adaptive Systems." *Daedalus* 121, no. 1 (1992): 17–30.

Mishel, Lawrence, and Jori Kandra. *CEO Pay Has Skyrocketed 1,209% since 1978*. Washington, DC: Economic Policy Institute, 2023.

OECD. *Corporate Tax Statistics*, 4th ed. Paris: OECD Publishing, 2022.

Ostrom, Elinor. *Governing the Commons: The Evolution of Institutions for Collective Action*. Cambridge: Cambridge University Press, 1990.

Piketty, Thomas. *Capital in the Twenty-First Century*. Cambridge, MA: Harvard University Press, 2014.

Pistor, Katharina. *The Code of Capital: How the Law Creates Wealth and Inequality*. Princeton, NJ: Princeton University Press, 2019.

Saez, Emmanuel, and Gabriel Zucman. *The Triumph of Injustice: How the Rich Dodge Taxes and How to Make Them Pay*. New York: W. W. Norton, 2019.

Schelling, Thomas C. "Dynamic Models of Segregation." *Journal of Mathematical Sociology* 1, no. 2 (1971): 143–86.

Simon, Herbert A. "The Architecture of Complexity." *Proceedings of the American Philosophical Society* 106, no. 6 (1962): 467–82.

Sornette, Didier. *Why Stock Markets Crash: Critical Events in Complex Financial Systems*. Princeton, NJ: Princeton University Press, 2003.

Wu, Tim. *The Curse of Bigness: Antitrust in the New Gilded Age*. New York: Columbia Global Reports, 2018.

## Strange Things That Happen in Economic Evolution: From Market Volatility to Institutional Collapse

Arthur, W. Brian. *The Economy and Complexity: Selected Works*. Oxford: Oxford University Press, 2015.

Kauffman, Stuart. *At Home in the Universe: The Search for the Laws of Self-Organization and Complexity*. New York: Oxford University Press, 1995.

Lorenz, Edward N. "Deterministic Nonperiodic Flow." *Journal of the Atmospheric Sciences* 20, no. 2 (1963): 130–41.

Schumpeter, Joseph A. *Capitalism, Socialism, and Democracy*. New York: Harper & Brothers, 1942.

Stengers, Isabelle, and Ilya Prigogine. *Order Out of Chaos: Man's New Dialogue with Nature*. New York: Bantam Books, 1984.

Strogatz, Steven H. *Nonlinear Dynamics and Chaos: With Applications to Physics, Biology, Chemistry, and Engineering*. Boulder, CO: Westview Press, 2014.

Taleb, Nassim Nicholas. *The Black Swan: The Impact of the Highly Improbable*. New York: Random House, 2007.

## Meta-Stable Democracies: Mapping the Chasm between Pluralism and Authoritarianism

Acemoglu, Daron, and James A. Robinson. *Why Nations Fail: The Origins of Power, Prosperity, and Poverty*. New York: Crown, 2012.

Levitsky, Steven, and Daniel Ziblatt. *How Democracies Die*. New York: Crown, 2018.

Müller, Jan-Werner. *What Is Populism?* Philadelphia: University of Pennsylvania Press, 2016.

Piketty, Thomas. *Capital in the Twenty-First Century*. Cambridge, MA: Harvard University Press, 2014.

Sunstein, Cass R. *#Republic: Divided Democracy in the Age of Social Media*. Princeton, NJ: Princeton University Press, 2017.

Tajfel, Henri, and John C. Turner. "An Integrative Theory of Intergroup Conflict." In *The Social Psychology of Intergroup Relations,* edited by William G. Austin and Stephen Worchel, 33–47. Monterey, CA: Brooks/Cole, 1979.

# Chapter 2

## Chaos Theory and the Dynamics of Democratic Instability: Political Polarization and Income Inequality

Farmer, J. Doyle. *Making Sense of Chaos: A Better Economics for a Better World,* New Haven, CT: Yale University Press, 2024.

Gleick, James. *Chaos: Making a New Science.* New York: Viking, 1987.

Lorenz, Edward N. "Deterministic Nonperiodic Flow." *Journal of the Atmospheric Sciences* 20, no. 2 (1963): 130–41.

Stengers, Isabelle, and Ilya Prigogine. *Order Out of Chaos: Man's New Dialogue with Nature.* New York: Bantam Books, 1984.

Strogatz, Steven H. *Nonlinear Dynamics and Chaos: With Applications to Physics, Biology, Chemistry, and Engineering.* Boulder, CO: Westview Press, 2014.

## A Chaos Theory Perspective on Monopolies, Market Concentration, and Income Inequality in American Society

Autor, David, David Dorn, Lawrence F. Katz, Christina Patterson, and John Van Reenen. "The Fall of the Labor Share and the Rise of Superstar Firms." *Quarterly Journal of Economics* 135, no. 2 (2020): 645–709.

Lynn, Barry C. *Cornered: The New Monopoly Capitalism and the Economics of Destruction.* Hoboken, NJ: Wiley, 2010.

Piketty, Thomas, Emmanuel Saez, and Gabriel Zucman. "Distributional National Accounts: Methods and Estimates for the United States." *Quarterly Journal of Economics* 133, no. 2 (2018): 553–609.

Stiglitz, Joseph E. *People, Power, and Profits: Progressive Capitalism for an Age of Discontent.* New York: W. W. Norton, 2019.

Tepper, Jonathan, and Denise Hearn. *The Myth of Capitalism: Monopolies and the Death of Competition.* Hoboken, NJ: Wiley, 2018.

## The Political Economy of Cognitive Capture

Bourdieu, Pierre. *Distinction: A Social Critique of the Judgment of Taste.* Cambridge, MA: Harvard University Press, 1984.

boyd, danah. "Social Media and the Transformation of Public Space." *Social Media + Society* 1, no. 2 (2015).

Gramsci, Antonio. *Selections from the Prison Notebooks.* Edited and translated by Quintin Hoare and Geoffrey Nowell Smith. New York: International Publishers, 1971.

Herman, Edward S., and Noam Chomsky. *Manufacturing Consent: The Political Economy of the Mass Media.* New York: Pantheon Books, 1988.

Kahneman, Daniel. *Thinking, Fast and Slow.* New York: Farrar, Straus and Giroux, 2011.

Piketty, Thomas. *Capital in the Twenty-First Century.* Cambridge, MA: Harvard University Press, 2014.

Zuboff, Shoshana. *The Age of Surveillance Capitalism: The Fight for a Human Future at the New Frontier of Power.* New York: PublicAffairs, 2019.

## Inequality as a Unique Attractor: A Chaos-Theoretic Framework for Wealth Concentration

Arthur, W. Brian. *The Economy and Complexity: Selected Works.* Oxford: Oxford University Press, 2015.

Gleick, James. *Chaos: Making a New Science.* New York: Viking, 1987.

Piketty, Thomas. *Capital in the Twenty-First Century.* Cambridge, MA: Harvard University Press, 2014.

## Self-Organized Criticality in Capitalist Economies

Arthur, W. Brian. *Complexity and the Economy.* New York: Oxford University Press, 2014.

Bak, Per. *How Nature Works: The Science of Self-Organized Criticality*. New York: Springer-Verlag, 1996.

Farmer, J. Doyne, and John Geanakoplos. "The Virtues and Vices of Equilibrium and the Future of Financial Economics." *Complexity* 14, no. 3 (2009): 11–38.

Haldane, Andrew G., and Robert M. May. "Systemic Risk in Banking Ecosystems." *Nature* 469 (2011): 351–55.

Mandelbrot, Benoit. *The (Mis)Behavior of Markets: A Fractal View of Risk, Ruin, and Reward*. New York: Basic Books, 2004.

Scheffer, Marten. *Critical Transitions in Nature and Society*. Princeton, NJ: Princeton University Press, 2009.

Stiglitz, Joseph E. *The Price of Inequality: How Today's Divided Society Endangers Our Future*. New York: W. W. Norton & Company, 2012.

Taleb, Nassim Nicholas. *Antifragile: Things That Gain from Disorder*. New York: Random House, 2012.

## Political Polarization as a Chaotic Divergence in Democratic Systems

Achen, Christopher H., and Larry M. Bartels. *Democracy for Realists: Why Elections Do Not Produce Responsive Government*. Princeton, NJ: Princeton University Press, 2016.

Benhabib, Jess. "Cycles, Chaos, and Bifurcations in Economics." *Economic Journal* 98, no. 392 (1988): 38–48.

Carothers, Thomas, and Andrew O'Donohue, eds. *Democracies Divided: The Global Challenge of Political Polarization*. Washington, DC: Brookings Institution Press, 2019.

Cramer, Katherine J. *The Politics of Resentment: Rural Consciousness in Wisconsin and the Rise of Scott Walker*. Chicago: University of Chicago Press, 2016.

Iyengar, Shanto, Gaurav Sood, and Yphtach Lelkes. "Affect, Not Ideology: A Social Identity Perspective on Polarization." *Public Opinion Quarterly* 76, no. 3 (2012): 405–31.

Levitsky, Steven, and Daniel Ziblatt. *How Democracies Die*. New York: Crown, 2018.

Mason, Lilliana. *Uncivil Agreement: How Politics Became Our Identity*. Chicago: University of Chicago Press, 2018.

McCoy, Jennifer, and Murat Somer. "Toward a Theory of Pernicious Polarization and How It Harms Democracies." *Annals of the American Academy of Political and Social Science* 681, no. 1 (2019): 234–71.

Sunstein, Cass R. *#Republic: Divided Democracy in the Age of Social Media*. Princeton, NJ: Princeton University Press, 2017.

## The Edge of Chaos: Innovation, Instability, and the Collapse of Shared Reality

Gleick, James. *Chaos: Making a New Science*. New York: Viking, 1987.

Piketty, Thomas. *Capital in the Twenty-First Century*. Cambridge, MA: Harvard University Press, 2014.

## The Power–Capital Feedback Loop: A Lorenz Model of Oligarchy Formation

Arthur, W. Brian. *Complexity and the Economy*. New York: Oxford University Press, 2014.

Haldane, Andrew G., and Robert M. May. "Systemic Risk in Banking Ecosystems." *Nature* 469 (2011): 351–55.

Mandelbrot, Benoit. *The (Mis)Behavior of Markets: A Fractal View of Risk, Ruin, and Reward*. New York: Basic Books, 2004.

Scheffer, Marten. *Critical Transitions in Nature and Society*. Princeton, NJ: Princeton University Press, 2009.

Stiglitz, Joseph E. *The Price of Inequality: How Today's Divided Society Endangers Our Future*. New York: W. W. Norton & Company, 2012.

Taleb, Nassim Nicholas. *Antifragile: Things That Gain from Disorder*. New York: Random House, 2012.

# Chapter 3

## The Planetary Prisoner's Dilemma: Coordinating Climate and Energy Policy on a Global Scale

Keohane, Robert O., and David G. Victor. "The Regime Complex for Climate Change." *Perspectives on Politics* 9, no. 1 (2011): 7–23.

Nordhaus, William. *The Climate Casino: Risk, Uncertainty, and Economics for a Warming World.* New Haven, CT: Yale University Press, 2013.

Ostrom, Elinor. "Polycentric Systems for Coping with Collective Action and Global Environmental Change." *Global Environmental Change* 20, no. 4 (2010): 550–57.

Stern, Nicholas. *The Economics of Climate Change: The Stern Review.* Cambridge: Cambridge University Press, 2007.

## A Fair Social Contract and Rawls' Veil of Ignorance

Arneson, Richard. "Equality and Equality of Opportunity for Welfare." *Philosophical Studies* 56 (1989): 77–93.

Cohen, G. A. "Where the Action Is: On the Site of Distributive Justice." *Philosophy & Public Affairs* 26, no. 1 (1997): 3–30.

Daniels, Norman, ed. *Reading Rawls: Critical Studies on Rawls's A Theory of Justice.* Stanford, CA: Stanford University Press, 1975.

Freeman, Samuel. *Rawls.* New York: Routledge, 2007.

Nozick, Robert. *Anarchy, State, and Utopia.* New York: Basic Books, 1974.

Nussbaum, Martha C. *Creating Capabilities: The Human Development Approach.* Cambridge, MA: Harvard University Press, 2011.

Pogge, Thomas. *Realizing Rawls.* Ithaca, NY: Cornell University Press, 1989.

Rawls, John. *A Theory of Justice.* Cambridge, MA: Harvard University Press, 1971.

Rawls, John. *Political Liberalism.* New York: Columbia University Press, 1993.

Sen, Amartya. *The Idea of Justice*. Cambridge, MA: Harvard University Press, 2009.

## A Game Theory Examination of Competitive Authoritarianism: Strategic Threats to American Society, the Economy, and Democratic Institutions

Acemoglu, Daron, and James A. Robinson. *Why Nations Fail: The Origins of Power, Prosperity, and Poverty*. New York: Crown, 2012.

Bermeo, Nancy. "On Democratic Backsliding." *Journal of Democracy* 27, no. 1 (2016): 5–19.

Svolik, Milan W. "Polarization versus Democracy." *Journal of Democracy* 30, no. 3 (2019): 20–32.

Way, Lucan A., and Steven Levitsky. *Competitive Authoritarianism: Hybrid Regimes after the Cold War*. Cambridge: Cambridge University Press, 2010.

## Moral Signaling Games and the Erosion of Trust in Post-Truth Societies

Baudrillard, Jean. *Simulacra and Simulation*. Ann Arbor: University of Michigan Press, 1981.

Frank, Robert H. *Passions Within Reason: The Strategic Role of the Emotions*. New York: W. W. Norton, 1988.

Kuran, Timur. *Private Truths, Public Lies: The Social Consequences of Preference Falsification*. Cambridge, MA: Harvard University Press, 1995.

Nowak, Martin A., and Karl Sigmund. "Evolution of Indirect Reciprocity." *Nature* 437 (2005): 1291–98.

Sunstein, Cass R. *#Republic: Divided Democracy in the Age of Social Media*, Princeton, NJ: Princeton University Press, 2017.

Tufekci, Zeynep. *Twitter and Tear Gas: The Power and Fragility of Networked Protest*. New Haven, CT: Yale University Press, 2017.

## Behavioral Game Theory and the Fallacies of Equity in Income and Wealth Disparity

Bolton, Gary E., and Axel Ockenfels. "ERC: A Theory of Equity, Reciprocity, and Competition." *American Economic Review* 90, no. 1 (2000): 166–93.

Camerer, Colin. *Behavioral Game Theory: Experiments in Strategic Interaction.* Princeton, NJ: Princeton University Press, 2003.

Fehr, Ernst, and Klaus M. Schmidt. "A Theory of Fairness, Competition, and Cooperation." *Quarterly Journal of Economics* 114, no. 3 (1999): 817–68.

Güth, Werner, Rolf Schmittberger, and Bernd Schwarze. "An Experimental Analysis of Ultimatum Bargaining." *Journal of Economic Behavior and Organization* 3, no. 4 (1982): 367–88.

Jost, John T., and Mahzarin R. Banaji. "The Role of Stereotyping in System-Justification and the Production of False Consciousness." *British Journal of Social Psychology* 33, no. 1 (1994): 1–27.

Kahneman, Daniel, and Amos Tversky. "Prospect Theory: An Analysis of Decision under Risk." *Econometrica* 47, no. 2 (1979): 263–91.

## The Dynamics of Multipolarity: Game Theory in a Post-American World System

Bull, Hedley. *The Anarchical Society: A Study of Order in World Politics.* 3rd ed. New York: Columbia University Press, 2002.

Keohane, Robert O. *After Hegemony: Cooperation and Discord in the World Political Economy.* 2nd ed. Princeton, NJ: Princeton University Press, 2005.

Kindleberger, Charles P. *The World in Depression, 1929–1939.* Berkeley: University of California Press, 2013.

Mearsheimer, John J. *The Tragedy of Great Power Politics.* Updated ed. New York: W. W. Norton, 2014.

## How Game Theory Destroys Collective Illusions

Rose, Todd. *Collective Illusions: Conformity, Complicity, and the Science of Why We Make Bad Decisions.* New York: Hachette Books, 2022.

## An Interdisciplinary Analysis of Game Theory and Complexity Economics

Gleick, James. *Chaos: Making a New Science*. New York: Viking, 1987.

Piketty, Thomas. *Capital in the Twenty-First Century*. Cambridge, MA: Harvard University Press, 2014.

## A Game-Theoretic Model of Significance and Restraint in Asceticism and Affluence

Frank, Robert H. *Luxury Fever: Why Money Fails to Satisfy in an Era of Excess*. Princeton, NJ: Princeton University Press, 1999.

Sen, Amartya. *Development as Freedom*. New York: Alfred A. Knopf, 1999.

Weber, Max. *The Protestant Ethic and the Spirit of Capitalism*. New York: Routledge, 2001.

## Payoff Asymmetry and the Ethics of Inequality: The Evolution of Fairness into a Non-Equilibrium State

Frank, Robert H., and Philip J. Cook. *The Winner-Take-All Society: Why the Few at the Top Get So Much More Than the Rest of Us*. New York: Penguin Books, 1996.

Merton, Robert K. "The Matthew Effect in Science." *Science* 159, no. 3810 (1968): 56–63.

Piketty, Thomas. *Capital in the Twenty-First Century*. Cambridge, MA: Harvard University Press, 2014.

Rawls, John. *A Theory of Justice*. Rev. ed. Cambridge, MA: Belknap Press of Harvard University Press, 1999.

Schelling, Thomas C. *Micromotives and Macrobehavior*. New York: W. W. Norton & Company, 1978.

Stiglitz, Joseph E. *The Price of Inequality: How Today's Divided Society Endangers Our Future*. New York: W. W. Norton & Company, 2012.

Taleb, Nassim Nicholas. *Skin in the Game: Hidden Asymmetries in Daily Life*. New York: Random House, 2018.

Wright, Erik Olin. *Envisioning Real Utopias*. London: Verso, 2010.

## A Game-Theoretic Basis of Solidarity

Axelrod, Robert. *The Evolution of Cooperation*. New York: Basic Books, 1984.

Bowles, Samuel. *The Moral Economy: Why Good Incentives Are No Substitute for Good Citizens*. New Haven, CT: Yale University Press, 2016.

Fehr, Ernst, and Simon Gächter. "Altruistic Punishment in Humans." *Nature* 415, no. 6868 (2002): 137–40.

Ostrom, Elinor. *Governing the Commons: The Evolution of Institutions for Collective Action*. Cambridge: Cambridge University Press, 1990.

Schelling, Thomas C. *The Strategy of Conflict*. Cambridge, MA: Harvard University Press, 1960.

Young, H. Peyton. *Individual Strategy and Social Structure: An Evolutionary Theory of Institutions*. Princeton, NJ: Princeton University Press, 1998.

## The Game-Theoretic Foundations of the Importance of Collective Solidarity

Axelrod, Robert. *The Evolution of Cooperation*. New York: Basic Books, 1984.

Bowles, Samuel. *The Moral Economy: Why Good Incentives Are No Substitute for Good Citizens*. New Haven, CT: Yale University Press, 2016.

Fehr, Ernst, and Simon Gächter. "Altruistic Punishment in Humans." *Nature* 415, no. 6868 (2002): 137–40.

Ostrom, Elinor. *Governing the Commons: The Evolution of Institutions for Collective Action*. Cambridge: Cambridge University Press, 1990.

Schelling, Thomas C. *The Strategy of Conflict*. Cambridge, MA: Harvard University Press, 1960.

Young, H. Peyton. *Individual Strategy and Social Structure: An Evolutionary Theory of Institutions*. Princeton, NJ: Princeton University Press, 1998.

# Chapter 4

## Envisioning a Post-Capitalistic Economy for the United States: Achieving Economic Justice, Income Equality, and Social Mobility

Stiglitz, Joseph E. *The Price of Inequality: How Today's Divided Society Endangers Our Future.* New York: W. W. Norton & Company, 2012.

## The Military-Industrial Complex and Its Influence on American Geopolitics

Bacevich, Andrew J. *America's War for the Greater Middle East: A Military History.* New York: Random House, 2016.

Bacevich, Andrew J. *The New American Militarism: How Americans Are Seduced by War.* New York: Oxford University Press, 2005.

Eisenhower, Dwight D. "Farewell Address." January 17, 1961. Dwight D. Eisenhower Presidential Library, Museum & Boyhood Home.

Galbraith, John Kenneth. *The Culture of Contentment.* Boston: Houghton Mifflin, 1992.

Johnson, Chalmers. *The Sorrows of Empire: Militarism, Secrecy, and the End of the Republic.* New York: Metropolitan Books, 2004.

Melman, Seymour. *The Permanent War Economy: American Capitalism in Decline.* New York: Simon & Schuster, 1974.

Stanger, Allison. *Whistleblowers: Honesty in America from Washington to Trump.* New Haven, CT: Yale University Press, 2019.

Stockholm International Peace Research Institute (SIPRI). *SIPRI Yearbook 2024: Armaments, Disarmament and International Security.* Oxford: Oxford University Press, 2024.

## A Comparative Analysis of Neoliberal Capitalism and an American Variant of Democratic Socialism

Harvey, David. *A Brief History of Neoliberalism.* Oxford: Oxford University Press, 2005.

Piketty, Thomas. *Capital and Ideology.* Cambridge, MA: Harvard University Press, 2020.

Sachs, Jeffrey D. *The Price of Civilization: Reawakening American Virtue and Prosperity.* New York: Random House, 2011.

Wolff, Richard D. *Understanding Socialism.* New York: Democracy in Action, 2019.

## The Impact of Globalization on the American Middle Class

Autor, David H., David Dorn, and Gordon H. Hanson. "The China Syndrome: Local Labor Market Effects of Import Competition in the United States." *American Economic Review* 103, no. 6 (2013): 2121–68.

Bluestone, Barry, and Bennett Harrison. *The Deindustrialization of America: Plant Closings, Community Abandonment, and the Dismantling of Basic Industry.* New York: Basic Books, 1982.

Goldin, Claudia, and Lawrence F. Katz. *The Race Between Education and Technology.* Cambridge, MA: Harvard University Press, 2008.

Piketty, Thomas, and Emmanuel Saez. "Income Inequality in the United States, 1913–1998." *Quarterly Journal of Economics* 118, no. 1 (2003): 1–39.

Stiglitz, Joseph E. *Globalization and Its Discontents Revisited: Anti-Globalization in the Era of Trump.* New York: W. W. Norton, 2017.

U. S. Census Bureau. *Income and Poverty in the United States.* Washington, DC: U.S. Government Printing Office, various years.

## The Path to Anarchy: Economic Disparity and the Emergence of Authoritarian Influences

Acemoglu, Daron, and James A. Robinson. *Why Nations Fail: The Origins of Power, Prosperity, and Poverty.* New York: Crown, 2012.

Kunkel, Lawrence R. *Complexity Economics and Systems Humanism: Toward a Moral Ecology of Economic Prosperity and Human Flourishing.* Forthcoming.

Lorenz, Edward N. "Deterministic Nonperiodic Flow." *Journal of the Atmospheric Sciences* 20, no. 2 (1963): 130–41.

Piketty, Thomas. *Capital in the Twenty-First Century*. Cambridge, MA: Harvard University Press, 2014.

Prigogine, Ilya. *The End of Certainty: Time, Chaos, and the New Laws of Nature*. New York: Free Press, 1997.

Strogatz, Steven H. *Nonlinear Dynamics and Chaos: With Applications to Physics, Biology, Chemistry, and Engineering*. 2nd ed. Boulder, Co: Westview Press, 2015.

Tainter, Joseph A. *The Collapse of Complex Societies*. Cambridge: Cambridge University Press, 1988.

## An Examination of Gun Legislation Efficacy and Firearm-Related Violence via Phase Transition

Everytown Research. "Gun Law Rankings." 2024. https://everytownresearch.org/rankings.

Giffords Law Center to Prevent Gun Violence. "Annual Gun Law Scorecard." 2024. https://giffords.org/lawcenter/resources/scorecard/.

RAND Corporation. "Gun Policies: What Science Says About Their Effects." 2020. https://www.rand.org/research/gun-policy/key-findings.html.

The Guardian. "Federal Help Needed to Stop Mass Shootings in California, Gun Laws Experts Say." February 3, 2023. https://www.theguardian.com/us-news/2023/feb/03/california-gun-laws-federal-support.

## Ayn Rand's Wrong Ideas About Economics and the Rise of Our Hunger Games Economy

Greenspan, Alan, *The Age of Turbulence: Adventures in a New World*. New York: Penguin Press, 2007.

Mishel, Lawrence, and Jori Kandra. "CEO Pay Has Skyrocketed 1,460% Since 1978." Economic Policy Institute, August 2023.

Piketty, Thomas. *Capital in the Twenty-First Century*. Cambridge, MA: Harvard University Press, 2014.

Stiglitz, Joseph E. *The Price of Inequality: How Today's Divided Society Endangers Our Future.* New York: W. W. Norton & Company, 2012.

U.S. Federal Reserve. "Distribution of Household Wealth in the U.S. Since 1989." 2023.

## The Commoditization of Privacy: A Menace to Democracy

Stiglitz, Joseph E. *The Price of Inequality: How Today's Divided Society Endangers Our Future.* New York: W. W. Norton & Company, 2012.

## Why Countries Choose Collapse Over Reform: The Main Reasons for Decline

Acemoglu, Daron, and James A. Robinson. *Why Nations Fail: The Origins of Power, Prosperity, and Poverty.*. New York: Crown, 2012.

Diamond, Jared. *Collapse: How Societies Choose to Fail or Succeed.* New York: Viking, 2005.

Fukuyama, Francis. *Political Order and Political Decay: From the Industrial Revolution to the Globalization of Democracy.* New York: Farrar, Straus and Giroux, 2014.

Kennedy, Paul. *The Rise and Fall of the Great Powers: Economic Change and Military Conflict from 1500 to 2000.* New York: Random House, 1987.

Olson, Mancur. *The Rise and Decline of Nations: Economic Growth, Stagflation, and Social Rigidities.* New Haven, CT: Yale University Press, 1982.

Tainter, Joseph A. *The Collapse of Complex Societies.* Cambridge: Cambridge University Press, 1988.

Turchin, Peter. *End Times: Elites, Counter-Elites, and the Path of Political Disintegration.* New York: Penguin Press, 2023.

Zakaria, Fareed. *The Future of Freedom: Illiberal Democracy at Home and Abroad.* New York: W. W. Norton, 2003.

## Algorithmic Inequality: How Complexity Affects AI-Driven Economies

Benkler, Yochai. "Networks of Power, Degrees of Freedom." *Yale Law Journal* 130 (2021): 564–622.

Brynjolfsson, Erik, and Andrew McAfee. *The Second Machine Age: Work, Progress, and Prosperity in a Time of Brilliant Technologies.* New York: W. W. Norton, 2014.

O'Neil, Cathy. *Weapons of Math Destruction: How Big Data Increases Inequality and Threatens Democracy.* New York: Crown, 2016.

Pasquale, Frank. *The Black Box Society: The Secret Algorithms That Control Money and Information.* Cambridge, MA: Harvard University Press, 2015.

Zuboff, Shoshana. *The Age of Surveillance Capitalism: The Fight for a Human Future at the New Frontier of Power.* New York: PublicAffairs, 2019.

## The Economics of Perception and Epistemic Collapse

Arendt, Hannah. *The Origins of Totalitarianism.* New York: Harcourt, Brace & Co., 1951.

Han, Byung-Chul. *In the Swarm: Digital Prospects.* Cambridge, MA: MIT Press, 2017.

Husserl, Edmund. *The Crisis of European Sciences and Transcendental Phenomenology.* Evanston, IL: Northwestern University Press, 1970.

Prigogine, Ilya, and Isabelle Stengers. *Order Out of Chaos: Man's New Dialogue with Nature.* New York: Bantam Books, 1984.

Simon, Herbert A. "Designing Organizations for an Information-Rich World." In *Computers, Communications, and the Public Interest,* edited by Martin Greenberger, 37–72. Baltimore: Johns Hopkins University Press, 1971.

Zuboff, Shoshana. *The Age of Surveillance Capitalism: The Fight for a Human Future at the New Frontier of Power.* New York: PublicAffairs, 2019.

## Breaking the Balance in Very Connected Systems


Arthur, W. Brian. *Complexity and the Economy*. Oxford: Oxford University Press, 2014.

Bak, Per. *How Nature Works: The Science of Self-Organized Criticality*. New York: Springer-Verlag, 1996.

Barabási, Albert-László. *Network Science*. Cambridge: Cambridge University Press, 2016.

Helbing, Dirk. "Globally Networked Risks and How to Respond." *Nature* 497, no. 7447 (2013): 51–59.

Holland, John H. *Hidden Order: How Adaptation Builds Complexity*. Reading, MA: Addison-Wesley, 1995.

Minsky, Hyman P. *Stabilizing an Unstable Economy*. New Haven, CT: Yale University Press, 1986.

Simon, Herbert A. *The Sciences of the Artificial*. 3rd ed. Cambridge, MA: MIT Press, 1996.


## Fractured Abundance: The Ineffectiveness of Wealth as a Stabilizing Force in Promoting Prosperity


Kahneman, Daniel. *Thinking, Fast and Slow*. New York: Farrar, Straus and Giroux, 2011.

Ostrom, Elinor. *Governing the Commons: The Evolution of Institutions for Collective Action*. Cambridge: Cambridge University Press, 1990.

Piketty, Thomas. *Capital in the Twenty-First Century*. Cambridge, MA: Harvard University Press, 2014.

Putnam, Robert D. *Bowling Alone: The Collapse and Revival of American Community*. New York: Simon & Schuster, 2000.

Wilkinson, Richard, and Kate Pickett. *The Spirit Level: Why More Equal Societies Almost Always Do Better*. London: Allen Lane, 2009.

# The Thermodynamics of Power and the Distribution of Justice


Arendt, Hannah. *The Human Condition*. Chicago: University of Chicago Press, 1958.

Arthur, W. Brian. *Complexity and the Economy*. Oxford: Oxford University Press, 2014.

Foucault, Michel. *Power/Knowledge: Selected Interviews and Other Writings*. New York: Pantheon Books, 1980.

Habermas, Jürgen. *The Theory of Communicative Action*. Boston: Beacon Press, 1984.

Havel, Václav. *The Power of the Powerless*. London: Routledge, 1985.

Polanyi, Karl. *The Great Transformation*. Boston: Beacon Press, 1944.

Prigogine, Ilya, and Isabelle Stengers. *Order Out of Chaos: Man's New Dialogue with Nature*. New York: Bantam Books, 1984.

Sen, Amartya. *Development as Freedom*. New York: Alfred A. Knopf, 1999.

Taleb, Nassim Nicholas. *Antifragile: Things That Gain from Disorder*. New York: Random House, 2012.

Weber, Max. *Economy and Society*. Berkeley: University of California Press, 1978.


# The Tragedy of Transparency: How Too Much Information Reduces Collective Rationality


Benkler, Yochai. *The Wealth of Networks: How Social Production Transforms Markets and Freedom*. New Haven, CT: Yale University Press, 2006.

Habermas, Jürgen. *The Structural Transformation of the Public Sphere: An Inquiry into a Category of Bourgeois Society*. Cambridge, MA: MIT Press, 1989.

Kuran, Timur. *Private Truths, Public Lies: The Social Consequences of Preference Falsification*. Cambridge, MA: Harvard University Press, 1995.

Morozov, Evgeny. *The Net Delusion: The Dark Side of Internet Freedom*. New York: PublicAffairs, 2011.

Sunstein, Cass R. *Republic.com 2.0.* Princeton, NJ: Princeton University Press, 2007.

Tufekci, Zeynep. *Twitter and Tear Gas: The Power and Fragility of Networked Protest.* New Haven, CT: Yale University Press, 2017.

## Economic Externalities: Less Freedom and Negative Consequences for American Society

Ostrom, Elinor. *Managing the Commons: The Evolution of Institutions for Collective Action.* Cambridge: Cambridge University Press, 1990.

Piketty, Thomas. *Capital in the Twenty-First Century.* Cambridge, MA: Harvard University Press, 2014.

Stiglitz, Joseph E. *The Price of Inequality.* New York: W. W. Norton, 2013.

## The American Debt Overload: How Too Much Debt for People, Businesses, and the Federal Government Will Destroy Democracy

Congressional Budget Office. *Reports on the Budget and the Economy.*

Federal Reserve Bank of St. Louis. *FRED Economic Data.*

International Monetary Fund. *Fiscal Monitor Reports.*

Mian, Atif, and Amir Sufi. *House of Debt: How They (and You) Caused the Great Recession, and How We Can Prevent It from Happening Again.* Chicago: University of Chicago Press, 2014.

Piketty, Thomas. *Capital in the Twenty-First Century.* Cambridge, MA: Harvard University Press, 2014.

Streeck, Wolfgang. *Buying Time: The Delayed Crisis of Democratic Capitalism.* London: Verso, 2014.

# Chapter 5

## Aristotle and Modern Game Theory: A Philosophical Synthesis of Strategy and Virtue

Aristotle. *Nicomachean Ethics*. Translated by Terence Irwin. Indianapolis: Hackett Publishing, 1999.

Ibid. 1155a23.

Ibid. 1103a15–20.

Ibid. 1140b5–10.

Aristotle. *Politics*. Translated by Carnes Lord. Chicago: University of Chicago Press, 2013.

Ibid. 1280b5–10.

Ibid. 1140a24–26.

Ibid. 1256b25–35.

## Nietzsche and the Game of Becoming: Power, Chaos, and Creative Destruction

Deleuze, Gilles. *Nietzsche and Philosophy*. New York: Columbia University Press, 1983.

Kaufmann, Walter. *Nietzsche: Philosopher, Psychologist, Antichrist*. Princeton, NJ: Princeton University Press, 1950.

Nietzsche, Friedrich. *The Birth of Tragedy*. Translated by Walter Kaufmann. New York: Vintage Books, 1967.

Nietzsche, Friedrich. *The Will to Power*. Translated by Walter Kaufmann and R. J. Hollingdale. New York: Vintage Books, 1968.

Nietzsche, Friedrich. *Thus Spoke Zarathustra*. Translated by Walter Kaufmann. New York: Viking Press, 1954.

Prigogine, Ilya, and Isabelle Stengers. *Order Out of Chaos: Man's New Dialogue with Nature*. New York: Bantam Books, 1984.

Schumpeter, Joseph A. *Capitalism, Socialism, and Democracy*. New York: Harper, 1942.

## Aristotle's Virtue Ethics in a Nonlinear World: Stability, Reciprocity, and the Golden Mean as Dynamic Equilibrium

Aristotle. *Nicomachean Ethics*. 3rd ed. Indianapolis: Hackett Publishing Company, 2019.

Capra, Fritjof, and Pier Luigi Luisi. *The Systems View of Life: A Unifying Vision*. Cambridge: Cambridge University Press, 2014.

Holland, John H. *Complexity: A Very Short Introduction*. Oxford: Oxford University Press, 2014.

Mitchell, Melanie. *Complexity: A Guided Tour*. Oxford: Oxford University Press, 2009.

Nussbaum, Martha C. *The Fragility of Goodness: Luck and Ethics in Greek Tragedy and Philosophy*. Rev. ed. Cambridge: Cambridge University Press, 2001.

Sherman, Nancy. *The Fabric of Character: Aristotle's Theory of Virtue*. Oxford: Clarendon Press, 1989.

Waldrop, M. Mitchell. *Complexity: The Emerging Science at the Edge of Order and Chaos*. New York: Simon & Schuster, 1992.

## Cognitive Disequilibrium and the Moral Framework of Truth

Arendt, Hannah. *The Human Condition*. Chicago: University of Chicago Press, 1958.

Arthur, W. Brian. *Complexity and the Economy*. Oxford: Oxford University Press, 2014.

Foucault, Michel. *Power/Knowledge: Selected Interviews and Other Writings*. New York: Pantheon Books, 1980.

Habermas, Jürgen. *The Theory of Communicative Action*. Boston: Beacon Press, 1984.

Havel, Václav. *The Power of the Powerless*. London: Routledge, 1985.

Husserl, Edmund. *Ideas Pertaining to a Pure Phenomenology and to a Phenomenological Philosophy.* The Hague: Martinus Nijhoff, 1958.

Kahneman, Daniel. *Thinking, Fast and Slow.* New York: Farrar, Straus and Giroux, 2011.

Polanyi, Karl. *The Great Transformation.* Boston: Beacon Press, 1944.

Prigogine, Ilya, and Isabelle Stengers. *Order Out of Chaos: Man's New Dialogue with Nature.* New York: Bantam Books, 1984.

Taleb, Nassim Nicholas. *Antifragile: Things That Gain from Disorder.* New York: Random House, 2012.

## Ethical Entropy and the Fragmentation of Collective Accountability

Arendt, Hannah. *The Human Condition.* Chicago: University of Chicago Press, 1958.

Arthur, W. Brian. *Complexity and the Economy.* Oxford: Oxford University Press, 2014.

Foucault, Michel. *Power/Knowledge: Selected Interviews and Other Writings.* New York: Pantheon Books, 1980.

Habermas, Jürgen. *The Theory of Communicative Action.* Boston: Beacon Press, 1984.

Havel, Václav. *The Power of the Powerless.* London: Routledge, 1985.

Kahneman, Daniel. *Thinking, Fast and Slow.* New York: Farrar, Straus and Giroux, 2011.

Levinas, Emmanuel. *Totality and Infinity: An Essay on Exteriority.* The Hague: Martinus Nijhoff, 1961.

Polanyi, Karl. *The Great Transformation.* Boston: Beacon Press, 1944.

Prigogine, Ilya, and Isabelle Stengers. *Order Out of Chaos: Man's New Dialogue with Nature.* New York: Bantam Books, 1984.

Taleb, Nassim Nicholas. *Antifragile: Things That Gain from Disorder.* New York: Random House, 2012.

# Chapter 6

## A Look at Chaos Theory and the Abstract Impressionism Art Movement

Gleick, James. *Chaos: Making a New Science*. New York: Viking, 1987.

Lyotard, Jean-François. *The Postmodern Condition: A Report on Knowledge*. Minneapolis: University of Minnesota Press, 1984.

Mandelbrot, Benoît. *The Fractal Geometry of Nature*. New York: W. H. Freeman, 1982.

Micolich, Adam P., David Jonas, and Richard P. Taylor. "Fractal Analysis of Pollock's Drip Paintings." *Nature* 399, no. 6735 (1999): 422–23.

Rosenberg, Harold. *The Tradition of the New*. New York: Horizon Press, 1959.

Tuchman, Maurice, ed. *The Spiritual in Art: Abstract Painting 1890–1985*. Los Angeles: Los Angeles County Museum of Art, 1986.

## The Art of Instability: Joan Mitchell and the Beauty of Chaos

Albers, Patricia. *Joan Mitchell: Lady Painter*. New York: Alfred A. Knopf, 2011.

Danto, Arthur C. *After the End of Art: Contemporary Art and the Pale of History*. Princeton, NJ: Princeton University Press, 1997.

Fineberg, Jonathan. *Art Since 1940: Strategies of Being*. London: Laurence King Publishing, 2011.

Prigogine, Ilya, and Isabelle Stengers. *Order Out of Chaos: Man's New Dialogue with Nature*. New York: Bantam Books, 1984.

Sardar, Ziauddin, and Iwona Abrams. *Introducing Chaos: A Graphic Guide*. London: Icon Books, 1999.

Stevens, Mark. "Joan Mitchell and the Edge of Abstraction." *The New Yorker*, March 1994.

Varnedoe, Kirk. *Pictures of Nothing: Abstract Art After Pollock*. Princeton, NJ: Princeton University Press, 2003.

## The Renaissance as a Revolution of Complexity: The Emergence of Artistic Order and Economic Growth


Alberti, Leon Battista. *On Painting*. Translated by John R. Spencer. New Haven, CT: Yale University Press, 1966.

Braudel, Fernand. *Civilization and Capitalism, 15th–18th Century. Vol. 1: The Structures of Everyday Life*. Translated by Siân Reynolds. Berkeley: University of California Press, 1992.

Burckhardt, Jacob. *The Civilization of the Renaissance in Italy*. Translated by S. G. C. Middlemore. London: Penguin Classics, 1990.

Goldthwaite, Richard A. *The Economy of Renaissance Florence*. Baltimore: Johns Hopkins University Press, 2009.

Johnson, Steven. *Where Good Ideas Come From: The Natural History of Innovation*. New York: Riverhead Books, 2010.

Panofsky, Erwin. *Renaissance and Renascences in Western Art*. Stockholm: Almqvist and Wiksell, 1960.

Powell, Walter W., and John F. Padgett, eds. *The Emergence of Organizations and Markets*. Princeton, NJ: Princeton University Press, 2012.

Vasari, Giorgio. *The Lives of the Artists*. Translated by Julia Conaway Bondanella and Peter Bondanella. Oxford: Oxford University Press, 1998.

Wallerstein, Immanuel. *The Modern World-System I: Capitalist Agriculture and the Origins of the European World-Economy in the Sixteenth Century*. New York: Academic Press, 1974.


## Abstract Expressionism and the Geometry of Emotion: Pollock as a Cartographer of Economic Disorder


Arthur, W. Brian. *Complexity and the Economy*. Oxford: Oxford University Press, 2014.

Gleick, James. *Chaos: Making a New Science*. New York: Viking, 1987.

Goodwin, Richard M. *Chaotic Economic Dynamics*. Oxford: Clarendon Press, 1990.

Mandelbrot, Benoît B. *The Fractal Geometry of Nature.* New York: W. H. Freeman, 1982.

Rosenberg, Harold. "The American Action Painters." *Art News,* December 1952.

Shlain, Leonard. *Art & Physics: Parallel Visions in Space, Time, and Light.* New York: Quill, 1991.

Taylor, R. P., A. P. Micolich, and D. Jonas. "Fractal Analysis of Pollock's Drip Paintings." *Nature* 399, no. 6735 (1999): 422–23.

## Art as Epistemology: When Aesthetic Qualities Unveil a Systemic Framework

Dirac, Paul A. M. *The Principles of Quantum Mechanics.* Oxford: Oxford University Press, 1930.

Einstein, Albert. *Relativity: The Special and the General Theory.* Princeton, NJ: Princeton University Press, 1920.

Goodman, Nelson. *Languages of Art: An Approach to a Theory of Symbols.* Indianapolis: Hackett Publishing, 1976.

Kant, Immanuel. *Critique of Judgment.* Cambridge: Cambridge University Press, 2000.

Langer, Susanne K. *Feeling and Form: A Theory of Art Developed from Philosophy in a New Key.* New York: Charles Scribner's Sons, 1953.

Morrison, Toni. *Beloved.* New York: Alfred A. Knopf, 1987.

Scarry, Elaine. *On Beauty and Being Just.* Princeton, NJ: Princeton University Press, 1999.

Taylor, Richard P. "Fractal Analysis of Pollock's Drip Paintings." *Nature* 399, no. 6735 (1999): 422–23.

# Chapter 7

## A Social Psychological Examination of Collective Narcissism in American Politics and Society

Golec de Zavala, Agnieszka, Aleksandra Cichocka, and Mikolaj Winiewski. "Collective Narcissism: Political Consequences of Investment in a Grandiose Image of the In-Group." *Advances in Political Psychology* 40, no. S1 (2019): 37–74.

Golec de Zavala, Agnieszka, Aleksandra Cichocka, and Mikolaj Winiewski. "Collective Narcissism and Its Social Consequences." *Journal of Personality and Social Psychology* 97, no. 6 (2009): 1074–96.

Loewen, James W. *Lies My Teacher Told Me: Everything Your American History Textbook Got Wrong.* New York: The New Press, 1995.

Mason, Lilliana. *Uncivil Agreement: How Politics Became Our Identity.* Chicago: University of Chicago Press, 2018.

Marchlewska, Marta, Aleksandra Cichocka, and Agnieszka Golec de Zavala. "'In Trump We Trust': The Need for Collective Narcissism and the Rise of Authoritarian Populism." *Social Psychological and Personality Science* 9, no. 3 (2018): 302–10.

Sunstein, Cass R. *Going to Extremes: How Like Minds Unite and Divide.* New York: Oxford University Press, 2009.

Tajfel, Henri, and John C. Turner. "The Social Identity Theory of Intergroup Behavior." In *Psychology of Intergroup Relations*, edited by S. Worchel and W. G. Austin, 7–24. Chicago: Nelson-Hall, 1986.

## The Political Economy of Cognitive Capture: An Examination from a Social Psychology Standpoint

Akerlof, George A., and Robert J. Shiller. *Phishing for Phools: The Economics of Manipulation and Deception.* Princeton, NJ: Princeton University Press, 2015.

Baron, Jonathan. *Thinking and Deciding.* Cambridge: Cambridge University Press, 2008.

Cialdini, Robert B. *Influence: The Psychology of Persuasion.* New York: Harper Business, 2006.

Daniels, Norman. "Democratic Equality and Fair Opportunity." *Journal of Political Philosophy* 7 (1999): 91–111.

Haidt, Jonathan. *The Righteous Mind: Why Good People Are Divided by Politics and Religion.* New York: Vintage, 2012.

Iyengar, Shanto, and Donald R. Kinder. *News That Matters: Television and American Opinion.* Chicago: University of Chicago Press, 2010.

Kahneman, Daniel. *Thinking, Fast and Slow.* New York: Farrar, Straus and Giroux, 2011.

Lippmann, Walter. *Public Opinion.* New York: Harcourt, Brace and Company, 1922.

Rose, Todd. *Collective Illusions: Conformity, Complicity, and the Science of Why We Make Bad Decisions.* New York: Hachette Books, 2022.

Sunstein, Cass R. *#Republic: Divided Democracy in the Age of Social Media.* Princeton, NJ: Princeton University Press, 2017.

Tversky, Amos, and Daniel Kahneman. "Judgment under Uncertainty: Heuristics and Biases." *Science* 185, no. 4157 (1974): 1124–1131.

Zuboff, Shoshana. *The Age of Surveillance Capitalism: The Fight for a Human Future at the New Frontier of Power.* New York: PublicAffairs, 2019.

## Rawls' Veil of Ignorance and an Equitable Social Contract

Arneson, Richard. "Equality and Equality of Opportunity for Welfare." *Philosophical Studies* 56 (1989): 77–93.

Cohen, G. A. "Where the Action Is: On the Site of Distributive Justice." *Philosophy & Public Affairs* 26, no. 1 (1997): 3–30.

Daniels, Norman, ed. *Reading Rawls: Critical Studies on Rawls's A Theory of Justice.* Stanford, CA: Stanford University Press, 1975.

Freeman, Samuel. *Rawls.* New York: Routledge, 2007.

Nozick, Robert. *Anarchy, State, and Utopia.* New York: Basic Books, 1974.

Nussbaum, Martha C. *Creating Capabilities: The Human Development Approach*. Cambridge, MA: Harvard University Press, 2011.

Pogge, Thomas. *Realizing Rawls*. Ithaca, NY: Cornell University Press, 1989.

Rawls, John. *A Theory of Justice*. Cambridge, MA: Harvard University Press, 1971.

Rawls, John. *Political Liberalism*. New York: Columbia University Press, 1993.

Sen, Amartya. *The Idea of Justice*. Cambridge, MA: Harvard University Press, 2009.

## Collective Narcissism in American Politics and Society: A Social Psychological Perspective

Golec de Zavala, Agnieszka, Aleksandra Cichocka, and Mikolaj Winiewski. "Collective Narcissism: Political Consequences of Investment in a Grandiose Image of the In-Group." *Advances in Political Psychology* 40, no. S1 (2019): 37–74.

Golec de Zavala, Agnieszka, Aleksandra Cichocka, and Mikolaj Winiewski. "Collective Narcissism and Its Social Consequences." *Journal of Personality and Social Psychology* 97, no. 6 (2009): 1074–96.

Loewen, James W. *Lies My Teacher Told Me: Everything Your American History Textbook Got Wrong*. New York: The New Press, 1995.

Marchlewska, Marta, Aleksandra Cichocka, and Agnieszka Golec de Zavala. "'In Trump We Trust': The Need for Collective Narcissism and the Rise of Authoritarian Populism." *Social Psychological and Personality Science* 9, no. 3 (2018): 302–10.

Mason, Lilliana. *Uncivil Agreement: How Politics Became Our Identity*. Chicago: University of Chicago Press, 2018.

Sunstein, Cass R. *Going to Extremes: How Like Minds Unite and Divide*. New York: Oxford University Press, 2009.

Tajfel, Henri, and John C. Turner. "The Social Identity Theory of Intergroup Behavior." In *Psychology of Intergroup Relations*, edited by S. Worchel and W. G. Austin, 7–24. Chicago: Nelson-Hall, 1986.

## Jovon's Paradox: Contemporary Applications and Prevailing Misconceptions in the American Economy

Alcott, Blake. "Jevons' Paradox." *Ecological Economics* 54, no. 1 (2005): 9–21.

Binswanger, Mathias. "Technological Progress and Sustainable Development: What About the Rebound Effect?" *Ecological Economics* 36, no. 1 (2001): 119–32.

Greening, Lorna A., David L. Greene, and Carmen Difiglio. "Energy Efficiency and Consumption—The Rebound Effect—A Survey." *Energy Policy* 28, no. 6–7 (2000): 389–401.

Jevons, William Stanley. *The Coal Question: An Inquiry Concerning the Progress of the Nation, and the Probable Exhaustion of Our Coal-Mines*. London: Macmillan, 1865.

Schwab, Klaus. *The Fourth Industrial Revolution*. New York: Crown Business, 2017.

Smil, Vaclav. *Energy and Civilization: A History*. Cambridge, MA: MIT Press, 2017.

Sorrell, Steve. "Jevons' Paradox Revisited: The Evidence for Backfire from Improved Energy Efficiency." *Energy Policy* 37, no. 4 (2009): 1456–69.

U.S. Energy Information Administration (EIA). *Annual Energy Outlook*. Washington, DC: U.S. Department of Energy, various years.

# Chapter 8

## The End of Democratic Capitalism and Financial Feudalism

Brown, Wendy. *Undoing the Demos: Neoliberalism's Stealth Revolution*. New York: Zone Books, 2015.

Foroohar, Rana. *Makers and Takers: The Rise of Finance and the Fall of American Business.* New York: Crown Business, 2016.

Fraser, Nancy. "Legitimation Crisis? The Political Problems of Financialized Capitalism." *Critical Historical Studies* 2, no. 2 (2015): 157–89.

Hacker, Jacob S., and Paul Pierson. *Winner-Take-All Politics: How Washington Made the Rich Richer—and Turned Its Back on the Middle Class.* New York: Simon & Schuster, 2010.

Harvey, David. *A Brief History of Neoliberalism.* Oxford: Oxford University Press, 2005.

Kotz, David M. *The Rise and Fall of Neoliberal Capitalism.* Cambridge, MA: Harvard University Press, 2015.

Mazzucato, Mariana. *The Value of Everything: Making and Taking in the Global Economy.* New York: PublicAffairs, 2018.

Piketty, Thomas. *Capital in the Twenty-First Century.* Cambridge, MA: Harvard University Press, 2014.

Polanyi, Karl. *The Great Transformation: The Political and Economic Origins of Our Time.* New York: Farrar & Rinehart, 1944.

Rajan, Raghuram G. *Fault Lines: How Hidden Fractures Still Threaten the World Economy.* Princeton, NJ: Princeton University Press, 2010.

Saez, Emmanuel, and Gabriel Zucman. *The Triumph of Injustice: How the Rich Dodge Taxes and How to Make Them Pay.* New York: W. W. Norton & Company, 2019.

Stiglitz, Joseph E. *The Price of Inequality: How Today's Divided Society Endangers Our Future.* New York: W. W. Norton & Company, 2012.

Sunderland, Matthew. *Finance and the End of Democratic Capitalism.* PhD diss., University of California, Berkeley, 2020.

Tooze, Adam. *Crashed: How a Decade of Financial Crises Changed the World.* New York: Viking, 2018.

Varoufakis, Yanis. *And the Weak Suffer What They Must?: Europe's Crisis and America's Economic Future.* New York: Nation Books, 2016.

Zuboff, Shoshana. *The Age of Surveillance Capitalism: The Fight for a Human Future at the New Frontier of Power.* New York: PublicAffairs, 2019.

## Civilizational Risk in the Age of Nonlinear Geopolitical Power

Beck, Ulrich. *World at Risk.* Cambridge: Polity Press, 2009.

Bostrom, Nick. *Superintelligence: Paths, Dangers, Strategies.* Oxford: Oxford University Press, 2014.

Burgess, J. Peter, ed. *The Routledge Handbook of New Security Studies.* London: Routledge, 2021.

Diamond, Jared. *Collapse: How Societies Choose to Fail or Succeed.* New York: Viking, 2005.

Goldin, Ian, and Mike Mariathasan. *The Butterfly Defect: How Globalization Creates Systemic Risks, and What to Do About It.* Princeton, NJ: Princeton University Press, 2014.

Homer-Dixon, Thomas. *The Upside of Down: Catastrophe, Creativity, and the Renewal of Civilization.* Washington, DC: Island Press, 2006.

Knight, Frank H. *Risk, Uncertainty, and Profit.* Boston: Houghton Mifflin, 1921.

Meadows, Donella H. *Thinking in Systems: A Beginner's Guide.* White River Junction, VT: Chelsea Green Publishing, 2008.

Nye, Joseph S. *The Future of Power.* New York: PublicAffairs, 2011.

Parker, Charles F., and Eric K. Stern. "The September 11 Crisis and the World: A Study in Nonlinear Dynamics." In *The Routledge Handbook of Security Studies*, edited by Myriam Dunn Cavelty and Victor Mauer, 2nd ed. London: Routledge, 2020.

Slaughter, Anne-Marie. *The Chessboard and the Web: Strategies of Connection in a Networked World.* New Haven, CT: Yale University Press, 2017.

Tainter, Joseph A. *The Collapse of Complex Societies.* Cambridge: Cambridge University Press, 1988.

Taleb, Nassim Nicholas. *The Black Swan: The Impact of the Highly Improbable.* New York: Random House, 2007.

World Economic Forum. *The Global Risks Report 2023*. Geneva: World Economic Forum, 2023.

Zolli, Andrew, and Ann Marie Healy. *Resilience: Why Things Bounce Back.* New York: Free Press, 2012.

## An Economic History of the IMF and American Geopolitics: Financial Architecture, Power, and the Moral Ecology of Global Order

Babb, Sarah. *Managing Mexico: Economists from Nationalism to Neoliberalism.* Princeton, NJ: Princeton University Press, 2001.

Chang, Ha-Joon. *Kicking Away the Ladder: Development Strategy in Historical Perspective.* London: Anthem Press, 2002.

Eichengreen, Barry. *Globalizing Capital: A History of the International Monetary System.* 3rd ed. Princeton, NJ: Princeton University Press, 2019.

Helleiner, Eric. *States and the Reemergence of Global Finance: From Bretton Woods to the 1990s.* Ithaca, NY: Cornell University Press, 1994.

Kindleberger, Charles P. *The World in Depression, 1929–1939.* Berkeley: University of California Press, 1986.

Piketty, Thomas. *Capital in the Twenty-First Century.* Cambridge, MA: Harvard University Press, 2014.

Rodrik, Dani. *The Globalization Paradox: Democracy and the Future of the World Economy.* New York: W. W. Norton & Company, 2011.

Ruggie, John Gerard. "International Regimes, Transactions, and Change: Embedded Liberalism in the Postwar Economic Order." *International Organization* 36, no. 2 (1982): 379–415.

Stiglitz, Joseph E. *Globalization and Its Discontents.* New York: W. W. Norton & Company, 2002.

Strange, Susan. *States and Markets.* London: Continuum, 1994.

Vreeland, James Raymond. *The IMF and Economic Development.* Cambridge: Cambridge University Press, 2003.

# The Geopolitics of Inequality: How Internal Extraction Creates External Instability and the Dismantling of the Cooperative World Order


Acemoglu, Daron, and James A. Robinson. *Why Nations Fail: The Origins of Power, Prosperity, and Poverty.* New York: Crown, 2012.

Arrighi, Giovanni. *The Long Twentieth Century: Money, Power, and the Origins of Our Times.* 2nd ed. London: Verso, 2010.

Blyth, Mark. *Austerity: The History of a Dangerous Idea.* Oxford: Oxford University Press, 2013.

Boyer, Robert. "Long-Term Growth and Institutional Complementarity." *Socio-Economic Review* 16, no. 3 (2018): 463–86.

Buzan, Barry, and Ole Wæver. *Regions and Powers: The Structure of International Security.* Cambridge: Cambridge University Press, 2003.

Cingano, Federico. "Trends in Income Inequality and Its Impact on Economic Growth." OECD Social, Employment and Migration Working Paper No. 163, 2014.

Farrell, Henry, and Abraham Newman. "Weaponized Interdependence." *International Security* 44, no. 1 (2019): 42–79.

Gills, Barry, and Joel Rocamora. "Low-Intensity Democracy." *Third World Quarterly* 13, no. 3 (1992): 501–23.

Gilpin, Robert. *The Political Economy of International Relations.* Princeton, NJ: Princeton University Press, 1987.

Hobsbawm, Eric. *The Age of Extremes: The Short Twentieth Century, 1914–1991.* New York: Pantheon, 1994.

International Monetary Fund. *Fiscal Monitor: Tackling Inequality.* Washington, DC: IMF, 2017.

Kuznets, Simon. "Economic Growth and Income Inequality." *American Economic Review* 45, no. 1 (1955): 1–28.

Mearsheimer, John J. *The Tragedy of Great Power Politics.* New York: W. W. Norton, 2001.

Milanovic, Branko. *Global Inequality: A New Approach for the Age of Globalization.* Cambridge, MA: Harvard University Press, 2016.

Piketty, Thomas. *Capital in the Twenty-First Century.* Cambridge, MA: Harvard University Press, 2014.

Polanyi, Karl. *The Great Transformation: The Political and Economic Origins of Our Time.* Boston: Beacon Press, 2001.

Rodrik, Dani. *The Globalization Paradox: Democracy and the Future of the World Economy.* Oxford: Oxford University Press, 2011.

Stiglitz, Joseph E. *The Price of Inequality: How Today's Divided Society Endangers Our Future.* New York: W. W. Norton & Company, 2012.

Streeck, Wolfgang. *Buying Time: The Delayed Crisis of Democratic Capitalism.* London: Verso, 2014.

Wallerstein, Immanuel. *World-Systems Analysis: An Introduction.* Durham, NC: Duke University Press, 2004.

Zuboff, Shoshana. *The Age of Surveillance Capitalism: The Fight for a Human Future at the New Frontier of Power.* New York: PublicAffairs, 2019.

## The Multipolar Bifurcation: Phase Transitions in World Order

Arrighi, Giovanni. *The Long Twentieth Century: Money, Power, and the Origins of Our Times.* 2nd ed. London: Verso, 2010.

Boyer, Robert. "Long-Term Growth and Institutional Complementarity." *Socio-Economic Review* 16, no. 3 (2018): 463–86.

Farrell, Henry, and Abraham L. Newman. "Weaponized Interdependence: How Global Economic Networks Shape State Coercion." *International Security* 44, no. 1 (2019): 42–79.

Gilpin, Robert. *The Political Economy of International Relations.* Princeton, NJ: Princeton University Press, 1987.

Hobsbawm, Eric. *The Age of Extremes: The Short Twentieth Century, 1914–1991.* New York: Pantheon, 1994.

Kauffman, Stuart A. *At Home in the Universe: The Search for Laws of Self-Organization and Complexity.* New York: Oxford University Press, 1995.

Mearsheimer, John J. *The Tragedy of Great Power Politics*. New York: W. W. Norton, 2001.

Milanovic, Branko. *Global Inequality: A New Approach for the Age of Globalization*. Cambridge, MA: Harvard University Press, 2016.

Polanyi, Karl. *The Great Transformation: The Political and Economic Origins of Our Time*. Boston: Beacon Press, 2001.

Rodrik, Dani. *The Globalization Paradox: Democracy and the Future of the World Economy*. Oxford: Oxford University Press, 2011.

Stiglitz, Joseph E. *The Price of Inequality: How Today's Divided Society Endangers Our Future*. New York: W. W. Norton & Company, 2012.

Streeck, Wolfgang. *Buying Time: The Delayed Crisis of Democratic Capitalism*. London: Verso, 2014.

Strogatz, Steven H. *Nonlinear Dynamics and Chaos: With Applications to Physics, Biology, Chemistry, and Engineering*. 2nd ed. Boulder, CO: Westview Press, 2018.

Wallerstein, Immanuel. *World-Systems Analysis: An Introduction*. Durham, NC: Duke University Press, 2004.

Zuboff, Shoshana. *The Age of Surveillance Capitalism: The Fight for a Human Future at the New Frontier of Power*. New York: PublicAffairs, 2019.

## BRICS and the End of Dollar Hegemony

Arrighi, Giovanni. *The Long Twentieth Century: Money, Power, and the Origins of Our Times*. 2nd ed. London: Verso, 2010.

Eichengreen, Barry. *Exorbitant Privilege: The Rise and Fall of the Dollar and the Future of the International Monetary System*. Oxford: Oxford University Press, 2011.

Kindleberger, Charles P. *The World in Depression, 1929–1939*. Berkeley: University of California Press, 1986.

Strange, Susan. *States and Markets*. London: Continuum, 1994.

Wallerstein, Immanuel. *World-Systems Analysis: An Introduction*. Durham, NC: Duke University Press, 2004.